"If you believe that sports can be a lens for interpreting and understanding our world, then *The Heritage* is the Rosetta stone. Howard Bryant's latest explains so much about racism and the black athlete's place in US history that every chapter could be its own college course. But Bryant's book is less history than twenty-first-century prophetic fire: a polemic homing in on the ways that militarism, sports, and black athletic resistance have become volcanically explosive in the era of Trump. This is the book for explaining our times, whether you give a damn about sports or not."

—**Dave Zirin**, sports editor, *The Nation*, and author
of *Jim Brown: Last Man Standing*

"Bryant's account of this tradition is bracing. He's at his fiercest when he arrives at the present and exposes the fundamental hypocrisy of the *shut up and play* directive . . . In an era of controversial wars in multiple countries, why, Bryant asks, should we view these loud displays as 'patriotism' and Kaepernick's silent protest as unseemly politics?"

—**John Swansburg**, *The New York Times Book Review*

"A fascinating, insightful look at race, politics, and sport."

—*Booklist*

"A well-researched meditation on the historical pressures on African American athletes to embrace (or avoid) political engagement . . . An appealing blend of sports history and provocative discussion of race and success, respect, and representation in America."

—*Kirkus Reviews*

"Provides a comprehensive walk through American history, filtered through the lens of sports. History lovers will delight in the care with which *The Heritage* details the events leading up to today's impasse between players who speak out against injustice and those who prefer that they remain silent and 'play the game.'... This book will surprise, enlighten, and provide readers food for thought. *The Heritage* lingers in the consciousness — readers will find themselves revisiting its pages long after completing it."

—**Beverly Glass**, *The Los Angeles Review of Books*

"An immediate reminder of why athletes feel compelled to protest in the first place."

—**Chris Voghar**, *The Dallas Morning News*

"In this timely book, Bryant, senior writer for *ESPN Magazine*, astutely explains how sports serves 'as a barometer of blacks' standing in the larger culture.' . . . This indispensable book expertly chronicles a fractured nation dealing with black players who no longer want to (as *Fox News* host Laura Ingraham told LeBron James) 'shut up and dribble.'"

—*Publishers Weekly*

"That *The Heritage* so thoroughly deconstructs current controversy highlights Bryant's insight, foresight, and strong writing . . . essential [to] understanding this tumultuous moment at the intersection of sports, race, business and politics."

—**Morgan Campbell**, *The Toronto Star*

"Bryant keeps his eye on the ball. On top of that, Bryant writes with the kind of vim, in turns darkly comic and serious, that pulls you from page to page. It's a bracing analysis that brings clarity during a hazy season."

—**Brandon Tensley**, *Pacific Standard*

"Bryant's *The Heritage* is required reading for young people to realize what they're seeing isn't new, for current adults to understand the current climate in American sports and for older folks who lamented the lack of activist voices in the athletic ranks. The baton has been tossed."

—*New York Amsterdam News*

"Serious times call for serious action. After leaving a communist totalitarian country when I was eighteen, I was free to speak out, and I did. *The Heritage* gives the clearest breakdown I've read on why we athletes not only have the right to advocate for what we believe in—but oftentimes a duty."

—**Martina Navratilova**, eighteen-time tennis Grand Slam winner

"It may make people uncomfortable, but I'm pleased that Howard Bryant has chosen to tell the story of our heritage, and even more pleased that there are still ballplayers today who are willing to stand up for what they think is right."

—**Henry Aaron**, Major League Baseball Hall of Famer

"A fascinating and complex look at the role of black athletes as political activists. Bryant's analysis of the intersection of professional sports and promoting patriotism (or nationalism, depending on one's point of view) is especially enlightening."

—*Library Journal*

THE HERITAGE

THE
HERITAGE

BLACK ATHLETES,
A DIVIDED AMERICA,
AND THE POLITICS
OF PATRIOTISM

HOWARD BRYANT

BEACON PRESS
Boston

For Stephen Downes,

who told us so

BEACON PRESS
Boston, Massachusetts
www.beacon.org

Beacon Press books
are published under the auspices of
the Unitarian Universalist Association of Congregations.

22 21 20   8 7 6 5 4 3 2

This book is printed on acid-free paper that meets the uncoated paper
ANSI/NISO specifications for permanence as revised in 1992.

Text design and composition by Kim Arney

Library of Congress Cataloging-in-Publication Data
Names: Bryant, Howard, author.
Title: The heritage : Black Athletes, a divided America,
and the politics of patriotism / Howard Bryant.
Description: Boston : Beacon Press, 2018. | Includes bibliographical
references and index. | Description b
Identifiers: LCCN 2017053716 (print) | LCCN 2018009066 (ebook) |
ISBN 9780807027004 (ebook) | ISBN 9780807038086 (paperback)
Subjects: LCSH: African American athletes—History. | African American
athletes—Social conditions. | Sports—Political aspects—United States. |
Sports—Social aspects—United States. | Discrimination in sports—United
States. | BISAC: SPORTS & RECREATION / Sociology of Sports. |
POLITICAL SCIENCE / Civics & Citizenship. |
SPORTS & RECREATION / History.
Classification: LCC GV583 (ebook) | LCC GV583 .B735 2018 (print) |
DDC 306.483—dc23

LC record available at https://lccn.loc.gov/2017053716

CONTENTS

HERE I STAND

THIS IS A BOOK ABOUT COLLISION. It is a book about collision in sports. For all the clichés about *sudden death* and *there being no tomorrow*, sports is just entertainment, offering the illusion of being important. Red Sox-Yankees, Cowboys-Eagles, and Lakers-Celtics made us feel as if the fate of our universe hung on the final two minutes of the game, but sports was always supposed a substitute for reality, where Americans could fight for three hours and hug it out afterward. The newspapers used to call the sports pages the "toy department" for a reason. It was, after all, only a game.

But sports was always more than that for the black athlete. Despite its obvious legal and extralegal barriers to equality, in sports, the scoreboard served as a metaphor for the meritocracy America always considered itself, and sports was the barometer for where African Americans stood in the larger culture, how American they would be allowed to be. Of all black employees in the history of the United States, it was the ballplayers who were the most influential and most important, the ones who made the money. The black thinkers—the doctors, lawyers, scientists, and intellectuals— were roadblocked by segregation. Entertainers were a close second, but the athletes were different. Being a ballplayer was the first black occupation allowed in the mainstream, to attend the overwhelmingly white universities and join the white professional sports leagues. Ballplayers would be the first black professionals to integrate white neighborhoods—and have a chance at the full promise of the American Dream. Musicians were never proof that America was fair, because Lena Horne and John Coltrane didn't have a scoreboard, a final buzzer that told you coldly and definitively if you won. America liked that. Ballplayers were the Ones Who Made It.

And being the Ones Who Made It soon came with the responsibility to speak for the people who had not made it, for whom the road was still blocked. The responsibility became a tradition so ingrained that it hung over every player. The tradition became the black athlete's coat of arms, and the players who upheld it—Jackie Robinson, Muhammad Ali, Tommie Smith, John Carlos—were the ones who one day would be taught in the schools. The ones who did not—O. J. Simpson, Michael Jordan, Tiger Woods—no matter how great they were and how much money they made, could never escape the criticism that they shrank from their larger duty to the people. The tradition was so strong that it even had an informal nickname, *the Heritage*, exemplified that day in June of 1956, when Paul Robeson, the Rutgers All-America who played in the NFL in 1921 before the league barred black players from 1933 to 1946, the man who was once the most famous black man in America walked straight into hell.

Hell was the Eighty-Fourth Congress, where the House Un-American Activities Committee held hearings titled "Investigation of the Unauthorized Use of US Passports." The afternoon was going to be hell because so many of the years previously had been, when America actively sought to break him. Robeson appeared before the committee requesting a reissue of the passport the government had taken from him six years earlier.

The revoking of the passport wiped out Robeson financially, taking him from a person who would be a millionaire in today's dollars to one making about $60,000 annually. Jackie Robinson, the man who one day would replace Robeson as the most famous black man in America, had already testified against him years earlier to this same committee—an act Robinson would later come to regret. It was Robeson's commitment to black people, both in the United States and around the world, combined with his popularity in Russia and his belief in anti-capitalist economic systems that drew the suspicion of the committee.

"The reason I am here today, you know, from the mouth of the State Department itself is: I should not be allowed to travel because I have struggled for years for the independence of the colonial peoples of Africa," he told the committee. "I stand here struggling for the rights of my people to be full citizens in this country, and they are not. They are not in Mississippi. And they are not in Montgomery, Alabama. And they are not in Washington. They are nowhere, and that is why I am here today."

The committee asked if he was Communist. Robeson invoked his Fifth Amendment rights six times.

Robeson addressed the committee with the recklessness of the condemned. He was, as the kids like to say today, out of fucks to give. He laughed at them, these nine white men who had already made up their minds that he was the enemy of the state. They told him his appearance was not a laughing matter. "It is a laughing matter to me," Robeson said. "This is complete nonsense." They were disdainful of him ("The witness talks very loud when he makes a speech, but when he invokes the Fifth Amendment I cannot hear him."), and he was disdainful back ("I invoked the Fifth Amendment very loudly. You know I am an actor, and I have medals for diction."). The chairman was Francis E. Walter, the Pennsylvania Democrat. "You," Robeson said, "are the author of the bills that are going to keep all kinds of decent people out of the country."

"No," Walter responded. "Only your kind."

Robeson told the committee that while visiting the Soviet Union, he had never faced the type of discrimination he faced in Mississippi, or the type of hostility he now faced from them. The Ohio Republican Gordon Scherer, known for his racism, for being a committee pit bull, threw the old *America, love it or leave it* saw at Robeson, the line so many whites would use over the years to treat black American citizenship as a charity unearned, which they could revoke easily, and at their leisure. "Why," Scherer asked, "do you not stay in Russia?"

"Because my father was a slave, and my people died to build this country, and I'm going to stay right here and have a part of it, just like you," he responded. "And no fascist-minded people like you will drive me from it. Is that clear?"

The combat ended with Walter abruptly adjourning the hearing ("I've endured all of this that I can."), but not before Robeson told the committee, "You are the non-patriots, and you are the un-Americans, and you ought to be ashamed of yourselves."

The following year, Robeson began working on a book about his life and his politics and worldview, to say all the things he was not allowed to say that day in Washington, to reiterate his words that the committee dismissed. The first sentence of the book contained but four words, simple, defiant: "I am a Negro." The year after, in 1958, finally discredited,

McCarthyism waned, and the courts ruled that no American could have his passport revoked without just cause and due process. Robeson had won, but McCarthyism had destroyed him. His name, at least to the white mainstream, no longer carried the same financial cachet or respect. He could no longer make a living as Paul Robeson, the great singer, the great actor, or the former athlete. He was to mainstream America but one thing: a Communist. And for that he lost everything.

The book was titled *Here I Stand*.

THE ABNORMAL NORMAL

A new generation of black athlete awakened by the fatal confrontations between African Americans and law enforcement, accepting of a heritage that began nearly a century ago with Robeson, on its face would have appeared to be a welcome sight. For years, sports journalists and fans had complained the players had become too antiseptic, too distant, and so wealthy the money had turned them vulgar. Did Lou Whitaker of the Detroit Tigers show up to a negotiation during the 1994 strike wearing a fur coat? Yes. Yes, he did. Did Patrick Peterson of the St. Louis Cardinals *really* not cash a bonus check of $15.3 *million* in 2014 because he "hadn't gotten around to it yet"? Also, yes. The players lived the gilded life, too rich to care, and had drifted so far afield of the Heritage that in 1995, the *New York Times Magazine* wondered aloud on its front page, "Does Sports Matter Anymore?"

The 2012 killing of Trayvon Martin and the 2014 Ferguson unrest in the wake of Michael Brown's killing, followed by several high-profile killings of African Americans by police, brought the players, led by LeBron James, out from behind the tinted glass of their Escalades. But the America the activated players returned to was a wounded, post-9/11 America that had responded to the attacks on the World Trade Center with a militarized, authoritarian pageantry. While black athletes demanded through protest that the nation live up to its democratic ideals for its citizens, the sports industry took advantage of the national appetite for police and soldiers, and incorporated it all into its business model. In the years following the September 11 attacks, the toy department became an extension of the war department.

With the opportunistic demagoguery that won him the presidency, Donald Trump engaged in a twenty-first-century version of McCarthyism by demanding that protesters receive the Robeson treatment. "Wouldn't you love to see one of these NFL owners, when somebody disrespects our flag, to say, 'Get that son of a bitch off the field right now? Out. He's fired! Fired!'" Trump infamously said during a September 22, 2017, rally in Huntsville, Alabama. He threatened the NFL owners to blacklist any players who did not comply. "Make them stand," the president would repeat on social media. Within weeks, the NFL began discussing language making it mandatory that players stand for the anthem, a requirement not demanded of most federal employees.

Trump positioned dissenting views as unpatriotic at best, traitorous at worst, to both the United States in general and the country's armed forces in particular. Black players, such as Colin Kaepernick, enjoyed wide support from military members and nationwide black police organizations that were committed to eradicating police brutality, but it didn't matter. Sports, if not completely nonpartisan but famously ambivalent to overt political messages, was sending its own message through its fans, media, broadcast partners, teams, and leagues: The American flag did not represent ideals. It was supposed to be obeyed.

Yet these were the same people who apparently had never heard of the old saying, *You don't wear the flag.* They wore shorts and bikinis in the image of the American flag—flaying open the hypocrisies of a so-called culture war, and the racialized codes of to whom the flag really belongs. When the Houston Astros defeated the Boston Red Sox in the 2017 American League Division Series, right fielder Josh Reddick celebrated by dancing in the middle of the visitor's clubhouse at Fenway Park, doused by teammates in a beer shower—wearing nothing but bikini briefs with the American flag printed across the fabric. "He's got his sweaty balls against an image of the flag," one former major leaguer said, "but kneeling peacefully during the national anthem is disrespectful?"

Yet by advocating that dissent is cause for losing one's career, the sports industry and the president of the United States have returned America to Robeson's dark time. And the questions of dissent and patriotism, of race and speech, he faced then are the same the black athlete is fighting now. We have been here before. In a time of flag and flyovers, camouflage jerseys and a president calling his citizens un-American, authoritarianism as patriotism has become the abnormal normal.

BACK TO THE BEGINNING

The result is collision. Black athletes are now awake and find themselves in a fight for their voice against a president who demands their obedience, threatens their livelihood, reminds them that even the ones who think they have "made it," haven't. The president is emboldened by a post-9/11 sports industry that has commercialized nationalism through owners who now benefit by politicizing sports and fans who wear their replica jerseys and demand spectacular athletic performances—and political silence. During one contentious meeting between NFL owners and players, in which players admonished several owners for giving millions to Donald Trump's presidential campaign, NFL Players Association executive director DeMaurice Smith told NFL commissioner Roger Goodell, "You've hung our players out to dry on this, and it's inconsistent with our business model. Our business model is to make sure that America loves our players. This just happens to be OK with you politically."

In response, today's players wrestle with where they fit, feted with multimillion-dollar salaries, hamstrung by corporate entanglements—and by a public that expects the money to buy athletes fast cars and silence. Looming over them, when police kill innocent citizens and white nationalism becomes reaccepted, is the legacy of Robeson, Robinson, and the lesser-known members of that heritage who gave sports its special historical currency—and the expectation to speak out.

Robeson's entertainment career and activism during the Cold War overshadowed his football roots, so he has never received proper appreciation for his place alongside Muhammad Ali, John Carlos, Curt Flood, Tommie Smith, and other black athletes historically celebrated for taking a stand. But he is part of a national and Pan-African legacy with deep roots. By risking his enormous fame and wealth to advocate for improving the black condition, Robeson lost his money but gained his people. When it comes to the Heritage, Robeson was its charter member and first casualty.

Even as the civil rights and Black Power movements eventually vindicated his positions and made his roots within the American black and

Pan-African communities stronger, mainstream America shunned Paul Robeson. This pattern continues to repeat itself, emblematic today with Colin Kaepernick, who has discovered in a new century the suffocating weight of the power of absorbing the phenomenon of white revenge and emerging more relevant, more important, more influential.

What followed was the ongoing struggle over the meaning of patriotism: of who gets to be a patriot, of who gets to speak, of when black athletes are allowed to use their *voice*—especially in a time when the very word *patriotism* is being politicized, commercialized, and racialized in a time of questionable hero narratives and endless war. At least twice per game and three times on Sunday home games—during the national anthem, in the middle of the third inning, and during the singing of "God Bless America" in the middle of the seventh—the Washington Nationals ask fans to acknowledge the military and honor America.

It is a militarized time, one of kneeling and blacklisting, of patriotism and heroes, some real, many more contrived. For a nation willing to conflate patriotism with authoritarianism and unsure if its athletes are truly heirs to the Heritage or just like sporting provocative T-shirts for the cameras, it is also a time of *authenticity*, of figuring out just who we are. Sixty years after Robeson's electric defiance of McCarthyism, the Heritage found itself back where it started: at the center of a divided America, fighting battles the country wanted to desperately believe had already been won. The omnipresent racial and class divisions and creeping authoritarianism embedded within sporting events in post-9/11 America would collide with the most powerful black employees in the country recognizing their political power and showing a willingness to use it. Through the great unifier of sports, with the black players kneeling, the white players standing, the police heroes to one, center of protest to others, America would discover explosively and definitively just how severe its fractures truly were.

PART ONE

RISE AND FALL

1

STICK TO SPORTS

> I really don't care about boxing. Boxing is a stepping-stone
> just to introduce me to the audience. If I was still in Lou-
> isville, Kentucky, and never was a boxer, I might get killed
> next week in some type of little freedom struggle that you'd
> never read in the news. Now, if I even say the wrong thing, it
> makes news. So, boxing is just to introduce me to the strug-
> gle. When I speak, I draw people in the States to teach my
> people . . . to give them dignity, pride, and self-help.
>
> —MUHAMMAD ALI, 1971

LOOK AT THE UGLY FACES, twisted but not betrayed. The betrayed face
contains a hint of hurt, that layer of justified anger that makes you stop
and feel a little compassion. This is not that. These are the faces of rage.

They don't get it. Well, that part isn't *exactly* true. They get *some* of
it. They get half of it, *their* half, the half that convinces them they've always been the good guys, and when you're the good guys, then there *is*
no other half. When they look down from their seats at the football field,
they get the enormous American flag unfurled across the field bigger than
Rhode Island. They get the color guard, faces stoic, grimly professional,
the immaculate Navy uniforms, with the porcelain-white gloves holding
the massive flag. And the soldiers? They always get the soldiers.

"They" are typical American sports fans in general and paying customers in particular at Qualcomm Stadium in San Diego before the
Chargers play the San Francisco 49ers in a meaningless preseason game
on September 1, 2016. "They" are the fans who die a little when a receiver drops a pass, in part because it may have cost their fantasy team, or

maybe it turned a good call to the bookies into a bad one *from* the book-ies. They're the ones with the curious relationship to the golden youths on the field, whom they at once idolize and can't stand for making all those goddamned millions money *for playing a kid's game.* (That the own-ers make all those goddamned *billions* from that same kid's game, well, that's another story.) When things go sideways, they fume at the players ("*I* coulda made that play!"). Through all the wins and losses, wings, tail-gates and fantasy drafts, they resent the players. They resent the money, the fame, the seemingly easy life. Underneath the anger at the key fum-ble or joy at the last-second touchdown is the root of the resentment, so often racially tinged, toward the black players from the underprivileged backgrounds performing for the predominantly white ticket buyers. It's coded in the language of sports, this player "doesn't play the game the right way," while that one is "undisciplined." The words are repeated by the machine of fans, coaches, and, especially, by talk radio, creating the filter through which the majority-black sports of basketball and football are viewed. According to Barrett Sports Media, eighteen of the twenty sports-radio shows in the country were hosted by white men.

Yet for all the resentment, fans are quick to bathe in the hero worship, to tell the guys at work they met Von Miller at baggage claim. Thirty years past puberty, they're the ones in the stands wearing the size 52 Ju-nior Seau jersey. It's complicated.

The fans who can afford season tickets are predominantly white, and on this day and on virtually every day during the National Football League's 2016–2017 season, their faces are contorted into spit-cannons all pointed in the direction of the biracial, kneeling San Francisco quarter-back, Colin Kaepernick.

The half with the police singing the national anthem and the soldiers, that part they get. This other half, Kaepernick's half, the half that grew exhausted of video after dashcam video of unarmed African Americans being shot by police, the crumpled, defeated faces of families after expect-ing justice but receiving another jury acquittal of police, the inconceivable reality to these fans that for millions of people, police are not their friends or even positive elements of a community; that's the part they don't get. Two reasons especially stand out: the first is that they don't want to. They came to see football. They paid out huge dollars for sacks and intercep-tions, beer and bratwurst. They came to see twenty-two guys crash into each other, not Kaepernick or his teammates kneeling during the national anthem. To them, politics is irrelevant, or so they think. They don't care about Greenpeace, black lives mattering, or the teach-ins for the youth Kaepernick donates his money to. And they certainly don't care about the catchy name the mainstream now uses to describe the players' sudden rediscovery of a social conscience: *athlete activism*. They are here for one reason: to be entertained. The players may earn a hundred times more in salary, but the fans are the leisure class.

The second reason for fans' attitude is that they don't see the ubiquitous deference to the military—the camouflage-printed baseball caps, the police officers, or the fifty-foot American flag in the middle of a football field—as *politics* at all. Even though much of the escalation of the on-field military spectacle has taken place with two wars ongoing, since the September 11 attacks, the military-cop nexus in sports has rarely been framed as a political response to perhaps the worst day in modern American history. *Political* is a word describing something fans don't like, like that Sunday after Thanksgiving, when after a loss to the Miami Dolphins, Kaepernick wore a T-shirt of Malcolm X and Fidel Castro to his post-game press conference, two days after Castro died. *In Miami.* Now *that*, the fans surely understood, and it inflamed them, evidenced by a sign in the window in front of Cowboy Bill's Salsa Loca, a Key West sports bar on Duval Street that refused to let Kaepernick's face grace the flat screen, even in a game against the playoff-bound home team, the Dolphins.

To my valued customers,

Due to Colin Kaepernick's total disrespect for this countries [*sic*] national anthem, I will not televise a single game the 49ers play in. Sorry for the inconvenience [*sic*].

Thx,
Bill

Political, fans think, describes an individual act of dissidence, not a collective one perpetrated against the public by the state, the mainstream media or your local sports team. Kaepernick walking off the field after beating the Rams, raising a fist in the air, the "Power to the People" salute of the Black Panthers, as he entered the tunnel to the locker room?

Political. The Los Angeles Dodgers hosting "Law Enforcement Appreciation Night" in the scarred city of Rodney King and O. J. Simpson during a time of high racial tension between minority communities and the police? Not so much. John Skipper, the former president of ESPN, once hosted a focus group of Trump voters in New York with the Republican political consultant Frank Luntz. "They were quite clear that the flag, football, veterans, and the national anthem was not politics," Skipper said. "They were also clear they did not want politics in their sports, but they did make a distinction that was a little artificial that politics didn't include the flag or the military. That wasn't politics. That was patriotism."

After the Chargers preseason game, Colin Kaepernick received a phone call from Carmelo Anthony, at the time the star forward for the New York Knicks, who congratulated him on his stance. Anthony was undergoing a similar political awakening in the wake of the 2015 death of Freddie Gray at the hands of police in his hometown of Baltimore, but Kaepernick had been the most effective at coupling the anger and frustration over the lack of police accountability in the streets to the fundamental American ideals of justice and fairness by challenging the country's most powerful symbol—the flag. Soon, Kaepernick was on the cover of *Time* magazine, kneeling in his red 49ers uniform, the background completely black, a metaphor for his isolation. He now symbolized a movement.

Anthony told him he was "courageous." He also cautioned Kaepernick that an isolated gesture would nullify his message and quite possibly do more harm than good. The communities that needed his leadership would expect this protest to be just the beginning. Now that Kaepernick had walked through the door, he couldn't stop. "If this is just a one-time thing," Anthony says he told Kaepernick, "you're fucked."

Kaepernick was not vague or reckless in his indictments. He said he had no conflict with veterans or the military, ostensibly the honorees of the national anthem and the patriotic ritual at ballgames. While cultivating a response to the police, he spoke with Nate Boyer, the former long-snapper for the Seattle Seahawks who was also a Green Beret. Kaepernick told Boyer that he wanted to make a public stand against police killings but also wanted to be respectful of the military. Boyer suggested quietly taking a knee during the national anthem.

Kaepernick also consulted with Dr. Harry Edwards, the legendary sociologist and activist who organized the iconic Olympic protest in 1968 that culminated with Tommie Smith and John Carlos raising their fists, black gloves high in the thin Mexico City air, on the medal stand. "For me, I just got to a point where I wasn't concerned about myself or what would happen in my future," Kaepernick said. "I got to the point where I knew this was the right thing to do. I knew I had to stand up for people who aren't being treated fairly, and I felt strongly enough about that to be willing to take that risk."

It was the gesture that directed the country's attention toward the police and a justice system completely unwilling to convict officers whose use of deadly force seemed to be the first and only option in confrontations with African American citizens. "I am not going to stand up to show pride in a flag for a country that oppresses black people and people of color," Kaepernick said, before adding, "There are bodies in the street and people getting paid leave and getting away with murder." Kaepernick did not advertise his protest. He knelt far behind his teammates, inconspicuously behind the coolers of Gatorade—and he'd done it for three games before anyone even noticed.

WIDE AWAKE IN AMERICA

The angry faces at the Chargers' stadium wanted to know just who the hell Kaepernick thought he was challenging their comfort, even while they celebrated the life of Muhammad Ali, who died three months before the start of Kaepernick's protest. ESPN covered Ali's funeral procession and service with eleven consecutive hours of live coverage. The tone was perfect, respectful of the remarkable life of the great champion who had, in the sports world, become a virtual head of state. Celebrating Ali was easy. The mainstream—media, fans, players—could roast all the old chestnuts that made it feel good about itself. It could talk about *progress* and *courage* and *how far we've come*. It could talk about Ali because it believed his grievances were in the past.

Ali was also safe. He had been older and infirm. For more than three decades, he had suffered from Parkinson's disease, which had robbed the great man of a wit and tongue so quick that only his hands were faster—maybe. He was a sympathetic figure. He couldn't even talk and hadn't taken a controversial public position since before most fans in those coveted age demographics were born. Mom and Dad, Grandma and Grandpa may have wanted Ali to do all five of the years in prison he was sentenced for refusing to serve in Vietnam back in 1967, but they'd lost that battle. In the new America, Ali was a vindicated symbol of peace to two generations of white America who saw themselves on his eventually victorious side. His indictment wasn't an indictment of them, per se, but of a history long ago, at a harmless remove, where the villains were someone else's parents and grandparents. The issues, too, belonged if not to the same US government and culture Kaepernick was challenging, then to another time detached from theirs. There was no reason *not* to celebrate Ali. That movie was over; everyone already knew who the hero would be and wanted to see the hero in themselves.

In 2013, Legendary Pictures released *42*, the Jackie Robinson biopic that offered a similar dynamic. The film highlighted Robinson's gallantry against an almost cartoonish racism that had once been the majority norm, and white, mainstream audiences across America identified with Jackie, laughing at the absurdity of the hatred and accepted racism he faced without connecting their bloodlines—their favorite cousins, uncles, and beloved grandparents, all of them—to the ones doing the taunting on the screen before them. The white audience was the progeny not of the film's hero, but its villains. Detachment, however, was a convenient, special dance, a privilege of power and a dangerous (for black people) example of white escapism. It was a phenomenon Elif Batuman captured in her novel *The Idiot*:

> I found myself remembering the day in kindergarten when the teachers showed us *Dumbo*, and I realized for the first time that all the kids in the class, even the bullies, rooted for Dumbo, *against* Dumbo's tormentors. Invariably they laughed and cheered, both when Dumbo succeeded and when bad things happened to his enemies. But they're *you*, I thought to myself. How did they not know? They didn't know. It was astounding, an astounding truth. *Everyone thought they were Dumbo.*

Kaepernick wasn't so easy. He wasn't a piece of history. His grievances weren't theory or grainy footage whose violence could be attributed to a previous generation. They were happening. *They were you.* Fifteen days after Kaepernick began his protest, Tulsa police officer Betty Shelby shot and killed Terence Crutcher, an unarmed black man, during a traffic stop.

Crutcher's hands were in the air. Shelby said she believed Crutcher was reaching into his car. Carmelo Anthony watched the video on his phone and said, "That's an execution." That all the messy pieces of his protest couldn't be foisted off on dead ancestors and strangers meant Kaepernick was indicting the present, and sports journalism, never known for an abundance of courage or independence, reached a similar consensus to the fans': shut up and play.

KNIGHTS OF THE KEYBOARD

And here they came, a parade of outraged voices that had previously never taken an interest in the concerns of the black community, had never written a word about police brutality, excessive force, or jury trials of indicted officers. Apart from employing the typical "dead or jail if not for sports" narrative seemingly reserved solely for black athletes, media took virtually no interest in the black athlete after the buzzer sounded.

So where did the talkers, honkers, and scribblers turn when Colin Kaepernick knelt? They talked to each other about what was important to them. And what was important to them wasn't the incident of April 4, 2015 (which just happened to be the forty-seventh anniversary of Martin Luther King Jr.'s assassination), when Walter Scott, an unarmed black man, was shot in the back and killed by Officer Michael Slager in North Charleston, South Carolina, following a traffic stop for a malfunctioning brake light. Nor did they turn to the November 23, 2014, video of police gunning down twelve-year-old Tamir Rice for holding a toy gun. What was important to them was the flag.

The punditry relied on the old saws, first by offering the platitude that Kaepernick as an American had a right to speak, then demanding that he shut his mouth. They attacked his salary, a particularly galling tactic that represented more racial coding, that players shouldn't just shut up and play because fans were not interested in their politics but also because these rich, black players had *made it*, and *making it* meant forfeiture of voice. They no longer had the right to speak about grievance because they now had money. Fans viewed players as ingrates insufficiently appreciative to the public for their good fortune.

Successful black people had been there before. "From an early age I had come to accept and follow a certain protective tactic of Negro life in

America, and I did not fully break with the pattern until many years later," Paul Robeson wrote in *Here I Stand*. "Always show that you are *grateful*. (Even if what you have gained has been wrested from unwilling powers, be sure to be grateful lest 'they' take it all away). Above all, *do nothing to give them cause to fear you*."

Money was the American lifeblood. Ronald Reagan and Arnold Schwarzenegger both won the governorship of California by being rich and famous. Sonny Bono, Clint Eastwood, Bill Bradley, Jim Bunning, Kevin Johnson, Dave Bing, and a host of others traded their celebrity for politics. The billionaire Michael Bloomberg was elected mayor of New York by having a lot of money. Money and fame made people listen to you. Nobody listened to poor people. By 2016, money could even win you the presidency. Rich black ballplayers needed to be quiet. They had made it. Stick to sports.

"I guess no one bothered to tell the guy who went 2-for-6 for 14 yards that the country he's protesting has had an African-American as its publicly elected president the last eight years," *Houston Chronicle* columnist Brian T. Smith wrote. "America allows Kaepernick to make a base salary of $11.9 million by sitting on the bench and failing to deliver on his athletic promise. The safety our flag provides also gives Kaepernick the right to defy it. The freedom so many have died for and will continue to sacrifice their lives for—the America Kaepernick so ignorantly takes for granted—allows him to be an idiot in the USA."

The television and radio commentator Doug Gottlieb did the same, tweeting out, "$61 million guaranteed . . . very oppressed. #Colinkaepernick." The *Houston Chronicle*'s Smith then attacked Kaepernick's decline from Super Bowl quarterback to reserve. It was an old ploy used by old white men of yesterday and the new white men of today. "When it was said (and it was said many times) that Paul Robeson had shown himself to be ungrateful to the good white folks who had given him wealth and fame, and that he had nothing to complain about," Robeson wrote, "the statement was bound to rub Negroes the wrong way. They know that nothing is ever 'given' to us, and they know that human dignity cannot be measured in dollars and cents."

Using money or diminished performance to silence an athlete is an old trick, but Smith was so far out of his depth, so without professional gift, that he simply sounded mad, a just-another-guy at a keyboard. He resembled an unlicensed dentist extracting the wrong tooth. "That's the thing about sports media, and all media, really," said ESPN host Bomani Jones. "Your simple desire to discuss something does not mean you have the qualifications to do so."

Smith and Gottlieb were in lockstep with a frothing mainstream machine whose sentiments underscored both the resentment toward the rising voice of the black athlete's political sentiment and the post-9/11 attitude that dissent, regardless of the subject, was disrespectful to the armed forces. "The commentariat paid tribute to Ali with one hand and slapped Kap with the other," Dave Zirin of the *Nation* said. During the first three quarters of the 2016–2017 NFL season, so many pundits advertised their ignorance and incuriosity that they were indecipherable from one another. They mourned Ali (even though he, too, was rich and famous when he refused induction into the army) yet could not comprehend the growing unrest in their own time that would prompt Kaepernick to feel compelled to take a political position, even though a year earlier, the US Department of Justice published *Federal Reports on Police Killings*, a disturbing, 585-page book detailing the routine manner in which police departments across the country violate the rights of citizens.

Many black people, fans, and even some players didn't get it either. Despite the YouTube videos of police shootings, the viral Twitter posts of young people blocking the freeways, the acquittals of officers caught killing suspects on video that left families stunned once again, they could not consider one basic possibility: Kaepernick's motives were authentic. They believed that he was engineering some kind of elaborate charade to get out of his massive six-year, $114 million contract—while keeping the money. The thinking went, he knew he couldn't play anymore, so he needed an outrageous public position that would force the 49ers to cut him and allow him to save face. Recovering from three surgeries, he had already lost his starting job to a nobody former-first-round bust named Blaine Gabbert, so clearly he was being insubordinate as a way to simultaneously disrupt the 49ers, show displeasure at being made a backup, and force his release. Ali hadn't been buried six months, and yet the sports machine could not envision an athlete taking a stand based on principle.

That left only a one-lane highway, full of nonstop debate about the American flag, patriotism, and "the right way" to protest. All the white guys who had been in the game for decades and never offered a peep of insight on race relations or public support for a black teammate on a single issue of any social significance were suddenly tripping over themselves to see who could sound the most patriotic. This was in line with a sports world that had embraced jingoism in the aftermath of the September 11 terrorist attacks but was unequipped to deal with complexity at home. It was easy to throw the word *patriotism* around but not quite so easy to tell just who the heroes really were.

"I cannot say it in the strongest, most direct way, that it's an embarrassment and it's about as disrespectful as any athlete has ever been," said Boomer Esiason, an NFL lifer who as a player and game-day commentator for CBS had never in his life said a memorable word on any of the issues of Kaepernick's protest, who now took it upon himself to be the prominent voice in the pile-on. Esiason used his massive reach working for CBS and the New York radio giant WFAN to crush Kaepernick.

"And I don't care what the cause is!" Esiason thundered. "The NFL football field is not a place for somebody to further their political ambitions."* Esiason even challenged Kaepernick to do a ride-along with police so he could become more informed about the heroism of those wearing "that blue uniform" who made "$35,000 or $40,000 a year, as opposed to the $11 million he's making."

Since Esiason knew and cared so much, where was he, for example, on September 27, 1994, when two days earlier he was sacked twice as quarterback of the New York Jets in a 19-7 loss to Chicago? That day, there was this kid, Nicholas Heyward Jr., who, having celebrated his thirteenth birthday a month earlier, did what thirteen-years-olds do and played cops and robbers with two other friends at the Gowanus Houses in Brooklyn, Heyward racing around, laughing and joking, carrying his brown toy guy with the plastic orange tip pointed in the air. Heyward bounded down a stairwell, where twenty-three-year-old policeman Brian George was making his rounds for the Housing Authority. George turned, saw Heyward, and fired, shooting the boy through the stomach, killing him.

---

*Since sports was not a place to further one's political ambitions, the New York Jets owner Woody Johnson should have had much explaining to do after accepting an ambassadorship to the United Kingdom in the Trump administration. Esiason said nothing about Johnson's appointment. The outrage must have cooled.

Another one who knew nothing about black people but had much to say was John Tortorella, the loudmouth coach of the National Hockey League's Columbus Blue Jackets, where he did not have to deal with even a moderate number of powerful African American athletes, never mind an entire industry of black players, like, say, the National Basketball Association, with its guaranteed contracts and players with far more power than most coaches. In discussing Kaepernick, Tortorella played the tough guy, the Good American, pandering to the fans who wanted their players to be grateful. Tortorella then threatened his players: any of his players on the US World Cup team who didn't stand for the national anthem would be benched.

"If I was ever involved in a situation where someone is trying to make a point, and they have a perfect right to do that, but to disrespect our flag and anthem, as I said yesterday, they would not play," Tortorella told ESPN's Linda Cohn. "If that ever happened, there's no question, it's just not right. And it's not black, white, blue, red. It has nothing to do with the politics of all of this. It's just not right. This is our country. Our people are fighting for our country, our flag, and our anthem. That shouldn't come into this equation at all. There are other ways of doing things."

Then, there was Tony La Russa, the former Major League Baseball manager, who had nothing to say but couldn't help but get into the act anyway. La Russa found himself talking to *Sports Illustrated* as an authority on patriotism, by way of Kaepernick. "I think that's disrespectful, and I really question the sincerity of somebody like Kaepernick," he said. "I remember when he was on top. I never heard him talk about anything but himself. Now all of a sudden he's struggling for attention and he makes this big pitch. I don't buy it. And even if he was sincere, there are other ways to show your concern. Disrespecting our flag is not the way to do it."

The message being sent by the Esiasons, Tortorellas, and La Russas, each a white player or coach with no stake in the issues that motivated Kaepernick yet were asked their opinion anyway, was shut up and play, and it was a message that largely resonated with the ticket buyers and the talk-radio honkers, who did not make up the demographic for whom police brutality was actually a personal issue. It was a charade of platitudes to democracy, the old lines of "You can speak out, but there are other ways to protest," which naturally was shorthand for the white mainstream still making the rules, of telling the players what they could do and when they could do it, which naturally defeated the entire purpose of protest. Protest didn't ask permission.

The authority figures demonstrated another privilege: the privilege of never being the target of the kind of abuse that drove Kaepernick and thousands of young people into the streets blocking traffic. Boomer Esiason and Tony La Russa weren't the ones getting their asses kicked. They had the luxury of being able to critique others and felt they should determine what time was the right time and which method of protest was the proper one. Protest was *just a topic* for them, something to be debated but never lived. So the talkers talked, as did the athletes who had never had anything to say but now felt emboldened to volunteer opinions that never addressed the forces that were contributing to the nation's simmering tensions. The media's responses to Kaepernick exposed its role in shaping how the public would view Kaepernick's protest.

Something else was happening in plain sight: America's racial framework was being exposed through sports, the one place that was supposed to be a meritocracy. The players were expected to perform, and just as the black Americans toiling without million-dollar contracts were expected to work, they weren't supposed to challenge or dispute the world in which they lived either. The white majority, whether the fans in the stands or in the break room, or behind the laptops and microphones or in front of the cameras, would decide what could be discussed and how. While this was hardly a revelation in the real world, it was supposed to be different in sports because there, status and salary ostensibly bought the players a freedom the rank-and-file workers never had. Like the military, sports was also supposed to be the place where race was secondary to the battle effort, and for years, sports had profited from the gauzy little lie that teammates battled together, understood each other, lived in such close proximity that maybe the rest of the country could learn from the game's *brotherhood*. What Kaepernick revealed was that sports was no less divided along racial lines than the rest of the country, even if its workforce comprised a black majority. The only difference was, the players were black millionaires.

During the 2016–2017 season, Kaepernick would weekly turn his chest into a bumper sticker, wearing designer T-shirts to troll his critics without speaking. Sometimes the T-shirts showed the faces of famous black leaders, like Malcolm X. Sometimes the T-shirts contained only phrases, like "I Know My Rights." One week, after the latest parade of experts was done telling him about the drawbacks of his actions, Kaepernick was spotted wearing a T-shirt that read

WE MARCH,
Y'all mad.
WE SIT DOWN,
Y'all mad.
WE SPEAK UP,
Y'all mad.
WE DIE,
Y'all silent.

And yet, despite the noise from Esiason and Tortorella and La Russa during the preseason of protest, when the national anthem played on the first weekend of the 2016 regular season, Colin Kaepernick took a knee and—*he wasn't alone.* Kaepernick's San Francisco teammates Eric Reid and Eli Harold, Kenny Britt of the Los Angeles Rams (whose activism during the Ferguson protests when the team played in St. Louis preceded Kaepernick's), Kenny Stills of the Miami Dolphins, and several other NFL players also knelt during the national anthem. It created a powerful visual for television. White US Soccer star Megan Rapinoe joined the protest during the playing of the anthem in a match against the Netherlands. In addition to Carmelo Anthony, two other NBA stars, LeBron James and Chris Paul, voiced support for Kaepernick.

Team owners scrambled behind the scenes, concerned that Kaepernick was not only starting a movement but could overshadow the September 14 schedule of games, when the NFL had planned special ceremonies for the fifteenth anniversary of the September 11 attacks. Jerry Jones, owner of the Dallas Cowboys, ordered his players to have their hands on their hearts during the national anthem. The Kansas City Chiefs sent out a press release on September 11 that read like a negotiated agreement:

STATEMENT FROM KANSAS CITY CHIEFS PLAYERS REGARDING TODAY'S REPRESENTATION DURING THE NATIONAL ANTHEM
After having a number of thoughtful discussions as a group regarding our representation during the National Anthem, we decided collectively

to lock arms as a sign of solidarity. It was our goal to be unified as a team and to be respectful of everyone's opinions, and the remembrance of 9/11. It's our job as professional athletes to make a positive impact on our communities and to be proactive when change is needed. Together we are going to continue to have conversations, educate ourselves and others on social issues and work with local law enforcement officials and leaders to make an impact on the Kansas City community.

Ownership had obviously gotten to the players.

Pregame, an American flag as large as the football field was held aloft by local law enforcement, but Chiefs Pro Bowl cornerback Marcus Peters, not quite on the team's public relations spinning team, wore a black glove on his right hand, and when the national anthem began, shot his fist straight into the air.

HIDING IN PLAIN SIGHT, OR SOMETHING LIKE THAT

While the media machine accused Kaepernick of staging a publicity stunt without action behind it, he organized a Know Your Rights Camp for youngsters in Oakland, a daylong workshop on healthy eating habits, how to deal with potential confrontations with local police, and how to be financially responsible. It was an adaptation of the Black Panther Party for Self-Defense's blueprint in the 1960s, which held similar seminars for people of color and which also originated in Oakland. Kaepernick wasn't throwing money at a problem from the comfortable remove of being rich but was showing his face in poor communities, as a member of a league whose players were often better known off the field for their luxurious lifestyles or arrest records.

And among the fans and media, there the issue sat, an elephant in America's living room. Where there was Boomer ("And I don't care what the issue is.") Esiason wearing blinders to Kaepernick's rationale, there was also Bart Scott, the black former Baltimore Ravens and New York Jets linebacker who happened to work alongside Esiason at CBS, on the same set in studio during games.

"I'm in support of anybody who has convictions to believe in something and willing to pay the price and take the lumps and take the hits, and the backlash that's coming from it," Scott said. "I think the death of

Muhammad Ali has stirred the pot. It has moved the needle to where athletes are becoming socially conscious. They're not concerned about the bottom line. They're not concerned with their dollars. They understand that they have a voice and [they're] almost ashamed of how they used their voice in the last twenty years since Jim Brown, Lew Alcindor, Muhammad Ali stepped up for social change. Now guys are ashamed and I think they're going to try to do something about it."

The fault lines of the divided America were all on full display. Two dozen black athletes protesting police brutality on the field, black commentators, whether ex-player or journalists, understanding and supporting not only the protest but the reason behind it. In the WNBA, the Minnesota Lynx connected as a team, defying its league's order when the women wore "Black Lives Matter" T-shirts during warm-ups, showing direct and unequivocal support for Kaepernick's political stand. With far more financial stability at risk (the WNBA paid its players an average salary of $60,000 per season while the average NBA salary was just under $6 million), the women nevertheless connected with their black teammates on an issue that required solidarity, sympathy, and action in a way the NBA players, for all the tough talk about "brotherhood" and "us against the world," never did.

Meanwhile, the white members of the sports world (with the exception of three NBA head coaches—Stan van Gundy, Steve Kerr, and Gregg Popovich—and a couple of football players, namely Chris Long of the Philadelphia Eagles) were either unsupportive or completely silent. The sports industry had laid bare the country's racial divisions, but the "dialogue" the punditry said was so desperately needed was never pursued. Instead, the mainstream media detoured from a discussion on police misconduct to showing the images it was actively selling to the public on game day: patriotism, the police, and the military.

It wasn't as if the players were ever going to get a fair hearing from the Big Media platforms anyway. The networks were business partners with the leagues, not the players. In 2011, the NFL signed an eleven-year contract extension with its broadcast partners that saw ESPN, Fox, NBC, and CBS pay the league a combined $3 billion to broadcast games. According to Forbes, that number was more than a 60 percent increase. That same year, ESPN signed an eight-year, $15 billion extension with the league that paid the NFL $1.9 billion annually. Forbes reported that the NFL also received $1 billion annually from the satellite television provider DirecTV for its exclusive rights to the NFL Sunday Ticket, which allowed consumers to turn their living rooms into a sports bar and watch games from every market.

No wonder Boomer Esiason so expertly regurgitated the talking points. It's why he was there. Since 9/11, professional sports and the NFL in particular sold patriotism to the public, but only patriotism of a particular kind. It sold the idea of a childlike obedience to symbols without giving much thought to their meaning. Through its mighty broadcast partners and massive commentary reach into America's computers and living rooms, sports, ostensibly the American pastime and our great unifier, and sports media were actively complicit in pitting protest against its armed forces and what it meant to be an American. Invariably, that division existed along the racial and class lines that have always defined sports—white owners, white coaches, white media, white season-ticket buyers, black players—but were conveniently ignored in favor of myth.

And it wasn't as if the punditry or the leagues could not find voices that understood and supported the protest elements embedded within the definition of patriotism. After Kaepernick began his protest, in the summer of 2016, a group calling itself Veterans for Kaepernick took to social media with an open letter to the NFL that was signed by more than two dozen veterans of the Iraq and Afghanistan Wars. "Far from disrespecting our troops, there is no finer form of appreciation for our sacrifice than for Americans to enthusiastically exercise their freedom of speech," the group wrote. "Far too often, people of color are dying at the hands of law enforcement personnel in the streets, our jails, and their homes. Indictments are rare and convictions are essentially nonexistent."

But most fans found it hard to view veterans as pro-First Amendment soldiers. Troops provided the perfect wedge between the players and the public. The soldiers were portrayed as selfless defenders of American freedom, the players as moneyed and selfish people who forgot where they came from and didn't know how good they had it. The troops also provided the perfect wedge between the players and owners, who could now turn the public against any protesting player by negatively comparing him to the men in uniform, the real heroes. Even though the truth was that the soldiers and the players likely had more in common with one another: both were generally from poorer communities and sought a better life in

America through their bodies. The players' access to education and riches came through their superior athletic ability, while the soldiers' access to higher education through the GI Bill came from offering their lives to the military. These calculations were never discussed on broadcast television. If the players were stereotyped for profit by the Big Media machine and the leisure class that tailgated every Sunday, so too were the soldiers.

"People can't seem to accept that protest is patriotic. And this obsession with the flag—I didn't serve twenty years in the military for the flag. I served for my friends, family, and country, and to myself, to be honest," said William Astore, an Air Force veteran and military historian. "I was honored to serve. I did so to uphold the Constitution, which grants us a protected right to protest."

Meanwhile, NBA commissioner Adam Silver saw disaster. A few Kaepernicks kneeling on Sunday was one thing. A league whose players were 80 percent black and kneeling *every night* in protest of American policing was something else, something potentially catastrophic for a league that had worked hard to escape the Larry Bird-Magic Johnson-Michael Jordan era of the late 1970s and 1980s when nobody wanted the league, when the NBA finals were so low-rated the networks ran championship games on tape delay, after the eleven o'clock news. The league that was considered too black, too predictable, and too coked-out for mainstream America had made a remarkable transition, and in the coming decades, fans embraced the game. So, with the airwaves talking only about patriotism and not Sandra Bland, a woman who mysteriously died in police custody in Texas after a traffic stop, a nightly show of black players kneeling during "The Star-Spangled Banner" threatened to lose the public the NBA had spent thirty-five years cultivating. Silver negotiated with the NBA players' union executive director Michele Roberts, as well as player representatives LeBron James and Chris Paul, to urge players to temper their political demonstrations in exchange for a promise from Silver to not further restrict their identities.

Why did the women seem to stick together better? Billie Jean King answered this for me years ago when I was interviewing her for the HBO documentary *Billie Jean King: Portrait of a Pioneer*. Recalled former tennis pro and broadcaster Mary Carillo: "I took her back to the meeting she held at the Gloucester Hotel in London with dozens of other women players—the meeting that formed the WTA [Women's Tennis Association] and forged the way for all of us who came after her. Billie was pushing to create the Women's Tennis Association, damn the ITF [International Tennis Federation] and everyone else, knowing that in doing so the women would likely be banned from all the majors and criticized heavily for wanting 'even more' than they had.

"Some in the room were wary," Carillo said. "One of them said to her, 'If we do this we could lose everything.' Billie won the room, won the fight, with this: 'We have *nothing*. Don't you see that? We have *nothing to lose*.' And all these years later, women athletes are still feeling the same things. They are marginalized, mistreated, misunderstood. Their only chance is to stick together for what they believe in."

Dialogue sounded like a nice goal, but what came from the Big Boys in the media establishment was a sledgehammer. When the soccer player Megan Rapinoe knelt in solidarity with black people and Kaepernick, her alliance was blindsided by black ESPN commentator Michael Wilbon, who essentially called her a tourist. "Rapinoe?" Wilbon snorted. "What was she going to do? What was she backing, what was she saying, what was she sacrificing? What was she giving herself over to? Just sort of being able to take a knee and have people watch her? . . . People thought what she did was incredibly distasteful. So now we're at the part where we have a lot of posing." Meanwhile, Rapinoe's league, US Soccer, attempted to silence her protest by playing the national anthem *before* the players took the field.

Though high-profile figures seemed dubious of his intentions, Kaepernick pledged $1 million of his salary to social justice agencies across the country. He continued to hold workshops and meetings with Bay Area community organizations dedicated to grassroots organizing, and he donated his sneaker collection, worth thousands, to homeless shelters in San Francisco. When he spoke of the black communities oppressed by a justice system imbalanced against them, he showed his face, going to where the people were, into the community, instead of just writing a check and hanging out behind the velvet rope—checkbook activism. Still, the Big Media machine did its part, waiting for him to stumble, salivating for the chance to call him a hypocrite, which would confirm that he was the fraud they always believed him to be. Nearing the end of the 2016 presidential campaign, Kaepernick gave it to them. Or, at least they thought he did.

A TRAP FOR FOOLS

All voting is a sort of gaming, like chequers or backgammon, with a slight moral tinge to it, a playing with right and wrong, with moral questions; and betting naturally accompanies it. The character of the voters is not staked. I cast my vote perchance, as I think right; but I am not vitally concerned that that right should prevail. I am willing to leave it to the majority. Its obligation, therefore, never exceeds that of expediency. Even voting for the right is doing nothing for it. It is only expressing to men feebly your desire that it should prevail. A wise man will not leave the right to the mercy of chance, nor wish it to prevail through the power of the majority.

—HENRY DAVID THOREAU, "Civil Disobedience," 1849

The date was September 27, 2016, the day after the first presidential debate between Hillary Clinton and Donald Trump. The 49ers had completed practice at their complex in Santa Clara, and the writers gathered around Colin Kaepernick's locker. Kaepernick told reporters that he watched "a little bit" of the debate but was hardly impressed by either Clinton or Trump.

"It was embarrassing to watch that these are our two candidates," Kaepernick told the scrum around his locker. "Both are proven liars and it almost seems like they're trying to debate who's less racist. And at this point . . . you have to pick the lesser of two evils. But in the end, it's still evil."

After the election, Kaepernick dropped an atom bomb on reporters: he hadn't voted. The papers dug a little deeper, and it turned out that Kaepernick not only wasn't registered to vote in 2016 but had *never* been registered to vote. Ever.

"You know, I think it would be hypocritical of me to vote," Kaepernick said. "I said from the beginning I was against oppression, I was against the system of oppression. I'm not going to show support for that system. And to me, the oppressor isn't going to allow you to vote your way out of your oppression."

San Francisco Chronicle columnist Ann Killion felt that by not voting, Kaepernick "lost a lot of support" from people who were genuinely sympathetic to his cause, especially because several ballot measures in California—from a repeal of the death penalty to gun control to education funding—affected the communities for whom Kaepernick was fighting.

ESPN's Stephen A. Smith, who supported Kaepernick's right to protest, found his reveal unforgivable. "I thought it was egregious to the highest order," Smith said, adding that Kaepernick was a "flaming hypocrite." And George Skelton of the *Los Angeles Times* was obviously not in the mood for the theories of Thoreau:

> What really fries me, however, is that Kaepernick—the supposed committed idealist—didn't bother to vote Nov. 8. In fact, he didn't even get off his butt to register to vote. He never has anywhere he lived, the Sacramento Bee reported last week. So Kaepernick is the classic hypocrite. And a bad role model. He hasn't been connecting the dots between griping and voting to fix what he's griping about. Yes, he has a constitutional right to refuse to stand during the anthem. Yes, he has a right to say a pox on politics and not vote. But no, he doesn't have a moral right to both disrespect the country and not exercise his fundamental birthright—and duty—to help change it.

And this is where the high-minded, frothy outrage, the talk of hypocrites and voting supposedly being the most important act a citizen owns sounded great in theory but, in the real world, was just another lazy talking point to discredit dissent the punditry could not handle. According to the US Elections Project, 94.2 million eligible voters—42 percent—did not vote in what was considered to be one of the most important elections in years, proof that Kaepernick wasn't a hypocrite but that something had gone terribly wrong with our democracy. For his age group, the percentage of those not voting shot to 50.

Further, approximately 147 million voters—or 65 percent of the electorate—lived in "non-battleground states whose electoral votes were pre-ordained." Kaepernick, a Californian, would have been one of them. In 2012, 52.9 percent of television ad spending was allocated by both parties in Florida, Ohio, and Virginia. The remaining 47.1 percent covered *all* the other forty-seven states. In 2016, Florida, North Carolina, Ohio, and Pennsylvania received more ad spending than the other forty-six states combined. Since the 2000 election, each presidential campaign has hinged upon essentially four states: Ohio, Virginia, Florida, and North Carolina, and in the 2016 presidential election, $1.7 billion of outside money was raised by Super PACs. Yet the sports world concluded that

Kaepernick was a hypocrite for not voting in a country whose entire political system had been overrun and corrupted by money. There was no room to discuss the disaffected American voter or the place of politics or the money, not in the world of the sports machine.

Maybe it was all too much to ask that an industry that bathed in the cliché of "taking it one game at a time" be expected to analyze political trends and parse analytics, whether the topic was patriotism and dissent or the values and flaws of the electoral college. Maybe most of the writers were in over their heads. ESPN's Bomani Jones was not.

"He thinks the system is busted, therefore dropping a ballot within that system isn't going to be something that is going to change anything," Jones said. "So, he's adopted a different take, and the idea that he is disqualified because he didn't vote is a lazy outlook to me because it doesn't even bother to take a moment to appreciate where it is that he is coming from. Rather than 'Why did you not vote?' it was 'How dare you not vote.' Maybe it's the economist in me, but the individual vote does not sway anything, and that's the paradox of voting. It's actually more costly to the individual than the payoff you'll ultimately receive."

Kaepernick had exposed the sports world's collective limitations in scope, curiosity, and critical thinking. He also had the giants of the philosophical canon on his side. Some of the greatest theorists took the position that the true dissident should not participate in the voting process. "In any case," wrote the French philosopher and Nobel Prize winner Jean-Paul Sartre in his 1973 essay "Elections: A Trap for Fools," "the revolution will be drowned in the ballot boxes—which is not surprising, since they were made for that purpose."

Like Thoreau before him, Sartre concluded that the true dissident surrenders his power to the state by participating in the political ritual that has created the very conditions for his dissidence. When Thoreau says, "Voting *for the right* is *doing* nothing for it," he is saying that voting is the most passive of acts, the very *least a person could do*. More important were the actions Kaepernick had begun to undertake through community programs, putting his hands in the soil, organizing workshops, donating money. Sartre concurred with Thoreau:

> Why am I going to vote? Because I have been persuaded that the only political act in my life consists of depositing my ballot in the box once

every four years? But that is the very opposite of an act. I am only revealing my powerlessness and obeying the power of a party. Furthermore, the value of my vote varies according to whether I obey one party or another. For this reason the majority of the future Assembly will be based solely on a coalition, and the decisions it makes will be compromises which will in no way reflect the desires expressed by my vote.

Kaepernick could have made different choices. He could have voted. He chose not to. Yet by merely voting, other people were deemed more competent, more responsible, more engaged, more committed to the democracy just because they stuffed a ballot box and for the next four years did nothing else. In the land of systematic gerrymandering, the influence of the oil mogul Koch brothers, and Super PACs, whose billions secretly controlled state, local, and national political races and left would-be voters resigned that voting didn't matter, Big Sports Media reached a different verdict: Colin Kaepernick was the problem.

THE BLIND SQUIRREL

Maybe it really was all a big con. Maybe Kaepernick really was just another spoiled athlete, too rich to care, someone who got lucky and found himself swept up in the zeitgeist. Maybe he closed his eyes, swung hard as he could, and, as they say in baseball when a slap hitter goes yard, "ran into one"—right into Thoreau and Sartre and MLK and all the other Big Thinkers with the Big Ideas about dissidence and civil disobedience. Maybe Kaepernick revealed, however unintentionally, that the high-minded talk of voting or not voting meant nothing compared to the billion-dollar power of the Koch brothers. Maybe all he was really trying to do, as Kaepernick's most dismissive critics in San Francisco suggested, was impress his girlfriend, Nessa Diab. Maybe his intentions were initially good and then he discovered that he was in over his head and, as Carmelo Anthony cautioned, couldn't turn back.

Nothing in Kaepernick's actions during 2016, however, suggested any of this to be true. Instead, something else was happening: Kaepernick saw the killing and was moved by injustice, and the simple act of standing up to it scared the hell out of the white mainstream, its fans, its jock pundits, and compromised talkers, who were more comfortable with celebrating dead martyrs than dealing with live issues. Kaepernick exposed other black athletes to be so far removed from their roots as political figures that they had forgotten their inheritance. In his landmark book *Forty Million Dollar Slaves*, Bill Rhoden referred to the African American athlete as suffering from "the loss of mission." It was Colin Kaepernick who began to return them home.

2

THE GOOD AMERICANS

> We are adamant: we intend to use every means at our dis-
> posal to smash segregation and discrimination wherever it
> appears. We are staring into the face of our oppressors and
> demanding by what right of skin coloration do they consider
> themselves our superiors. . . . We clearly understand that the
> falsehoods about our supposed inferiority have taken deep
> root in the minds of white Americans. These lies are now
> being exposed for what they are. They must be destroyed.
>
> —JACKIE ROBINSON, 1964

BLACK PLAYERS, POLITICS, AND patriotism have *always* been linked.
Fans telling Colin Kaepernick to stick to sports was their way of saying
they didn't want their fun and games interrupted by the real world, but
black athletes never knew such a luxury. That Kaepernick could pierce
the American psyche so deeply underscored how long it had been since
athletes had spoken on anything important. Two generations of fans had
gotten comfortable with the ballplayer as touchdown maker and sneaker
salesman.

The more revealing question was why the Heritage was so important
in the first place. For the other races and for the immigrants, access to the
America story came through education and the entrepreneurial spirit, yet
the most well-known black people were famed for running the fast break.
How did the athlete become the most influential and important black
employee of the twentieth century?

Black people were no different than all the rest. African Americans
sought education, but America did not want the black brain. It wanted

the black body. As segregation tightened, Booker T. Washington, W. E. B. Du Bois, Anna Julia Cooper, Frederick Douglass, and other notable members of the black intelligentsia set out to prove that they had brain power equal to whites' and should be accorded full citizenship in their own country. Wendell Thomas Cunningham, the son of a slave and the first black man to graduate from Harvard Business School, in 1915, found after his graduation what they all found: impenetrable segregation once he left Harvard Yard. The rest, whether it was the Talented Tenth or an existence separate as the fingers of one hand, was just a question of navigation.

The insistence on racial segregation was the one ideology where Know-Nothings and Whigs, Democrats and Republicans, Unionists and Confederates could meet and agree. Even history's good guys believed it. Abraham Lincoln, who split with the Whigs to form the Republican Party in the mid-1850s, believed African Americans deserved the right not to live in bondage ("No man," Lincoln said in 1854, "is good enough to govern another man, *without that other's consent.*"), and the sentiment sounded great. It was the piece of Lincoln, the visionary Lincoln, that would survive the longest. It was the reason why the man could be dead for 150 years and still new books on him appeared like perennials. It was why so many black people of a certain generation across America often had photos of two white men in their house: Lincoln and John F. Kennedy. Lincoln personally praised the writings of Frederick Douglass, honored his intellect, befriended him, eventually met with him in the White House, and during the war years finally accepted Douglass's proposal that blacks be allowed to become Union soldiers to prove their loyalty to the United States and their mettle as enlisted fighting men, that didn't mean Lincoln believed they were entitled to the same aspirations of the white man. Consider Lincoln's speech from the 1858 senatorial campaign against Stephen A. Douglas, five years before Emancipation:

> I am not nor ever have been in favor of bringing about in any way the social and political equality of the white and black races. I am not nor have ever been in favor of making voters or jurors of Negroes, nor of qualifying them to hold office, nor intermarry with white people. . . . There is a physical difference between the white and black races which I believe will forever forbid the two races living together on terms of social and political equality.

Despising the institution of slavery while simultaneously despising the slave was a common attitude among abolitionists. Without slavery as an institution, abolitionist allies transposed into whites who believed in the inferiority of African Americans, a sentiment that intensified during Reconstruction. In response, the mission of black leadership in the years when the country distanced itself from Reconstruction aimed to prove the worthiness and upward potential of the people—to, in effect, prove Lincoln wrong. The black thinkers and the writers, the black doctors and the lawyers, were out there, all wanting to "become" American and gain respect through their brilliance. Du Bois dubbed this group the "Talented Tenth," or the top 10 percent of all black people in America who he estimated could become esteemed leaders.

The other 90 percent who used their hands, minds, and hearts to fight were there, too, proof that from Douglass's time to the present, the black soldier was willing to spill his blood to prove his patriotism for a country that did not want him, like the Harlem Hellfighters, the black army unit that fought under the French flag in World War I because American whites wouldn't fight side by side with them. "So here we are, just a hundred years ago, with an African American regiment fighting in French uniform," said Russel Honoré, the retired three-star army lieutenant general best known for his leadership and coordinating efforts in the wake of Hurricane Katrina. "And when they returned from the war and were downloading at Hell's Kitchen in New York, some whites saw them with medals on, indicating they'd been front-line troops, and they said, 'What are you all doing with those medals?' And the African American troops said, 'We were fighting in the war.' They said, 'No, you weren't.'"

Within days of each other in 1902, many states in the Deep South imposed segregation of public facilities, including streetcars. The Ku Klux Klan, whose numbers had dropped after its initial appearance during Reconstruction, resumed its infiltration of local, state, and national politics and law enforcement. Even the Yellow Pages were segregated. The accomplishments of African Americans existed largely within the black world. Douglass was once the most famous black man in the country, but black brilliance was not often mainstream brilliance. The writer and philosopher Alain Locke, the country's first black Rhodes Scholar, Harvard- and Oxford-educated, was considered the "father of the Harlem Renaissance." Locke was also something else: the scholar who could scarcely find work and who ultimately became a legendary educator at Howard University, the center of black higher education. Locke was a superior thinker in his world, but most white people at the time had no idea who he was, and to later generations, he was not taught alongside prominent white educators.

James Weldon Johnson was one of the first black US diplomats and another towering figure of the Harlem Renaissance. He had been appointed by President Theodore Roosevelt to serve as consul to Nicaragua and Venezuela. Johnson was also a novelist and songwriter who penned "Lift Ev'ry Voice and Sing," also known as the Negro national anthem. Yet, like Locke, for all of his fame in the black world, Johnson's successes did not translate to even a softening of rigid segregation and racist attitudes.

Even the sunburst of the arts was tinged as a shadowy place. The great writers and visual artists of the Harlem Renaissance lived in a certain type of limbo between respect and inferiority. The same was true for musicians, even though jazz was a black creation. Duke Ellington ruled the jazz world, headlining the famed Cotton Club, which was situated in the middle of Harlem but did not admit black patrons. Few jazz bands during the period were integrated. And plays performed during the Harlem Renaissance period were being recognized as valuable but not yet considered on par with whites'; good enough to be enjoyed, but not good enough to share the bookshelf or the stage with whites or be included in the pantheon. When H. L. Mencken said as much in a critique of black artistic contribution, Du Bois countered in a 1927 article in the *Crisis*:

> In music, Harry Dett has given the Negro spiritual another form and Harry Burleigh has done more than reproduce it. W. C. Handy is father of the "Blues." Coleridge-Taylor, if we may be permitted a journey overseas, stands manifestly the great creative artist with his "Bamboula" and "Take Nabandji"; and there is Roland Hayes—is he not an artist? There may, of course, be differing opinions about Negro poets, but in our opinion Paul Laurence Dunbar, Claude McKay, Countee Cullen and Langston Hughes stand far above "second rate." . . . On the whole then, despite a stimulating critic's opinion, we Negroes are quite well satisfied with our "Renaissance." And we have not yet finished.

The soldiers were just a bit less American—if they were black. The scholars were not quite scholarly enough to share the same canon with whites—if they were black. The Great Depression crushed the financial future of the Harlem Renaissance, denial of black employment in mainstream America grew more deeply entrenched, and the Du Bois vision for the black brain faded. With opportunities walled off by segregation, there would be no proving Lincoln wrong by producing generations of black professionals, and the black body, as it had been during slavery, continued to be the primary black currency. Unlike with slavery, however, the currency of the black body in the 1930s would be spent on sports, entertainment, and the military.

There was, however, one major problem: the foundation of segregation lay in the diminishing of the black contribution, and black fitness to join the mainstream on equal footing in sports was no different. "It is important to understand that in the melting pot theory, the question of what ethnic ingredients were being added to the brew of American civilization was as important as the capacity of the mixture to absorb those ingredients," wrote the historian G. Edward White in his history of the early roots of baseball. "The case of blacks demonstrated those dual preoccupations. Early twentieth-century stereotypes of black Americans treated them only as assimilable into mainstream American civilization in a limited fashion: as an underclass of dependent or despised persons."

The Negro Leagues, formed in 1920, would become one of the most successful predominantly black-owned businesses in America, and many of the white players who played against the great black players of the league knew the best black players could compete with white major leaguers. Thus, merit could not be used by organized baseball to justify segregation. A different, more debilitating measure was required: blacks were unsavory, inherently unfit, regardless of equal or superior ability. It was the Lincoln logic of 1856. White continued:

> When the Negro Leagues had come within the consciousness of those with Organized Baseball, they had been seen as a reverse mirror image. If Organized Baseball was free from gambling and corruption, the Negro Leagues were run by gamblers. If Organized Baseball was structured around the permanent franchise cities and regular schedules, the Negro Leagues were a kaleidoscope of changing franchises and

whimsical scheduling. If Organized Baseball was a clean, wholesome, upwardly mobile sport, Negro League games were the scenes of rowdy, disorderly, vulgar behavior. By being the opposite of Organized Baseball's idealized image, the Negro Leagues served as their own justification for the exclusion of blacks from the major leagues. They appeared to demonstrate just how "contaminated" major league baseball would become if blacks were allowed to play it.

This view of "contamination" was a universal attitude sold to the white mainstream, which bought it because it reinforced their existing worldview that segregation existed not because whites were unwilling to open society to African Americans but because blacks were too inferior for the invitation to succeed.

Once integration arrived in baseball, in 1947, the black brains of the Negro Leagues—its owners, trainers, managers, coaches, and executives—were excluded from the Major Leagues. Integration didn't come from proving Lincoln wrong, that blacks could be just as competent in the operating room as whites, but from the indefensible position that Jackie Robinson could play baseball for ten months with whites, even if he couldn't buy a house next to one of his white teammates.

So, though the black body entered the mainstream through sports, the black brain had to wait, even in sports. Robinson had already been retired and voted into the Hall of Fame when baseball hired its first black coach, Buck O'Neil of the Cubs—fifteen years after Robinson was signed. And Jackie had been dead two years when Cleveland hired Frank Robinson to be the first black manager in the game and a full *ten* when San Francisco hired Robinson to be the first black manager in the National League. What remained of value was the black body. Once Robinson arrived, the greatest influx of talent the game had ever seen followed: Robinson, Roy Campanella, Willie Mays, Henry Aaron, Ernie Banks, and Roberto Clemente. They and other elite athletes would immediately do what neither those in the Harlem Renaissance nor those coming through the classroom could: become the first fully mainstreamed black employees in the country.

Integrating team sports was the greatest threat to segregation. It was one thing to integrate individual sports such as track and field and boxing, where the combatants competed against one another. But sports, in which black and white players would travel together, room together, shower together, compete, have physical contact with one another, and live as a *team* was something altogether different. Team sports foreshadowed an integrated society, for if blacks and whites could live together during six weeks of spring training and six months of the baseball season, why not side by side in the classroom, the foxhole, or on Main Street? "We sent the Harlem Hellfighters to France to fight with General Pershing," Russel Honoré said. "And when they got there, the Congress of the United States said, 'Don't let them fight,' because if you do, they knew they'd want to come back and have social justice."

If blacks and whites could play as a team, or fight side by side with whites against the Nazis, segregation would eventually collapse. But when US society began to open, black advancement did not come through the sciences or the English department. Nor was it through the unions, where the white immigrant underclass began climbing out of poverty into the middle class through the trades. Nor was it in police and fire departments, or even the military, which allowed whites to leapfrog into the middle class through the GI Bill, which for years wasn't offered to black veterans. It was the black body, its willingness to be killed in battle for America and its ability to run really fast, that propelled African Americans into the American household.

THE GOOD AMERICAN

Nazi Germany grew tired of hearing America moralize about concepts of "good" and "evil," and reminded America, through newspaper articles and rhetoric, that for all the talk, the Land of the Free wouldn't let white and black people drink out of the same water fountain. So, when America needed its national ideals defended, it didn't *want to stick to sports*. It demanded the black athlete. Even before Jesse Owens stood down Adolf Hitler's white supremacy by dominating the 1936 Berlin Olympics, Owens had been asked by American Jews and the Communist newspaper the *Daily Worker* to consider boycotting the games in solidarity against Nazism on the grounds that Jews were suffering in Germany under the similarly legal and extralegal methods used to subjugate blacks in America. Owens refused. In order to claim a favorable contrast with Nazism, America needed Owens to be a spokesman on the black social condition. Owens would run for the United States and be an ambassador for its virtues.

America wasn't perfect, he would say, but at least it allowed the possibility of a meritocracy, especially through sports. "The Nazis often point out that American Negroes are victims of discrimination, but Negroes are not barred from our Olympic teams," wrote syndicated columnist Westbrook Pegler in the *Washington Post* in the summer of 1936. "Many of them have worn the American shield in the past, and some of the most formidable athletes on this year's squad are colored."

The black intelligentsia knew better, not easily swayed by claims of integration. Trotting out Du Bois as an example of the progress and goodness of America certainly was not going to work. Langston Hughes, the poet laureate of the Harlem Renaissance, was also free of the illusion and responded with something too true, too withering. A month before the 1936 summer games began, *Esquire* published his poem "Let America Be America Again" in which Hughes wrote that the immigrant—and by extension African Americans—found out that America gave you only the "same old stupid plan," that "of dog eat dog, of mighty crush weak."

Unlike the poet, the athlete was used to being managed. Athletes' schedules, meets, games, matches, and training regimens were set for them. They were also at a cultural disadvantage, for sports allowed athletes to compete and represent their country in a positive way, even though Owens couldn't eat in most restaurants in his home state of Alabama.

The excellence of Owens made America look good. "The Nazis face a delicate problem in the track and field events where the Hitler youth will doubtless be defeated by a group of Negro boys," Pegler wrote.

During World War II, when America was not quite the good guy as advertised, it turned to the emerging black athlete to rescue it, this time the boxing champ Joe Louis. Louis volunteered for the army, though he did not fight. He got the cushy ballplayer treatment Joe DiMaggio received; no combat, just touring to keep up morale for the boys on the bases. Maybe a lucky GI might even get to spar a couple of rounds with the champ, but Louis would not be a Warren Spahn or Ted Williams or Bob Feller, athletes who enlisted in the service and actually saw combat. Nearly a hundred years after Robert Gould Shaw's famed black regiment, the Fifty-Fourth Massachusetts Infantry, were martyred at Fort Wagner, the American military was still segregated, and many black enlistees were given menial responsibilities instead of being allowed to fight. More often than not, they were going to do their part with pots and pans, not rifles.

But there he was, Joe Louis, the Good American, the muscular, formidable world champ selling an image to potential recruits that couldn't have been more fictitious: Louis featured in an iconic army recruiting poster carrying a rifle, bayonet pointing forward with the caption "We're going to do our part . . . and we'll win because we're on God's side."

The poster, too, was reminiscent of Frederick Douglass's appeal to Lincoln eighty years earlier, more proof that black people were willing to die for American values they weren't allowed to share in. The poster was also disingenuous, for once blacks enlisted, they were not being trained to be fighting elite. Randy Roberts's biography of Louis examined the duplicity:

> The poster itself suggested Louis' iconic status. At a time when the government censored, and mainstream newspapers commonly refused to print pictures of black soldiers in uniform, let alone shots of them holding up rifles, Louis' image—in uniform, armed and aggressive— was slapped up on the walls of recruiting stations and government buildings in every section of the country. The tag line as well as his accepted persona had deracialized his image, transforming him into a symbol of patriotism. And not just black patriotism—American patriotism. Under the stress of a national emergency, for a brief period Joe Louis succeeded in erasing the color line.

That was one way to put it. Another way was to say that Louis succeeded in projecting the *idea* that segregation was being erased in favor of a wartime unity where people at long last joined together as Americans. Still another way to put it was that Louis was being used to encourage black enlistees to risk their lives without the return promise of freedom. However put, Louis, like Owens before him, had been positioned to speak about politics through sports.

THE BIRTH OF THE HERITAGE

The roots of the Heritage were not romantic. It did not arise from a black athlete epiphany, a Ferguson moment, nor from the recognition that his value over the black brain gave him a special platform to advocate for black people. Instead, the Heritage began from the responsibility of being the Good American. White America asked black athletes to defend its ideals and Owens and Louis obliged. This defense continued into the postwar era, as tensions rose with the Soviet Union. The black athlete wanted to stick to sports. It was white America that wouldn't let him.

As early as 1937, the Communist Party's *Daily Worker* ran a story quoting the great Satchel Paige saying that organized baseball should be integrated. Far more urgently and consistently than the American mainstream press, it was the *Daily Worker*, specifically its sportswriter Lester Rodney, who continued to press the argument that without integration, America was really no different than the regimes its soldiers were fighting. The Communists were calling America out on its racial hypocrisies. The Russians argued that the United States had a hell of a lot of nerve acting as the world's moral conscience when African Americans and whites often did not have their babies delivered in the same hospitals, and the same athletes honored for winning Olympic medals and lauded for defending American principles couldn't even play sports on the same field with whites within the borders of their own country. The government responded to Communist claims that minority groups in the country were growing impatient not because their basic rights were being denied them but because good, hardworking black communities comfortable with their place had been infiltrated by Communists—and would set out to prove it.

In 1948, the House Un-American Activities Committee (HUAC) held hearings on the Nixon-Mundt bill, which would require members of the Communist Party to register with the government. The bill had a more nefarious name: the Subversive Activities Control Act. The bill, authored by Republican congressmen Richard Nixon of California and Karl Mundt of South Dakota, met serious backlash from American intellectuals from Hollywood to Harvard. McCarthyism had dawned.

In the spring of 1949, Paul Robeson, radical, anti-capitalist, Pan-African, gave a speech at the Paris Peace Conference and dropped a bombshell that in many ways would change American history. If the United States were drawn into a war with the Soviet Union, he said, American blacks should not fight. "Why should the Negroes ever fight against the only nations of the world where racial discrimination is prohibited, and where the people can live freely? Never! I can assure you, they will never fight against either the Soviet Union or the peoples' democracies."

The *New York Times* picked up Robeson's comments. Robeson the Bad Negro had to be parried. Congress needed someone to assure it that despite the lynchings, the segregation, and the injustices that black Americans could still be counted on. So where did it turn? It didn't turn to the black brains. It turned to sports. It turned to Jackie Robinson.

If there was a moment when a romantic narrative of the Heritage could have been woven, it would have been during the spring and summer months of 1949, when Robinson appears and defends Robeson's staunch Pan-Africanism, linking African Americans to the African independence movements that swept the continent in the 1940s. Instead, the opposite occurred.

Robinson arrived with marching orders from HUAC. He was there to discredit Paul Robeson. It was midseason, July 18, 1949, to be exact. Robinson was in his third year in the majors and having his best season when he appeared before the committee to refute Robeson's claim. Jackie Robinson knew better. He didn't want to do it. He may not have agreed with Robeson, but he also knew a trap when he saw it. "I didn't want to fall prey to the white man's game and allow myself to be pitted against another black man," Robinson would later write in his autobiography. "I knew that Robeson was striking out against racial inequality in the way that seemed best to him." Besides, Robinson knew America firsthand. Five years earlier, in the army, he had been on trial for refusing segregated seating on a bus. When he was a teenager, his brother Mack ran with Jesse Owens in Berlin, winning a silver medal in the 200 meters. Mack Robinson made America proud, and when he came home, he got the best job he could find—as a janitor.

Robinson could have demurred, as did many players who came after and said, "I'm an athlete, not a politician," but that would have thrown Robinson's credentials as a patriot into question and exposed both him and the larger black public to the charges that maybe Robeson was right. A century's worth of dying to prove black Americans were as loyal to the United States as any other group may have been jeopardized. *Stick to sports* wasn't an option. So Robinson testified, got political, because that's what his country was asking him to do.

> The white public should start toward real understanding by appreciating that every single Negro who is worth his salt is going to resent any kind of slurs and discrimination because of his race, and he is going to use every bit of intelligence such as he has to stop it. This has got

absolutely nothing to do with what Communists may or may not be trying to do. And white people must realize that the more a Negro hates communism because it opposes democracy, the more he is going to hate any other influence that kills off democracy in this country— and that goes for racial discrimination in the Army, and segregation on trains and buses, and job discrimination because of religious beliefs or color or place of birth.

During his testimony, Robinson was addressed by the Missouri Democrat Morgan Moulder. Finding a prominent black person to denounce another was an old strategy, one that would be employed to great effect over future decades whenever some African American went off script and threatened the mainstream. When addressing Robeson directly, Robinson did exactly what the committee had brought him to Congress to do. He played the Good American.

> MOULDER: Mr. Robinson, this hearing regarding communist infiltration of minority groups is being conducted to give an opportunity to you and others to combat the idea Paul Robeson has given by his statements.
>
> ROBINSON: Thank you, Congressman Moulder, for this opportunity. Paul Robeson's statement in Paris to the effect that American Negroes would refuse to fight in any way against Russia . . . sounds very silly to me. . . . I've got too much invested for my wife and child and myself in the future of this country . . . to throw it away because of a siren song sung in bass.
>
> MOULDER: I think you have rendered a great service to your country and to your people and we are proud of you and congratulate you upon being the great success that you are in this great country of ours.

Robinson's testimony would commence the economic destruction of Paul Robeson, and Jackie Robinson would forever be lauded as an American hero for standing up for America. Robeson would lose his passport and livelihood less than a year later.

Yet, buried inside that testimony, were seeds of the other Jackie Robinson, the fierce Robinson, the radical Robinson who never backed down, the Robinson of the Heritage. While America was busy patting him on the back for crushing the Bad Negro Robeson, Robinson left a clue of how formidable he would be embedded in his testimony:

> And one other thing the American public ought to understand, if we are to make progress in this matter: The fact that it is a Communist who denounces injustice in the courts, police brutality, and lynching when it happens doesn't change the truth of his charges. Just because Communists kick up a big fuss over racial discrimination when it suits their purposes, a lot of people try to pretend that the whole issue is a creation of Communist imagination.
>
> But they are not fooling anyone with this kind of pretense, and talk about "Communists stirring up Negroes to protest" only makes present misunderstanding worse than ever. Negroes were stirred up long before there was a Communist Party, and they'll stay stirred up long after the party has disappeared—unless Jim Crow has disappeared by then as well.

There it was: The black athlete using public testimony, under oath, to denounce police brutality, lynching, and the injustices of the legal system and the Jim Crow laws that America accepted. An athlete telling white America that he didn't turn double plays simply for its enjoyment. Naturally, these were not the comments that received play in the papers the next day, but they were the first indications, on the road to the Heritage, that sticking only to sports was never going to be acceptable. Each piece, from Owens and Louis defending American values to Robeson openly challenging them, and to Robinson doing both, contributed to an expectation that the black athlete take an active role on political issues when asked, and that expectation soon grew into a responsibility. If at first it appeared that the country was getting a steal—prominent black players defending the country as a promising work in progress, even when they knew it was treating them as half a person—Robinson's testimony served notice, that he had also purchased the right to hold his country up to its promise, and he intended to collect. For most white fans, this bargain was only supposed to be one-way, and players were to be quiet until America needed them. On that day in Washington, DC, Robinson announced that it would definitely be two-way. After his testimony, Robinson returned to Brooklyn. That night at Ebbets Field, he hit a triple in a 3–0 win over the Cubs to raise his batting average to .363. The Heritage was officially born.

In the postwar years, sports, often by its very nature, had been positioned in rhetoric as the antidote to American racism by media and popular culture, which understood the hypocrisy of declaring victory over fascism in World War II while practicing segregation in the United States. Sports provided the opportunity to prove that there were no boundaries to one's ability. It was an attractive sell: color, height, background didn't matter. Highest score wins. White America believed it, and in the immediate aftermath of the war, blacks did too. Sports was the arena with reduced racial opposition, growing evidence that the races were coexisting; most importantly, sports had the scoreboard that kept tapping into that American vein of a meritocracy: if your score is higher than mine, you win.

It was also another lie America would tell itself to sleep better at night. On those college campuses, black players were accepted grudgingly, if at all. The Boston Red Sox, New York Yankees, Philadelphia Phillies, and Detroit Tigers stood out as racist teams in a game full of racists. So did the Washington Redskins. The great Jim Brown, a founding member of the Heritage, had a coach at Syracuse University, Ben Schwartzwalder, who refused until he could no longer to have black players. So, too, did those college legends Adolph Rupp and Bear Bryant.

Basketball would soon be a black game, but for years the unwritten codes of the game maintained that three of the five players on court had to be white to maintain the optics of a majority, a rule Red Auerbach broke with the Boston Celtics by playing five black players at once.

Coaches cared only about winning was pabulum repeated ad nauseam in sports, but coaches around the country didn't want a player like Jim Brown or couldn't handle more than two black guys dribbling a basketball on the same team. The meritocracy has been treated like a basic, obvious concept in sports, and yet Auerbach was treated like Abraham Lincoln for having the courage to play his best players. The real American vein wasn't a meritocracy. Sports was just too visceral a place to maintain white hypocrisies. It was one thing to segregate a classroom, quite another to put Bill Russell on a basketball court and argue he wasn't good enough.

A. S. "Doc" Young, the leading columnist for the Chicago *Defender*, the nation's preeminent black newspaper, referred to sports as the "door-breaker to progress [for] Americans of color" and "proof to the world that democracy can work." It was where black people like Jackie Robinson could be told by white congressmen like Morgan Moulder that they were proud of their citizenship, even though Robinson wasn't protected by the full extent of the law. Being an excellent trumpeter like Dizzy Gillespie was not considered a barometer of citizenship, but Joe Louis was a "credit to his race." Some of the geniuses of the Harlem Renaissance may have had trouble finding work, but when America needed to extol its promise, sports would be its bullhorn, and its scoreboard-meritocracy metaphors would be so appealing they would become baked into the language. Eradicating inequality was a concept now literally part of the American language. Society's goal was to *level the playing field.*

THE VERY CENTER OF THE CULTURE

Paul Robeson was the original conscience and soul of the Heritage, but Jackie Robinson became its godfather. For the remainder of his life, Robinson created the obligation of the modern black political athlete both within the framework of team sports and by using his power to challenge other players. Of course, Jackie had been fighting long before baseball, refusing to abide by segregation at Ft. Hood as an army man in 1944, leading to his court-martial. For the schoolbooks, it was Robinson who gifted the legacy of the black athlete as central to the social progress of black people, and generations would love and honor him for that. When Robinson testified to Congress in 1949, Major League Baseball comprised more than four hundred players, only seven of whom were black. In both the 1952 and 1953 World Series, each between the Brooklyn Dodgers and New York Yankees, Robinson criticized the dominant Yankees for being the only one of the three New York baseball teams (including the New York Giants) to have not integrated. Unlike other athletes, Robinson may once have been asked by the public and the politicians to denounce Robeson, but now he was speaking out on a host of social and political issues—and he wasn't asking permission. It was Robinson earlier who had used his influence to integrate the Chase Hotel in St. Louis, which began the integration of hotels across the country, and it was the desire to follow his lead (and not disappoint him) that encouraged other black players to use their voice as Robinson had used his.

The Heritage was also born out of something else: money and opportunity. It was sports where suddenly and almost overwhelmingly, the black labor and employee aspiration was rooted. But music and entertainment weren't far behind. During the 1950s and first years of the 1960s, the entertainers Fats Domino, Chuck Berry, Sammy Davis Jr., Johnny Mathis, Harry Belafonte, John Coltrane, and Miles Davis, were everywhere. The same was true for women. Where there were Ella Fitzgerald and Billie Holiday and Eartha Kitt, there were also Wilma Rudolph and Althea Gibson. The baseball journalist Leonard Koppett credited Robinson with moving the black person from the invisible background of white culture into the foreground, because now Robinson stood side by side with white players in an institution of vast cultural importance. As David Halberstam wrote:

> With the coming of television, professional sports, particularly football and basketball, had a far greater national impact than they had ever had before. What had once happened before relatively small crowds now happened simultaneously in millions of American homes; in effect, it was going from the periphery to the very center of the culture.

It was a phenomenon that accelerated integration, making white America aware of the black cultural presence, but the exposure also had a profound effect on black culture and professional aspiration. If Harriet Tubman, Booker T. Washington, Du Bois, and Douglass were the most visible black faces in the late nineteenth century, a half century later, the black faces in white living rooms were ballplayers (and singers). This sent another message, more chilling, to black kids around the country: as a generation of frustrated black Americans ran into limited opportunity, they saw their path to the American Dream passing not through education but through sports and entertainment. They were not only exciting and glamorous fields but also what the mainstream culture was encouraging black kids to enter into.

It was also the anti-Robinson message. In 1948, a fourteen-year-old Henry Aaron met Jackie Robinson in Aaron's hometown of Mobile, Alabama. Robinson advised the youngster to stay in school. (He didn't.) Finding success in playing professional sports was only slightly less probable than winning the lottery, and steering black kids into thinking they would win it posed devastating consequences, but the payoff was intoxicating.

In 1957, when President Eisenhower sent federal troops to enforce a school desegregation order in Little Rock, Arkansas, the median annual income for a black male in America was $2,069; for a woman, it was $745. The city of Birmingham, Alabama, would not hire its first black police officer for another ten years. Alain Locke, the first black Rhodes Scholar back in 1907, would be the only one for the next fifty-five years, until 1962. Edward Brooke, the first black US senator since Reconstruction, wouldn't be elected until 1966.

Yet Aaron, who never graduated high school and bet on his talent, earned nearly twenty times hitting home runs what the average black man was earning as a twenty-three-year-old, at $35,000 per year with the Milwaukee Braves. In 1956, Jackie Robinson was offered $50,000 to come out of retirement to play for the New York Giants after he was traded by the Dodgers and left baseball.

It was clear the money was in sports. The attention was on sports. The pathway to college for families who lacked the financial resources to send their children to the white universities that were now slowly admitting blacks increasingly ran through sports scholarships. In a culture of legal segregation, sports were seen as the place where African Americans could compete with whites without significant disadvantage, especially when college athletic programs began placing greater emphasis on winning and were willing to relax segregation to recruit prized black talent. Elite athletes became the growing power of the black American workforce, the visible sign of success. Sports seemed to represent the occupation with a real upward trajectory, which was not a compliment, for it ignored the racial obstacles for black people without the talent of Wilt Chamberlain—and what would become of them? All of these factors increased the importance of the black athlete to adopt a voice of influence, to be heard as well as seen. Whether fans accepted it or not, and whether or not they wanted to hear it, Robinson's legacy would be that black athletes were expected to be more than just ballplayers. Robinson called it "first-class citizenship."

Left unspoken was the effect of the black body's rise not simply on the lagging opportunities for the black brain but also the economic effect on the black economy from siphoning off its greatest asset. Integration was great for the black players who knew being a true legend meant competing with white players on the white, mainstream stage. But the departure of Robinson, Mays, Aaron, and Campanella from the black leagues—because baseball would not integrate its front offices with even remotely equal enthusiasm—killed the Negro Leagues. The white universities that would finally integrate college sports with the great black bodies—the Jim Browns and Bill Russells, the Ernie Davises, Wilt Chamberlains, and Lew Alcindors—on the way to becoming a billion-dollar industry, undermined the economic power of the traditionally black colleges, which would have been able to compete with North Carolina and Kansas and UCLA had it maintained its superstar black talent. The commodities—the black players—were taken, but the black brains in sports—the coaches, athletic directors, and executives—were left behind.

There was another difference that elevated sports and separated it from entertainment: the requirement of a political movement in order for entry. Unlike the arts and entertainment, in those days, professional sports was an entity in which white society did not welcome blacks. In 1943, Paul Robeson and a black delegation met with Kenesaw Mountain Landis, the notoriously racist commissioner of Major League Baseball, at the Roosevelt Hotel in New York City. They told Landis that the time had come to integrate.

"The meritocracy is absolutely first, but the other thing is, the only reason you could play professional sports was because there was a movement. That was the *only* reason," civil rights activist Al Sharpton said. "There was always a Nat King Cole or some other entertainer that could always break through. Even when they were not allowed to stay in the hotel, they could get on the stage. They *always* allowed us to entertain them. They *never* allowed us to play pro ball. We could add a Negro League, but we never could [have played] pro ball without that movement. So you owe, because you received."

DON'T RUIN IT

Even into the 1960s, opportunities for the black body far surpassed the open doors for the black mind. When Jackie Robinson wrote the words that began this chapter in his 1964 book *Baseball Has Done It*, black aspirations in the mainstream were limited by the realities of politics (no major city in the United States had yet elected a black mayor), journalism (no major newspaper had yet hired a black columnist, and even though sports was trending toward becoming a predominantly black workforce, virtually no newspapers sent black reporters to travel with the team), law enforcement (the first black chief of police for New York City or Chicago was twenty years away, and in Los Angeles, nearly thirty), and a host of other fields that a white immigrant class would enter to achieve the American Dream. No African American woman had yet graduated from Harvard Business School. Los Angeles would not hire its first black fire chief until 2011. It would be another decade before enrollments at colleges and universities that were not historically black institutions of higher learning would begin to rise.

But for black men, sports was not as promising an employment opportunity as it appeared. Their bodies were valuable, but beyond playing, chances to coach, evaluate personnel, or run or own teams were as remote as they were in the non-sports world. And as for the Heritage, Robinson had created the template of the black political athlete, but it was still a game, and employees were still just ballplayers, with plenty of visibility but not nearly enough security (the million-dollar, guaranteed contract was a decade and a half away), so the tolerance for speaking out about social issues was low. Even during the obvious inequality of the Jim Crow era, the white mainstream was still confounded by the black demand for equality. Some whites admired Robinson. Many more simply admired his playing, and most of the public had forgotten he had done the government the solid of testifying against Robeson and wanted him to shut up about politics and the constant demands of black people (*"What do they want now?"*). This prompted resentment from whites and wariness from the black establishment: pull back; don't rock the boat, lest we risk everything being taken away.

By 1964, Robinson had already been retired nearly a decade. Two years earlier, he had been enshrined in the Baseball Hall of Fame. He was a living legend. Robinson's face was heading for the immortality of an American stamp, with streets and schools, scholarships and highways, to be named after him.

Yet to the young people who were emerging as the activists of the era, Jackie Robinson was a fossil, too old, too establishment to reach anyone under the age of forty. He was their parents' age, and no self-respecting radical listened to his parents. In retirement, though, Robinson was more radical than he'd been as a player, all of which burnished the future legend, but at that time, Robinson was seen as an out-of-step old man. He was a Nixon supporter during the 1960 presidential election and remained a moderate Republican for the rest of his life. Younger blacks thought the times had passed him by, even as Robinson traveled to the Deep South to stand with the civil rights movement, marching side by side with Martin Luther King Jr., registering people to vote, showing his face. Robinson also never quite lived down his role in HUAC's takedown of Paul Robeson, an infamous moment Malcolm X never let him forget in their public war of words. By today's mild standards of dissent, Robinson sounds like Malcolm X, but at the time, Malcolm X referred to Jackie Robinson, who carried America on his shoulders until it broke him, as an Uncle Tom. Robinson already knew what America's African American youth thought of him, and Malcolm was unrelenting in his criticism of Jackie's moderation: "They see me in a suit and tie and they look at my white hair and they're too young to remember what I did, or they don't care. I began to talk and some shouted 'Oreo.' You know, the cookie that's black outside and white underneath."

The Heritage formed because athletes had no choice. Bill Russell, the Boston Celtics great, was often surrounded by people who did not support him or who did so while lacking the courage to join him publicly, or who simply found him unnecessarily distant, overly sensitive to *the way things are*. They felt this even though they did not have to live with his indignities, like the time vandals broke into his home in Reading, Massachusetts, and not only ransacked his property but left feces in his bed and smeared on the walls of his house. Bill Russell, the greatest champion in American team sports history, came home to the place where he had won all those championships, and while the white mainstream was telling him to stop being so moody, someone broke into the man's house and *took a shit in his bed*.

Curt Flood found dealing with the white world was like learning a foreign language: there were the rules of the language and then the unwritten rules that became custom to the native speakers, impossible to know for everyone else. Flood had to learn the game, the secrets to the foreign language. In the minor leagues, he wore Jackie Robinson's number 42. When he got to the big leagues, hoping to be half the man Jackie was, he selected 21. In 1962, his fifth year in the majors, he accompanied Robinson to Mississippi for several civil rights demonstrations. He saw firsthand how deference to power, whether calculated or not, undermined whatever collective strength ballplayers might have, and when he was traded in 1969, he realized that for all the money players made, when it came to power, they had none. Deference only worked if you were one of the chosen ones, a realization Flood came to after sharing the St. Louis Cardinals clubhouse for eight years with one of the all-time greats, Stan Musial:

> Stan was one of the outstanding players of all time. He was so exceptionally talented, popular and durable that he played for twenty-one seasons, amassed substantial wealth and became a member of the Cardinal management. As an authentic superstar, he lived remote from the difficulties encountered by lesser athletes. Like [Willie] Mays, he saw the world entirely in terms of his own good fortune. He was convinced that it was the best of all possible worlds. He not only accepted baseball mythology but propounded it. Whereas the typical player all but choked while reciting the traditional gibberish of the industry, and whereas Bob Gibson, superstar of another hue, would simply change the subject, Musial was a true believer. Gibson and I once clocked eight "wunnerfuls" in a Musial speech that could not have been longer than a hundred words.
>
> "My biggest thrill is just wearing this major-league uniform," Stan used to say. "It's wunnerful being here with all these wunnerful fellas."
>
> On such occasions, Gibson would hang his head in embarrassment and mutter "Shitfuckpiss." We admired Musial as an athlete. We liked him as a man. There was no conscious harm in him. He was just unfathomably naïve. After twenty years of baseball, his critical faculties were those of a schoolboy. After twenty years, he was still wagging his tail for the front office, not because he felt it politic to do so, but because he believed every word he spoke.

At Speed City, the nickname of San Jose State University and its powerful track program, the young sociology graduate student Harry Edwards envisioned a complete boycott by black athletes of the 1968 Mexico City games for the purpose of drawing attention to black inequalities in America and also, as Paul Robeson had, to the Pan-African struggle. "Black" wasn't just African American, but Ghanaian and Ethiopian, Cuban and Dominican and Haitian, encompassing the independence movements that had swept across Africa and the Caribbean in the two decades following World War II. America had stripped Ali of the heavyweight title because he refused to be inducted into the army, an issue directly affecting college students who feared being drafted and fighting a war that lacked credibility. The inclusion of South Africa to the Olympics activated athletes, including Lew Alcindor, the best college basketball player in the country. Tommie Smith, Lee Evans, and John Carlos were track and field stars who grew in conscience. "The word of the day was boycott and anyone who was either a black athlete or sympathetic to the cause of black athletes was well-versed in the arguments on both sides," Carlos said. "And it was clear you couldn't be a bystander in this struggle. Black, white or brown, we needed to know which side you were on."

The white mainstream reaction was confounded, hostile, wounded. On July 15, 1968, *Newsweek* put Smith on its cover, with the headline "The Angry Black Athlete." Two years earlier, when Jim Brown quit football, *Time* magazine ran a picture of him in fatigues, on the set of *The Dirty Dozen*, the World War II movie Brown was filming. Instead of comparing Brown to an American soldier, the magazine compared him to Che Guevara, the murdered Cuban revolutionary. Brent Musburger, who would go on to have a legendary broadcasting career despite harboring racist attitudes toward the very players he glamorized every weekend, would refer to Smith and Carlos as "two dark-skinned storm troopers." Alcindor, who had already converted to Islam by 1968 but did not officially change his name to Kareem Abdul-Jabbar until 1972, supported Edwards's idea of a total boycott as the most effective way for black athletes to express the level of their discontent with black conditions. On July 20, 1968, he appeared on *Today* with Joe Garagiola, the former big-league catcher. Alcindor, the best college basketball player in America, did not try out for the Olympic team. Garagiola asked him why.

ALCINDOR: Yeah, I live here, but it's not really my country.
GARAGIOLA: Well, there's only one solution: maybe you
    should move.
ALCINDOR: Well, you see, that would be fine with me, you know;
    it all depends on where we are going to move.

Jesse Owens, who came home from the 1936 Olympics a hero, found all those promises of the Olympics to be an illusion and *still* denounced

Edwards and the boycott, fearing that athletes who pushed too fast, too hard would compel the powers that be to take away athletics as an opportunity for black people, closing the one door that had opened faster than the rest—all for a strategy that in Owens's mind couldn't work. *Don't ruin it.*

To the older black generation, the only way to gain rights was through the benevolence of whites, to lift the race by winning white respect through good behavior, otherwise known as "respectability politics," which reinforced their patriotism and ownership of the land to be as strong and as deserved as white citizens'. Even Paul Robeson maintained the position that the blood of his ancestors made him an American. But the new black protest position did not ask for partnership: that had been tried and had failed. "It's not our country," Ali would often say. It was time to fight, an attitude famously captured by activist Stokely Carmichael ("All the scared niggers are dead"). So much of the battle was generational and tactical, age-old issues of strategy that had been part of the struggle for decades, and the old guard responded uncharitably to its new revolutionaries, to the very heritage it had begun. John Carlos, connected to Robeson's Pan-Africanism, was convinced the boycott was "the perfect tactic" and saw the attitudes carried by Owens as out of touch, unaware that now was the time to act. Wrote Carlos:

> You had a lot of the elder African American "statesmen" and mainstream civil rights leaders hating this kind of plan. You had the older athletes, like Jesse Owens, shocked that we would even consider such a thing. You also had young Caucasian individuals like the rowers from Harvard University lending us some serious support. The movement had gained steam because in February 1968 the president of the IOC [International Olympic Committee], Avery Brundage, the man who delivered the 1936 Olympics to Hitler's Germany, readmitted apartheid South Africa to the Olympic community—as if that racist state had somehow reformed. It gave us focus, energy and a very clear demand to put on the table: if South Africa was in, we were out.

THE FIGHTERS FIGHT

The old guard may have been cautious, but two men in particular understood what the young people were doing and approved. The first was

Martin Luther King Jr., who, according to Carlos, personally put Edwards, then twenty-six years old, in charge of the boycott. Edwards was already the boycott's author, but there could be nothing greater than being anointed its leader by Dr. King himself. King confirmed their vision, their wildest ambitions. "He said that our strongest leverage was that an Olympic boycott could have a global reach. We could shock the world and we could do it by also adhering to the principles of nonviolence that he held so dear," Carlos said. "We could bring attention to the problems of society, but we did not have to throw a rock or burn a building in order to do so."

The second to offer support was that white-haired, unhip "Oreo," Jackie Robinson, still in the fight after twenty years despite—or because of—his profound disillusionment with the pace of civil rights. It was Robinson who stood in complete, if not fatalistic, support. Robinson, the patriot, the veteran, the black conservative Uncle Tom, had become so cynical that he no longer stood for the flag. "I know very well this is not going to work," he said. "However, I have to admire these youngsters. I feel we've got to use whatever means, except violence, we can to get our rights in this country. When, for 300 years, Negroes have been denied equal opportunity, some attention must be focused on it."

Alcindor stayed true to his word and did not play in the 1968 Games, but the black boycott never materialized. Smith won the 200-meter race and before the medal ceremony, he improvised, determined to see some portion of the vision through. Now was the time. He pulled out two black gloves, one for him, one for Carlos, who had won the bronze. The white, Australian silver medalist, Peter Norman, wanted to wear a glove in solidarity, but Smith only had one pair. As the American national anthem played, Smith and Carlos drove their gloved fists into the air. The gesture didn't have the seismic effect of a total black boycott, but the two athletes had made history. As the world watched, and Jesse Owens, once a hero and an important member of the Heritage, referred to the black gloves as "false props," Smith recalled the specific purpose of each of their gestures: "My raised right hand stood for the power in black America. Carlos's raised left hand stood for the unity of black America. Together they formed an arch of unity and power. The black scarf around my neck stood for black pride. The black socks with no shoes stood for black poverty in racist America. The totality of our effort was the regaining of black dignity."

Even though his short time as a professional athlete in favor of an entertainment career decoupled him in some ways from its lineage, Paul Robeson had poured the foundation. Jackie Robinson shaped it, and a heritage followed. Henry Aaron fought for integrated spring-training housing in Florida with the Milwaukee Braves and integrated seating at Fulton County Stadium when the Braves moved to Atlanta in 1966. In 1960, pitcher Jim "Mudcat" Grant once left the ballpark in protest after absorbing racial slurs from one of his teammates. In baseball, the Heritage did not only refer to black players being provocative on political issues but, thanks to the Robinson legacy, it also created a tradition of black players connecting as a brotherhood in sports, supporting each other in a game each knew only accepted them reluctantly. After Robinson, other black veteran players would mentor the younger ones, on the same and even opposing teams. When a black player would come to Atlanta, it was Henry Aaron's responsibility to reach out, Ernie Banks's in Chicago, Richie Allen's in Philadelphia, Willie Mays's in San Francisco, Jim "Junior" Gilliam's in Los Angeles, and so on. Black players on opposing teams shared information about cities, which ones were hostile or more welcoming to blacks, which schools and neighborhoods were preferable, which managers and players were rednecks and which would give them a fair shake. And it was generational. At second base with the Dodgers, Jackie Robinson gave way to Junior Gilliam, and when the time came for a young Davey Lopes to enter the system, it was Junior Gilliam who took him under his wing, drove him around the city, showed him the game. "You have no idea what that meant to a young player," Lopes said. "Invaluable. That's the game."

And there was another unspoken compact that, since 1947, has rarely been discussed and rarely violated: African Americans on opposing teams did not fight each other on the diamond, even in the case of bench-clearing brawls. Take the Dodgers and Giants and their infamous brawl of 1965, when Giants pitcher Juan Marichal hit Los Angeles catcher Johnny Roseboro in the head with a bat, fracturing his skull. It was Willie Mays, the black Giants centerfielder who carried Roseboro, the black Dodgers catcher, off the field.

The Robinson influence on the baseball traditions of the Heritage led to a tightly knit network of African American players that would span generations, both leagues, and the entire country. "We had to take care of each other," Dusty Baker said. "There weren't that many of us. You knew the game didn't always want you. You had to pass on what you knew, like, prepare the ones that were coming. That was your responsibility."

The spirit of activism defined sports in the 1960s. In 1964, NBA players—the league of Russell and Chamberlain, Jerry West and Elgin Baylor—nearly boycotted the All-Star Game over the pension policy. In 1965, after being treated with racial hostility in New Orleans, black AFL players boycotted the game. In 1966, Major League Baseball players hired labor negotiator Marvin Miller and built the most powerful union in the history of professional sports, a model for athletes coming to understand their rising power in the workforce. The 1968 Olympics were seismic and could have been more so if the athletes had decided to push further and not gone to Mexico City. In 1969, Curt Flood took the first step toward defying baseball at the Supreme Court when he refused to be traded from St. Louis to Philadelphia, challenging the reserve clause, baseball rules that teams owned players for life. Along with artists in the fast-growing music industry, black athletes were the most visible black professionals in the world. The public wanted them to be grateful for their talent, but athletes didn't just have talent; they had power. If the best prospect for black America was not going to be education but the lottery ticket of sports, body over brain, then the most physically gifted African Americans were bound to interrupt America's fun and games when the times demanded their political participation. This was the Heritage. It was the special inheritance of the black athlete. It belonged to them now, even if it was a burden the next several generations of athletes did not always seem to want.

For all the gauzy tributes and reflections of the 1960s, there was no mistaking a central fact: the Heritage and all of its political strains, from the conservative push of moderate integration to radical wings of the movement, were never welcome by the suits who signed the checks or the executives who picked the talent. Jim Brown told his biographer Dave Zirin that he considered Paul Robeson his "number-one guy, a great man . . . who was doing it, fighting, for decades before anyone knew Dr. King." Robinson was a Republican, an integrationist, but never shied from asserting his rights.

In response, teams understood that integration was inevitable, but they attempted to avoid players with a Robinson-Brown-Russell-Ali attitude toward civil rights. When it came to scouting black players, the fiction that teams always looked for the best players was again being exposed. Teams wanted the best player *who would not make a big deal out of civil rights*—or of not having any. There was a reason the Yankees, notoriously and openly racist, chose mild-tempered Elston Howard as its first black player. The same was true for the racist Boston Red Sox, who signed Earl Wilson in part to its scouting report describing him as a "well-mannered colored boy, not too black, pleasant to talk to." Wilson would be traded to Detroit years later for standing up for himself during a racist incident in Florida. As a matter of survival, the team's first black player, Pumpsie Green, avoided virtually all racial topics. Even the legendary Dodgers signed a great catcher in Roy Campanella but also knew that Campanella was not going to demand justice for black people. The difference in their politics always came between Robinson and Campanella. "There's a little 'Tom' in Roy," Robinson once said of the catcher.

3

JUICE

AMERICANS HAVE SHOWN THEY can only discuss race within two frameworks: *Things are better than they were* or *Get over it.* So what exactly happened to the Heritage in the 1970s that began a nearly half-century slide into dormancy, when protest was transformed from noble to toxic? O. J. Simpson happened to it.

These two racial frameworks defined the 1970s well, and OJ was the perfect embodiment of both. The country was tired, tired of war, tired of race, tired of fighting—and definitely tired of black people asking for stuff. America wanted to call itself colorblind (an odd aspiration for a place that also prided itself on being a "melting pot"), and Simpson represented the future, the hope, the American dream for both races.

He was the anti–Jim Brown, the anti–Harry Edwards, which for black people meant that he was the symbol of long-promised equality and for whites, proof of their goodness and willingness to finally open the door, proof that black people could finally, at long last, stop bitching about race. All they had to do was work hard, like OJ, and if they had the goods, the rewards would come, just like they would for OJ. Across many a dinner table in white America, the frustration of *"What do these people want?"* was assuaged by the clean-cut, wholesome, and uncontroversial figure of O. J. Simpson. *If they could only all be like him.* Black people, tired of being represented by the Bad Negro (Sonny Liston, villainous boxer, line 1) or the Mad Negro (Jim Brown, rich, famous but always angry, line 2), desperate for the formula that would coax white society into accepting black people, were saying it too. "Give me a guy like O. J. Simpson, who is neat and clean and well-spoken," wrote the longtime *Chicago Defender* columnist Doc Young. "You take all those guys who are too lazy to get a haircut, who foul the air with curses and other dirty words each time they have an audience, who talk about killing humans like the deed is no worse than swatting flies, all the while bemoaning 'whitey's' brutality." None of this would age well.

Simpson was postracial before that became a thing. He benefited from the battles and the boycotts and the protests without having participated in them. In the 1970s, mainstream popular culture began to slowly permit an increasing black presence in television and movies, and commercial endorsements, and sports was already ahead of other industries in featuring African Americans. Someone was going to profit from this new day, especially if he was willing to leave the confrontation behind and make America feel good about itself, and O. J. Simpson was the one uniquely positioned to take full advantage of the exciting and lucrative new doors that were opening.

PAYING THE PRICE

Before Simpson could truly become the face of sports in the 1970s, however, the Establishment first had some unfinished business: it had to punish the Heritage. As the years went by, its charter members were like those one-name rock stars: Smith and Carlos, Ali and Jackie. Even if you didn't know the whole story, you knew the deeds.

Smith and Carlos were never stripped of their Olympic medals, though that was a rumor left intentionally uncorrected by the IOC for a specific purpose: to scare off any would-be heroes thinking of further challenging the system. IOC president Avery Brundage said, according to Carlos, that he and Smith had embarrassed him and the Olympic community in Mexico City, and though both were an inspiration to athletes around the world, John Carlos always said Brundage vowed to make them pay. Their opportunities to make a living in sports disintegrated. Smith never raced again. Carlos ran in his final year of eligibility, ran well, and in need of an option, following the steps of the great sprinter turned Dallas Cowboys star receiver Robert "Bullet Bob" Hayes, turned to the NFL. It didn't last. During a short stint with the Philadelphia

Eagles, Carlos tore up his knee, and the avalanche continued. His marriage collapsed. Wrote Carlos:

> By 1969 and into 1970, my life was beg, beg, borrow, and steal. If I had $100, I would leave my family and hightail it to Vegas and hit the crap tables to see if I could score us up some money. I just felt like the hustle was the only way to solve the most immediate problems: food and shelter. The hustle is what I did when I wasn't working. Whatever jobs I had to take, I wasn't too proud or too ashamed to do it. I had a job as a security guard at a nightclub, wearing this brownstone ranger uniform. Many people used to come in the club and say, "Hey! Aren't you John Carlos?" They were shocked that I would be doing work like that. But I did what I had to do. I put out the word that I would take whatever job was necessary to make sure my family was able to eat.

Tommie Smith's marriage also ended. The supportive allies weren't so supportive after all, he found. That included some of his fellow warriors in the struggle. Smith, too, tried the NFL. A famous fallout with Jim Brown was particularly personal. Brown, the icon everyone looked up to, lent Smith money for a tryout with the Los Angeles Rams. When the tryout fell through, Smith, just hanging on financially, was stunned to see the great, rich, and famous Jim Brown demanding his money back. Smith languished on the taxi squad of the Cincinnati Bengals. In his autobiography, he dedicated a chapter to this period, calling it "Paying the Price."

> After the silent protest, though, there was never a chance that I would earn anything from track and field. Just as important, I never would know how fast I could have become. I was 24 years old in Mexico City, and I was running at 28 miles an hour then. I would have just turned 28 by the time of the 1972 Olympics in Munich, and everyone has seen what runners like Carl Lewis and Michael Johnson have done as they matured. . . . Yet with all the components of the system lined up against me, punishing me for the sin I committed against their values and beliefs, the treatment I received from black folks hurt even worse. I was looking up to them for support, but I found out that there were more blacks than whites who didn't want anything to do with me.

CURT FLOOD KNEW SOMETHING the rest of the world would sadly learn: he couldn't play anymore. He had been out of the game a year and a half, and physically had nothing left. The arm was shot, and the legs that, for a time in the 1960s had made people believe he was a better defensive centerfielder than even the great Willie Mays, had slowed. The authority Flood once possessed at the plate, that produced consecutive two-hundred-hit seasons in 1963 and 1964, well, that was gone too.

And Flood wasn't just thirty-three years old in 1971. He was an *old* thirty-three. Besides that, he was an alcoholic, and in those days, before the massive improvements in work-out regimens and nutrition, muscle turned to flab overnight, especially when mixed with scotch. Even though his playing had stopped, the responsibilities of life had not. Flood owed money on his failing businesses. He owed alimony to his ex-wife. Moreover, he had virtually no support from the public, which had no time for a guy who'd been making $110,000 referring to himself as a "slave." Nor did he have widespread support from his fellow players. Some, like Boston's Carl Yastrzemski (who had two residences, his home and in owner Tom Yawkey's pocket), called him an ingrate. Willie Mays didn't back him. The truth was, even if Flood had been making half that amount, the public was never going to back him because he was still making significantly more than they were—and for *playing a kid's game.*

The writers, owned by ownership and siding with the power, commissioner Bowie Kuhn, were ruthless. Now Flood was attempting a comeback in Washington, playing for a hard-ass, Senators manager Ted Williams, the old Red Sox legend best known for being the last man to hit .400, lesser known for being the man who wanted to drop a nuclear bomb on Korea. Williams never wanted Flood and would never be an ally. The strain of a Supreme Court challenge to one of the most powerful institutions in America broke him. He was going, in his words, insane, and as his comeback further revealed everything he had lost as a ballplayer, Curt Flood snapped. The Senators had given him a chance. But the walls were closing in, and one day during the season, Flood didn't show up to the ballpark. He had fled the country.

STILL, ON EVERY FRONT LINE, it seemed, was Jackie Robinson. In 1970, he had testified at the Supreme Court hearing on Flood's behalf, noting that though sports was a game to the fans, players, for whom it was their livelihood, should have rights. Robinson told the court of Flood's courage of risking reputation and livelihood for a cause that wasn't particularly supported by his fellow players.

> It takes a tremendous amount of courage for any individual—and that's why I admire Mr. Flood so much for what he is doing—to stand up against something that is appalling to him, and I think that they ought to give a player a chance to be able to be a man in situations like this, and I don't believe this is what has happened. Give the players the opportunity to say to themselves, "I have a certain value and I can place it on myself."

By challenging the reserve clause, Flood had used the inheritance of Robinson, just as Smith and Carlos and Ali had done before, and at enormous cost to himself, one that would never be recouped. Flood would lose his Supreme Court challenge, much of the goodwill from the people who had attempted to give him a chance to return to the game, and all of his money, as biographer Brad Snyder noted, refusing to file for bankruptcy even as creditors closed hard around him. Like Smith and Carlos, Flood was paying the price for challenging the institution.

"It seems clear rather than letting down the players, as many members of the press have reported," Marvin Miller told a group of players, "Curt's problems were compounded because of his awareness of his responsibilities to the rest of the players."

Save for a short-lived TV gig with the Oakland A's and other small, unfulfilled flashes of reconciliation with Major League Baseball, there was nothing left in baseball for Curt Flood. What Flood didn't lose, baseball took by making sure he could never get back into the game long enough to retrieve it. The words were always there, whenever the latest hotshot would score a contract worth tens of millions, invariably Flood's name would be mentioned, the original sacrifice, a lifetime membership to the Heritage. There was no better way to illustrate the point than the time Bobby Bonds, the great right fielder and father of Barry Bonds, received a phone call from me, at the time a frightened young *Oakland Tribune* reporter doing a story on Flood. "What did Curt Flood lose?" Bonds repeated the question with incredulity and increasing hostility, bitter both at what the game took from Flood and the injustice that what Flood started made everyone in the game that had barred him richer.

Bonds finally answered: "Everything."

And then he hung up.

ON OCTOBER 26, 1970, in the Atlanta Auditorium, Muhammad Ali beat Jerry Quarry in a third-round TKO, the result of Ali slicing open the left side of Quarry's face. After more than three years away from being stripped of his title and license to box after refusing induction in to the army, Ali was back in the ring. He was still appealing his conviction for draft evasion, which carried a five-year prison term and ten-thousand-dollar fine. But the political maneuvering of state senator Leroy Johnson had secured Ali a boxing license in Georgia when most states wouldn't budge. Ali, the undefeated champion without a championship belt, had returned. Joe Frazier was the champion, but Ali was the number-one contender, and Quarry looked like a tomato can by the time Ali was finished with him.

Unlike Smith, Carlos, and Flood, the Ali who entered the ring against Quarry was not spent. He was not the same Ali as he was when he had last fought, in 1967—beautiful, mesmerizingly quick for a six-foot-three-inch fighter, with those hands and the unlined face. This Ali was twelve pounds heavier, nearly four years older. He was still strikingly fast compared to his peers but demonstrably slower compared to his old self. Ali's quest to regain his title spoke for the people, for the protesters and the underdog, and when he lost in his first attempt to regain his heavyweight title, March 8, 1971 against Joe Frazier, it felt as if the Heritage and its supporters had lost as well. It was as if everything the fight was all about had been taken away by the government, and the Bowie Kuhns and Avery Brundages of the world, that they had won again.

Banned from his sport, Ali likely lost hundreds of thousands of dollars in prize money, so the Ali who returned to the ring in 1971 was not always the same political Ali, at least not publicly. He did not as often mention Vietnam or the American racial condition. He attempted to regain financially what had been taken from him through the ban, officially unfairly when the Supreme Court overturned his conviction in August 1971. It wouldn't be for another three years, in 1974, that Ali was made whole again, beating George Foreman in Zaire for the heavyweight title and becoming a worldwide symbol that made every attempt to ruin him look that much smaller. Ali was indomitable, in many ways no different than Tommie Smith, John Carlos, and Curt Flood—except he was the one who survived. Unlike the rest, Ali had a second act after they tried to destroy him. The architects of the Heritage would own the images. They would own the history and win the day, but what the power had taken from them was time—and that could not be recovered.

History writes people out of the story. On January 23, 1976, in Philadelphia, Paul Robeson died. He was seventy-seven and decidedly not, in the eyes of the American mainstream, a hero. The United States would never forgive him for his sentiments toward the Soviet Union, and his *New York Times* obituary read as though it was written through gritted teeth, observing, "Although Mr. Robeson was unwelcome in many quarters, except in the black community, during the cold war, he was widely recognized abroad." He was the living embodiment of the Heritage, by using his talent to amplify the causes of his people around the world, by using excellence in sports for access to education and the larger world denied less athletically gifted black people that made the Heritage relevant, and in the enormous price he paid for an unwavering fidelity to his people.

Robeson's obituary in the mainstream media said as much about the white media lens through which it was written as it did about him, a staggering list of accomplishment embedded in a grudging retelling. "He stood more as a symbol of black attainment, it was said, and of black consciousness and of pride," read the *Times* obituary.

But where Robeson mattered most, among the laborers, the blacks and browns and underdogs of the world who would never forget what Robeson had and what was taken from him, his was the story of a towering life. "Inevitably, like a mountain peak that becomes visible as the mist is blown away, the towering figure of Paul Robeson will emerge as the thick white fog of lies and slanders is dispelled," wrote Lloyd Brown, Robeson's original collaborator on his autobiography five years before Robeson died. "Then he will be recognized and honored here in his homeland, as he is throughout the world, as Robeson the Great Forerunner."

At the end of the era, was the beginning of it all: Jackie Robinson. Robinson stood alone, anguished, a fifty-three-year old man who looked seventy, ravaged by sadness, pessimism, and diabetes. He was legally blind, his hair snow-white. He was the possessor of a broken heart and a pioneer's disillusionment. Robinson knew he had made history and understood that he was a seismic figure not only in sports but in American history. Like Ali would one day, Robinson had dwarfed all his enemies, the ones who over the years had nipped at him, wounded him, and at a certain moment believed they had beaten him. The imperious Dodgers owner Walter O'Malley was one who thought he had won when he and the rest of baseball—including Branch Rickey, who ran front offices in Pittsburgh and St. Louis but never offered Robinson a post-playing job— kept Robinson out of the game after retirement. Omitted from the history books and the retellings of the Jackie Robinson legend was that baseball couldn't wait to get rid of him.

There would be no second act in baseball for Jackie Robinson. So much of his pessimism, despite the obvious fallacy of his belief that he hadn't made a dent in society, was that he often felt like failure. In 1972, baseball had still not hired its first black manager and showed no signs of doing so. The energy and commitment to civil rights of the 1960s had felt transformative, and objectively he had been part of the generation that changed America, but nevertheless he was utterly disillusioned not only by the glacial pace of change but the speed in which the pushing stopped. He had trusted men who had betrayed him, who said they were committed to equal rights, but were not. Richard Nixon, now president, was one of them. Jackie Robinson no longer stood for the national anthem because he felt betrayed. He was the army veteran who thought the anthem's words sounded hypocritical. He had outlived Malcolm X by seven and a half years and now saw that Malcolm's acidic realism was neither hysterical nor hyperbolic after all. It was just based on the facts of his life as he saw them. Robinson now saw it too.

Robinson knew now, in the case of Paul Robeson, that Nixon and HUAC had used him to play the role he feared then, the worst role a black man could ever play in America: the safe, establishment black alternative to counter a legitimate black demand for fairness. As Malcolm X once charged, he had been pitted against his own. He knew it then, and stood by his testimony, but only now did he doubt that testifying had been the right thing. "That statement was made over twenty years ago and I have never regretted it," he said. "But I have grown wiser and closer to truths about America's destructiveness, and I do have an increased respect for Paul Robeson, who over the span of that twenty years, sacrificed himself, his career and the wealth and comfort he once enjoyed because, I believe, he was sincerely trying to help his people."

On October 24, 1972, before Game 1 of the World Series in Cincinnati, Robinson gave his most famous speech, using their commemoration of his twenty-fifth anniversary of integrating the big leagues to admonish baseball for having never hired a black manager or even a third-base coach, even though Bill Russell had already won two championships as coach of the Boston Celtics. Robinson spoke while his enemies clapped politely, all except Joe Cronin, Robinson's nemesis who took the coward's way out, choosing not to appear on the field with the man he had humiliated during Robinson's infamous tryout with the Boston Red Sox back in 1945. Cronin was manager of the Red Sox when the team had an opportunity to be the first to integrate but would become the last. Robinson was shut out of baseball while Cronin had not only made a living in the game before, during, and after Robinson's time but was now American League president. Jackie Robinson understood it now. He was the Heritage, but they were the power, and the power could do whatever it wanted. Nine days later, he was dead.

Ali's talent had allowed him to outrun his enemies into the vindicating arms of history, but Jackie, too, had a secret weapon, and her name was Rachel Robinson. She had been the stabilizing force for him during the years of humiliation and frustration. The concept of *first-class citizenship* had been as much hers as his, as they built a post-playing life of service to others. Now, with his death, Rachel Robinson did not take the widow's walk to obscurity, allowing herself to disappear and the deeds, memory, and name of Jackie Robinson to fade or be left to chance. Rachel Robinson took her legendary name into the coming decades and forced baseball to do with her husband in death what they would not do with him in life: incorporate him into the game as a living, undying reminder of the Heritage and baseball's eternal responsibilities to it. Rachel Robinson did not let Jackie die. If the game was going to profit from his name, as it certainly would in the years ahead, it was Rachel who made sure baseball was going to live up to his principles as well—or be exposed for the hypocrisy of using his name while erasing his legacy.

FASCISM, NO DOUBT ABOUT IT

The police and the Heritage were never far apart. Police brutality had been a part of the black community's grievance since Emancipation. Jackie Robinson mentioned police misconduct to Congress during his HUAC testimony in 1949. When explaining their reasoning for the proposed Olympic boycott, Smith, Carlos, and Edwards did too. During the 1960s, the tension between black residents and law enforcement was the spark for civil disturbances in Newark, Watts, Detroit, and Philadelphia. While the black community saw police as a hostile force in their communities, mainstream America did not, and that other diversion, Hollywood, was a big reason why. During a time of deep animosity between minority communities and law enforcement, Hollywood introduced a new genre to the popular culture: the renegade hero cop.

Two days before Christmas 1971, Warner Brothers released *Dirty Harry*, a repudiation of the dissent of the time and a metaphor for the political pivot toward authoritarianism's softer semantic cousin, law and order.

Through the film's eyes, it wasn't the system that oppressed the poor and the powerless and needed reform but the exact opposite. The system had been overtaken by liberal politicians who turned strong law enforcement officers into weaklings who couldn't stand up to the criminal element, which incidentally just happened to be inner-city blacks and the hippie radicals depicted in the film, the very people the Nixon White House had targeted throughout the 1968 presidential campaign. The city needed someone moral enough to ignore immoral laws. The film promotes the Nixonian attitude that the courts had emboldened killers and rendered police forces too weak to stop them. What the country really needed, was a little more authority, somebody willing to kick a little ass. The judicial system was feeble and ineffectual, bleeding with too much compassion after civil rights laws that enabled the murderers and could not be counted on. The only hope was the renegade cop—always white and educated but fearless and moral enough to be trusted by the audience—who broke the law in order to aid justice. The genre introduced to the American mainstream the idea of the policeman as patriot.

Dirty Harry did not hide its intentions. The film opened with a shot of the memorial in the city's Hall of Justice that read "In Tribute to the Police Officers of San Francisco Who Gave Their Lives in the Line of Duty," followed by a panning shot of the names of the city's fallen officers, beginning in 1878 and ending in 1970 before the film begins with a tight shot of a sniper's silencer and scope about to kill an innocent blond woman swimming in a rooftop pool. In the film, the tribute to police is celebrated by Dirty Harry's illegal methods and dismissal of the law—the abandonment of Miranda rights in particular, whose enactment were a response to the abuse of police power—which minority communities had long complained about in their treatment by law enforcement.

In the *New Yorker*, Pauline Kael referred to the film as a "right-wing fantasy," and critic Roger Ebert wrote, "The movie clearly and unmistakably gives us a character who understands the Bill of Rights, understands his legal responsibility as a police officer, and nevertheless takes retribution into his own hands. The movie's moral position is fascist. No doubt about it."

The role made Clint Eastwood, already famous, into an American box-office icon. *Dirty Harry* spawned three sequels, but the film's legacy would be an everlasting industry of propaganda for police sold to American homes, one that reinforced both the goodness and righteousness of police power, lampooned the academics and the eggheads who only could see law in theory, and confirmed and escalated the fears and distrust white Americans may have had of shadowy minority communities. It was a formula that would be repeated through so many countless imitations, both on television and on screen, that the depictions of all three—cops, liberals, blacks—became stereotype. Whether violent or comedic, the police would have a permanent vehicle in pop culture to burnish their image, no matter how different the reality may have been on American streets. In turn, the grievances of the communities walled off from the mainstream would seem to the millions of Americans who knew nothing of the ghettoes just that much more illegitimate, their charges against law enforcement that much more difficult to prove to a public that identified with a hero seeking vengeance and law enforcement as just and moral. The popular culture sent the message to a middle America that often feared cities as too crime-ridden, too black, that it could take comfort in the (albeit fictional) presence of a white cop willing to ignore the rules and the soft-willed liberals to protect them, to put them first. Hollywood had created a genre of the state as protagonist and, whether directly or as an unintended consequence, also created a natural antagonist: the black and the poor as villain, an eternal threat to the comforts of the white mainstream.

"*Dirty Harry* is obviously just a genre movie, but this action genre has always had a fascist potential, and it has finally surfaced. If crime were caused by super-evil dragons, there would be no Miranda, no Escobedo; we could all be licensed to kill, like Dirty Harry," Kael wrote in the *New Yorker*. "But since crime is caused by deprivation, misery, psychopathology and social injustice, 'Dirty Harry' is a deeply immoral movie."

Walled off from the mainstream by race, class, and geography, the mainstream did not have its ideas of the black community shaped by personal interaction with African Americans but through films such as *Dirty Harry*. Through the pop culture, the black community had been demonized as the enemy of law enforcement, but Hollywood wasn't done. By the middle of the 1970s, its new villain was a charter member of the Heritage itself.

In 1976, Sylvester Stallone wrote and starred in *Rocky*, the account of an under-talented Italian American underdog who improbably lands a shot at the heavyweight boxing title. The film pulled at the sports clichés of hard work and determination, aspiring to an opportunity that appeared, without sufficient heart, to be beyond reach.

If *Dirty Harry*'s message to the white mainstream was that it needed a hero to restore order against the encroaching black community, *Rocky* sent a similar message with the hero's antagonist, reigning heavyweight champion Apollo Creed, played by Carl Weathers: the black athlete threatened what Americans held dear about sport.

The Creed character was, essentially, a fictional version of Muhammad Ali, containing the stereotypes the white mainstream fan (and many black fans, as well) would come to dislike about the modern black athlete in the post–civil rights age of rising salaries and free agency: brash and disrespectful of authority, arrogant, flamboyant in style and dress, fabulously wealthy but indifferent to the average fan. Many fans were in awe of black players' talent but resented their outspoken personalities, which created a cultural distance between black braggadocio and the humble intensity through which white fans saw white players, and by extension through which they saw themselves. These characteristics made Creed the perfect on-screen villain to Rocky Balboa's blue-collar aspirations, easy to dislike.

Through Creed, a fictionalized Ali represented the perfect sports villain, but only through the distortion of Hollywood's sleight-of-hand. If Apollo Creed contained the personality traits the white paying customer would resent about black athletes, it was only because *Rocky* stripped Creed of the one piece of Ali that redeemed and later deified him: his courageous, vindicated politics. Without the post–Vietnam War exoneration of his political stance and the principles that defined Ali as an international symbol of strength to all races, Creed was nothing but a black loudmouth, craven and empty. With those characteristics, the true hero of the film would possess talent and the depth of his convictions—and his name wouldn't have been Rocky Balboa.

Instead, *Rocky* cemented Stallone, like Eastwood, as a star. The film was a runaway hit and cultural phenomenon. It won three Academy Awards, including Best Picture and Best Director. Stallone was nominated for Best Actor and became only the third actor in history to be nominated for both acting and writing in the same year, after Charlie Chaplin and Orson Welles. Less heroic, the "Rocky" character became a physical, pop cultural face of the white hero who would protect it against the elements of black culture whites hated, a racialized dynamic lampooned harshly by the comedian Eddie Murphy. As *Dirty Harry* did for Hollywood's police-as-hero genre, *Rocky* founded what would become an enduring Hollywood archetype: the champion white American boxer. For Rocky to exist, Hollywood created an entire alternate reality. For in real life, Muhammad Ali was the most famous, important, and beloved boxer in history in a sport that was overwhelmingly dominated by black and Latino fighters, while the white American boxing champion, alive only to cheers on the silver screen, was well on his way to becoming extinct.

———

IT WAS IN THIS climate of backlash against protest, the Nixonian thirst for law and order that would soon create the war on drugs and the increasing militarization of the police, draconian elements that would soon be melded into the mainstream, elements that made protest more difficult. Even in film, a heroic figure such as Ali was being caricatured as a villain. The groundwork of transition was being laid. The soil was fertile for the emergence of O. J. Simpson. So, how, exactly did he begin the killing of the Heritage?

His first move was by simply being himself. Even before his endorsements machine kicked into high gear, Simpson was willing to disengage from the Robinson model of being on the front lines of social questions, precisely at the time when people began to believe what would become the Heritage's biggest problem: the idea there was no longer a need for it.

In the 1970s, with everyone able to drink from the same water fountain, civil rights legislation passed, and cities no longer rebelling, there was no need for athletes to speak—or so the players thought. There were plenty of issues that still required attention, especially from the highest-profile people, but that attitude, Harry Edwards believed, was a key reason why the black athlete began to drift from his political roots.

"The seminal issue, from about 1975 to 2010, some thirty-five years, was the absence of a defining ideology and movement that would frame and inform activist positions," Edwards said. Without an immediate issue accompanied by a public face, for example Jim Crow or a police shooting, the athlete could not see his place in confronting systemic conditions that were less explosive but equally as damaging to the black community. The ideology, Edwards believed, should always come before the event. One athlete, Jim Brown, was the only one whose ideology revolved around black economic empowerment. Brown would always frustrate his activist peers with what seemed to be odd alliances—with Richard Nixon and Ronald Reagan and later Donald Trump—but Jim Brown was not a marcher. He was a capitalist. Without a prevailing ideology and leaders to synthesize its importance, injustices that were not as obvious as segregation would be dismissed as too esoteric or too complicated.

Edwards's fears were realized in the 1970s. The Kerner Commission report, which examined the causes of the race riots of the 1960s across the US and sought to provide preventative solutions, foretold of the despair and lack of opportunities among African Americans and detailed the lack of hope and possibilities for economic stability. The report was released February 29, 1968, months after Willie Horton, the Detroit Tigers outfielder and Detroit native, stood in uniform on Twelfth Street and West Grand during the 1967 riots and tried to help quell what was, at the time, the largest civil disturbance in American history. The days of rioting left forty-three dead, hundreds injured, and more than a thousand buildings burned.

Martin Luther King Jr. called the Kerner Commission report "a physician's warning of approaching death, with a prescription for life." Within its conclusion, the report stated, "What white Americans have never fully understood—but what the Negro can never forget—is that white society is deeply implicated in the ghetto. White institutions created it, white institutions maintain it, and white society condones it."

That same year, *Sports Illustrated* published a groundbreaking five-part series by Jack Olsen titled "The Black Athlete: A Shameful Story," which recognized the responsibility black athletes took upon themselves to be politically active citizens. Within the eighteen months of the Detroit riots and the seminal Mexico City Olympics of Smith and Carlos, the Black 14—the fourteen black players on the 1969 University of Wyoming football team—were dismissed from the team by coach Lloyd Eaton for joining a student protest against the racial policies of Brigham Young University, whose parent, the Mormon Church, didn't allow blacks to join its priesthood. In a meeting, the players asked to protest silently with armbands. Eaton told them they could not, but defensive end Tony McGee remembered that Eaton told the players they *could* "go to Grambling State or Morgan State" or "back to colored relief."

Also in 1968, nine Syracuse University football players petitioned head coach Ben Schwartzwalder for changes—the same Schwartzwalder who didn't want Jim Brown playing for him. The players alleged the coach held separate rules for white and black players. The football team had black players but no black assistant coaches. The football team allowed white players advantages not available to black players, such as advanced course loads. The players were determined to use their power. The Syracuse 8, as they were called, boycotted the 1970 season and some players and fans threatened to boycott if the players were allowed to return.

In an editorial about the series, *Sports Illustrated* wrote:

Every Negro athlete is a potential messenger from the white world to the ghetto—a messenger who can help bridge the intolerable communications gap that exists today. Sport and the universities and business must all ask: What news do we want these messengers to deliver? News that in this field, at least, a black man is recognized as a man, that exploitation has been replaced by human consideration and that equality is more than just a word? Or do we want the message to be: burn, baby, burn?

The message, from Wyoming to Syracuse was that the players may have been the ones who made it from their communities, but they were mules, to perform and conform but not to believe they had earned the right to demand anything.

The riots stopped, but the issues did not. From economic inequities, to religious protest, to coaching hires, the issues surrounded the athletes, but without a synthesizing ideology, the players wouldn't know where they fit into the struggle. The incidents at Syracuse and Wyoming linked athletes to social issues that required a sustained presence, but without Edwards's notion of a sustained ideology, the players would be easy to divide, conquer, or otherwise be convinced by management (or coaches and athletic directors) that their job was to just play ball. It wasn't framed as such at the time, but the Wyoming players indirectly showed their power. Eaton flexed his muscles by kicking the Black 14 off the team, but the team lost its final four games. Eaton was fired after the Cowboys went 1–9 in 1970, and black players, the lifeblood of Division I college football, avoided attending Wyoming for the next twenty years. Player influence was strong, if they knew how to use it.

By 1976, congressional leaders were forced to face the foundations of the despair that existed within black communities and the consequences if left to later generations to confront. James Blair, US assistant secretary for fair housing and equal opportunity, held hearings on lending practices in black communities. The riots within the black community had ceased, the rich and famous actors such as Sammy Davis Jr., Marlon Brando, and Charlton Heston went back to Hollywood, and the athletes returned to the locker room—but the root issues that drew their attention remained.

Over two and a half days, fifty-eight witnesses and more than two thousand pages of submitted documents, the hearings, aptly titled "The Fair Housing Administrative Meeting on Redlining and Divestment as a Discriminatory Practice in Residential Mortgage Loans," commenced in Washington, DC. Its purpose was for the banking suits and Washington bureaucrats to discuss what residents and activists in DC, Chicago, San

Francisco, Boston, Oakland, and Milwaukee already knew: the state and financial institution machinery had worked to keep the slums exactly what they were during the years before the great federal legislative victories that were supposed to place America on the path toward equality. Blair wanted to know why ghettoes were not improving. The answer was the extralegal corruption of Great Society programs by local, state, and federal agencies—as well as mortgage lenders.

What was revealed over two remarkable days was the architecture of discrimination. The discriminatory practice of redlining—in which lenders literally outlined in red marker on maps the "undesirable" communities where they would discourage lending—was an old one. The key factor determining what was undesirable, beyond the age of the building, its infrastructure or location, or the borrower's income, was race. After the passage of the Fair Housing Act of 1968, the government was confident it would see improvement. When it did not, it concluded, as a result of the 1976 hearings:

> In attempting to reverse this past discrimination, FHA altered its policies and began to try to provide large amounts of mortgage money for these areas. Extremely lax underwriting, however, combined with maladministration and even fraud, contributed to the inundation in these areas of FHA mortgages followed by FHA foreclosures and FHA abandonment. As FHA-insured mortgages became the main source of home financing in these areas redlined by conventional lenders, the effects of the FHA programs were seen by many as part of the problem rather than part of the solution.

During the hearings, as well as in those held by the Senate Committee on Banking, Housing, and Urban Affairs on redlining a year earlier, the secrets were laid bare, from the nefarious methods lenders used to thwart the best intentions of the law, to the callous attitudes lenders had toward would-be borrowers who lacked sterling credit, to the lenders who dismissed customers solely on the basis of skin color, even if they had good credit. "Perhaps the most remarkable aspect of redlining and its devastating consequences is that it is, in a real sense, government sponsored," said committee member Frances Werner on the first day of the meeting.

"Most of the lenders accused of the practice depend on one or more of four federal regulatory agencies, either for their very existence or to facilitate mortgage lending. The agencies are the Federal Home Loan Bank Board, the Comptroller of the Currency, the Federal Reserve Board and the Federal Deposit Insurance Corporation."

All of which was fancy speak for "the fix was in": the mortgage lenders, government agencies, and real estate agents all conspired to undermine a landmark piece of legislation, the 1968 Fair Housing Act, designed to energize depressed black communities with the resources needed to turn ghettoes into thriving neighborhoods.

On its face, bank loans would seem to have nothing to do with a running back for the Dallas Cowboys, but these lending practices were the underlying issues that roiled the ghettoes. These were the subjects that players, many of whom came from these communities, were already familiar with as youngsters. Had the players embraced Harry Edwards's idea of a sustained ideology, meaning bonding together over issues of justice and fairness, the Heritage could have lent its considerable knowledge, resources, experiences, and *fame* to an issue that had personally thwarted so many of them. The players knew the frustration of being rich and famous—and *still* have whites petition against their right to move into white communities—but all accepted their individual situations without combining their strength as they had during the civil rights movement. Willie Mays, maybe the greatest baseball player of them all, was long denied housing in the supposedly tolerant San Francisco Bay Area, even as fans cheered him nightly. The same was true for Curt Flood, who tried to move in to the city's Alamo neighborhood. In 1970, while with the Milwaukee Bucks, white neighbors petitioned Oscar Robertson's move to the Glendale. Henry Aaron's neighbors welcomed him as the first black resident in the Milwaukee suburb of Mequon, but only because he was the Great Hank Aaron.

Some of it, the asking of players to be constant social advocates in addition to hitting home runs, was an impossible ask: ballplayers couldn't be expected to take a stand on all issues. They were point guards, not policymakers. But without a guiding principle, Harry Edwards concluded, players wouldn't even know when to join a battle that affected them directly. "I don't think anyone in or out of sports would accuse Willie Mays of offending white sensitivities," Jackie Robinson wrote of Mays in *Baseball Has Done It*. "But when he was in California, whites refused to sell him a home in their community. They loved his talent, but didn't want him as a neighbor."

Jackie and Rachel Robinson knew it firsthand. When they wanted to move to integrated communities in Connecticut, no realtors would help. "We answered ads for some places around Greenwich," Rachel Robinson told the writer Roger Kahn. "When the brokers saw us, the places turned out to be just sold or no longer on the market." Finally, it took a giant to intervene. Andrea Simon, wife of Dick Simon, the head of the mighty Simon and Schuster publishing house, got involved, and eventually the Robinsons were able to buy a house in Stamford.

The end result of these maneuverings was to further isolate both the ghettoes and the lower middle-class communities of color that teetered on the precipice of revitalization. Yet the glamour of sports offered a cruel tease, as many of the ballparks—in San Francisco, Detroit, New York, Chicago, and Miami—were situated in these impoverished communities. The erosion of educational infrastructure left little room for the black brain to flourish, leaving nothing left but the black body, hoping for the golden ticket and a chance for millions by running fast and jumping high or a greater chance of jail, as O. J. Simpson, from the black projects of Potrero Hill in San Francisco, soon discovered. It was the players who were raised in these places, where the combination of government incompetence and corruption from lenders ruined their possibilities for better, and placed an even greater premium on success through the physical skills of the black body and not the mind. All of it was a shell game that would eventually collapse on the black bodies who ran fast enough to get a college scholarship but not quite fast enough to make it in the pro game— and no one knew this better than the players themselves. Eventually, these players were going to be exposed for being uneducated, largely in part to the apparatus that was allowed to exist unchecked as the Heritage moved on. The "prescription for life" that MLK saw in the Kerner Commission had been thwarted by corruption, isolation, and a lack of educational and employment opportunities, combined with the ongoing tense relationship with law enforcement, only increased the potential with each passing decade of neglect for urban black communities to erupt once more.

"SHOW THEM YOUR HEELS!"

While the government held hearings on redlining, and white resistance over school desegregation ripped cities apart (and black frustration that black communities were denied resources to improve their schools *without* having to attend schools with white children), the good life awaited O. J. Simpson. There were opportunities for black athletes to join the mainstream world of endorsements and integration that had never existed before, and OJ took advantage of every one of them. The other great, top-shelf player during the early 1970s was Kareem Abdul-Jabbar, but the ad men and marketers of Madison Avenue weren't too keen on him. Kareem was too aware, too serious, and, most of all, too *political*. Simpson was by far the most attractive to the ad makers.

And OJ was in the perfect storm. The bidding war for players between the NFL and AFL before the 1970 merger increased salaries. Simpson's 1969 four-year contract was for nearly $400,000. It was once unheard of that a rookie would begin his career making $100,000 in a season, but the money was exploding in all sports. In the three seasons from 1972 to 1974, the Milwaukee Bucks paid Abdul-Jabbar $350,000, $378,000, and $399,000, respectively. In December 1975, what Curt Flood had started in baseball was finished when baseball arbitrator Peter Seitz ruled in favor of pitchers Andy Messersmith and Dave McNally. Both were granted free agency, and the reserve system was dead.

When players asked for salary increases, owners had forever told them the teams were broke, but the money following the Seitz ruling exploded. In 1972, the Atlanta Braves made Aaron the highest-paid player in baseball at $200,000 per season. In 1976, the Yankees signed Reggie Jackson to a five-year, $3 *million* deal—$600,000 per season. Three years after that, Nolan Ryan became the first player to earn $1 million per season. In 1981, the Yankees signed Dave Winfield to the biggest contract in professional sports history: ten years, and—wait for it—*$23 million*. The following year, George Foster signed a free-agent deal with the New York Mets that made him the first player (because Winfield's contract was backloaded) to earn at least *two million dollars* per season.

The money even came with some ceiling-shattering seats at the table that just five years previous appeared unlikely. In 1973, the Milwaukee Bucks made Wayne Embry the first black general manger in NBA history.

The next year, the Cleveland Indians hired Frank Robinson, the first black manager in baseball history. In 1977, Ted Turner, the new owner of the Atlanta Braves, made Bill Lucas, Henry Aaron's former brother-in-law, the first black general manager in baseball.

Less than a decade earlier, Bob Gibson, the legendary St. Louis Cardinals pitcher, had complained that his 1967 World Series MVP award may have come with a car but very few product endorsement opportunities. And that's where O. J. Simpson steered the black athlete, from the Heritage to the suburbs, from identifying with black issues to green ones. Simpson opened a word of financial possibilities to black athletes. The baseball player Reggie Jackson and basketball star Julius Erving served as pitchmen for everything from Coca-Cola to TV sets. Before Jackson joined the Yankees, he once boasted, "If I played in New York, they'd name a candy bar after me." And they did.

Simpson embodied the new mind-set of the advertising suits on Madison Avenue so much that in 1975, the rental-car company Hertz made Simpson the first black man to lead an advertising campaign. He was a national name, and his commercials became iconic in sports and marketing history. They made him the most visible black athlete in team sports, and in terms of overall name recognition in America, only Ali rivaled him. Simpson wore the face of possibility, proof to the corporate world that Nixon's notion of "black capitalism" could be profitable. In 1965, the mean average salary for black workers was $3,318 per year; by 1975, the figure had doubled. Black financial health was a concept attractive also to Jim Brown, and it would explain why over the years he would rather vigorously support a string of Republican politicians who ostensibly stood for positions anathema to the people who thought they knew the man. In the end, though, "black capitalism" was a clumsy, hopeful term that was essentially meaningless. While the players grew wealthy, the boon for the community in the face of redlining and illegal schemes to depress minority areas was nonexistent. This was illustrated in the far-away year of 2015, when the Federal Reserve Bank of Boston published a study titled *The Color of Wealth in Boston*, in which it calculated that the net worth of the average white Bostonian was close to $250,000. For non-immigrant African American Bostonians, nearly a half century after Nixon introduced black capitalism, the study found their next worth to total eight dollars.

While selling his products to the black community, which was a major part of his appeal to Hertz, Simpson himself spent as much time as he could avoiding the same black communities in which he was raised.

Meanwhile, in that same year, 1975, but in a different universe, Muhammad Ali, Pan-African, anti-capitalist despite earning $10 million the previous two years, the anti-OJ, sat down for an interview with *Playboy*: "I was driving down the street and I saw a little black man wrapped in an old coat standing on a corner with his wife and a little boy, waiting for a bus to come along—and there I am in my Rolls-Royce. This little boy had holes in his shoes and I started thinking that if he was my little boy, I'd break into tears. And I started crying. Sure, I know I got it made while the masses of black people are catching hell, but as long as they ain't free, *I* ain't free."

The Hertz campaign was brilliant, groundbreaking, and also sinister, proof that the right black face could sell not only to black consumers but also to white—with a catch. Black and white consumers could interact with Simpson the pitchman, but not with each other. In his Hertz commercials, Simpson was affable, appealing to white middle-class America, from Boy Scouts to grandmothers. He was seen racing through airports, cheered on only by white people. In fact, Simpson was often the only black person in his commercials, assuaging any white fear that the advertising industry was promoting integration. After all, one black person was acceptable. Two meant they were taking over.

Advertising Age named Simpson the 1977 Presenter of the Year, even as he suffered one of the worst seasons of his career on the field, his last with the Buffalo Bills. The commercials were historic successes, helping to make Hertz the top rental-car company in America and O. J. Simpson a superstar. Simpson was as far from the Heritage as he could possibly be: nonthreatening, friendly, the guy you wanted to live next door. (Note: *This* would not age well, of course.)

Simpson was also, in contrast to Abdul-Jabbar, a test case for a new conceit: the colorless black athlete. Where Abdul-Jabbar would feel socially isolated as a black man living in segregated Milwaukee, Simpson was attractive to the public, who liked to think of him (and themselves) as color-blind. The product-buying public loved Simpson precisely because he did not identify his blackness as a particularly obvious or important characteristic. That made him saleable in a way Kareem, Jim Brown,

Jackie Robinson, and Bill Russell would never be. If the athlete was the most powerful player in the black American workforce because his success in sports suggested a more equitable, less race-conscious society, Simpson was the model for how capitalism was seen by whites as a vehicle, in their eyes, to erase racism. As Simpson once famously told *New York Times* writer Bob Lipsyte, "I'm not black. I'm OJ." Black became green.

Simpson encouraged the erasure. He did not discuss politics, on camera or off. There was, for him, no Heritage. He did not make whites uncomfortable with demands on behalf of his people. Simpson did not use his power as the best football player in the game to demand the hiring of a black head football coach in the NFL, even though the league had nothing that resembled a pathway to head coaching in a sport that profited heavily from black labor. Despite its big-name, Super Bowl quarterbacks—Terry Bradshaw, Roger Staubach, Bob Griese—the biggest name in football was Simpson, a guy whose teams made the playoffs exactly once in his ten-year career. Nor did Simpson use his celebrity to attack discrimination as Abdul-Jabbar and Aaron did during the tense racial moments over segregation in housing in Milwaukee.

Hertz was just the start. Buy a comic book in the 1970s—Marvel or DC, Archie or Veronica—and invariably on the back cover was the image of Simpson, usually in a cartoonist's rendering. There he was, with the autograph across the page, telling you the way to be cool was to buy what Simpson was selling, whether it was a Hertz rental car or Dingo cowboy boots. One ad campaign for Spot-Bilt youth cleats implored kids to "Show them your heels," naturally because the heel of the shoe said "Spot-Bilt." That meant you were wearing Simpson's shoe, the same ones he purportedly wore to rip through the defenses of the Patriots and the Dolphins and the Jets. Spot-Bilt even called the shoes "Juicemobiles." At a time when few black Americans were featured in advertising, there was O. J. Simpson, selling Schick razors, R.C. Cola, Foster Grant eyewear, and, naturally, orange juice by TreeSweet.

The money and the visibility were available, but they weren't free. Part of the reason Simpson was so marketable was precisely *because* he was unwilling to be involved in social issues. In 1979, his final season in the NFL, Simpson earned a reported $806,000. According to the Bureau of Labor Statistics, that year, the average black male in the United States earned $9,265.

The issues that created the Heritage still existed, but the players had moved on. Simpson was a pivotal character in this history because, as they say in the clubhouse, "the smartest guy in the room is the guy with the most zeroes on his paycheck," and in the 1970s, that person was Simpson. Even before he retired, he had moved on from football—first to television and commercials, then movies. He had proven that the marketing opportunities long denied African American players were opening up and were available to certain black players with a certain appeal to whites. Other doors were also opening, and in the mid-1970s, Simpson purchased a house in Brentwood, an exclusive white enclave of Los Angeles. It was clear to Simpson and others that taking a stance on controversial issues, embracing blackness, was only going to cost players money. The players had made it, and it made sense why the athletes were not invested in redlining or blockbusting or failing schools in the same way Robinson and Aaron were—the new generation of athletes no longer lived in communities that were directly affected by those problems. For the emerging new wealthy athlete, these were just *topics*—unless the Heritage lived in your soul. While O. J. Simpson was selling "Juicemobiles," Muhammad Ali was giving television interviews like the one below indicting the Simpson–style abandonment of black advocacy:

> They go down in history for just being athletes. I'm getting more praise and credit for doing what I'm doing now on this show than . . . beating five of your English champions, because right now black people are at home shouting, at home jumping, because they don't have the nerve to say what I'm saying and nobody's never said it. And they're just so happy to see a black man who will stand up and jeopardize every quarter he's got to tell the truth. So, like Floyd Patterson and other fighters, they just don't take part. They make a million dollars, they get a Rolls Royce and a nice home and a white wife and think, "Well, I made it." But when one man of popularity can let the world know the problem, he might lose a few dollars himself. He might lose his life, but he's helping millions. But if I kept my mouth shut because I can make millions, that isn't doing nothing.

Maybe it was all too romantic an ideal, expecting ballplayers to adopt Harry Edwards's idea of a sustained ideology. America had valued the black body, certainly, and it was now worth millions to the machine of professional sports, and that made black athletes' voices lucrative. Assimilation became the new pathway—and the old ways of Robinson became history instead of inheritance.

Recalled Al Sharpton: "When I was about fourteen, Jesse [Jackson] was in town. I was youth director of Operation Bread Basket, and Jesse said, 'Al, I'm gonna take you tomorrow. Jackie Robinson's having a fund-raiser at his house for Daytop Village,' because his son had had a drug problem. 'Bring your momma.'" I got my mother. My mom was all excited. We were going to Jackie Robinson's house. I'd seen Jackie Robinson around the church. So we get there. They do the thing, and Jackie Robinson took pictures with my mother and all that. We get in the car and head back into the city. Jesse said, 'You don't seem all that excited, Al.' I said, 'It was all right.' He said, 'What do you mean "all right?"' That's Jackie Robinson, first black to ever play baseball.' But Jackie Robinson did that in the late '40s. I wasn't born until the '50s. So by the time I was born and got old enough, you had Hank Aaron. You had Al Downing. It wasn't no big thing.

"Then my mother explained to me how it changed the perception of blackness for this black man to play and mainstream black talent, and then come to New York; was an executive for Chock Full o'Nuts, and come to our churches. That was the impact. That was the Heritage. He was a big player with the NAACP and was on the founding board of Operation PUSH, the original founding board. Here's a black Republican, close to our churches, founding board of PUSH. We go from there to guys that want to do nothing? Nothing? We didn't ask you to be on the board of our organizations or come to our churches. Make a statement. Identify. Nothing? So he paved the way for y'all to do that? He took those insults for y'all to remain silent? It is an absolute disgrace to me."

O. J. Simpson had created a new template: the colorless black athlete. He opened the doors to the white world and other black players followed. Jim Brown preceded him, making movies and transitioning to Hollywood from sports, but Brown never possessed Simpson's marketing muscle. No one did—until Michael Jordan arrived. O. J. Simpson was the first true black athlete as celebrity and capitalist. After Simpson, endorsement and entertainment dollars and housing in communities once exclusively white became available to black players. The contrast between the opportunities athletes had before and after Simpson could not be starker. Simpson was the pioneer for money and mainstream social acceptance black players never envisioned—if they were willing to lay off the politics and the anger. Competing with the potential riches that followed, the Heritage never stood a chance.

4

JUMP, MAN

LIKE EVERY GOOD DRAMA, the story of the athlete in twentieth-century America comprises three acts.

The first was the immigrant story, where sports became the gateway for how to become a Real American. When scores of Italians, Irish, and Germans arrived to the United States in the late 1800s, the Land of the Free was hostile yet full of ideals, potential, and hope. To secure a foothold, many immigrants felt compelled to change their names to something more Anglo-Saxon, more "American," and if the grownups in the house didn't speak English, the kids did. And those first-generation American boys also played baseball.

Sports was the common language for kids who wanted to belong. All crammed together in the Bronx and on the South Side, the Flats and Fells Point, North Beach and the North End, it was the way to make America theirs without feeling like Old World refugees. For every ethnicity, their heroes obliged. The Germans had Babe Ruth, Lou Gehrig, and Honus Wagner. The Irish had Lefty O'Doul on the West Coast, a one-man dynasty in owner-manager Cornelius Alexander McGillicuddy (Connie Mack, to the uninitiated) in Philadelphia, and, especially, the boxers John L. Sullivan and Jack Dempsey, along with dozens of tomato-can pugs everybody loved but whose names nobody remembered.

The Italians had Tony Lazzeri, Yogi Berra, and, of course, the great DiMaggio boys, led, naturally, by Joe. Because of their Italian stars, the Yankees were for years the adopted team of Italian Americans everywhere. The Italians had their boxers, too, like the five-foot-four-inch New York Sicilian featherweight Johnny Dundee, whose real name was Giuseppe

Carrora but who was known in the ring for his 335 fights as the "Scotch Wop"—and then, of course, the LaMottas, the Grazianos, and the Marcianos. Even the Jews, long lampooned for having but a pamphlet's worth of sports greats, well before the Dodgers star Sandy Koufax had the great slugger Hank Greenberg in Detroit, the sprinter Marty Glickman, and the boxer born Jacob Finkelstein, who became an Olympic champion as Jackie Fields. For a boy, the road to assimilation in pre–Pearl Harbor America was clear: lose the accent, pick up a bat (or some boxing gloves), and learn how to read a box score.

The second act was the integration story, birthplace of the Heritage, of Jackie Robinson headlining with twenty million African Americans in tow. The second act was the historical ancestor of the black Union regiments of the Civil War and World War II, where sports substituted for a now-segregated military, another forum where black people had to prove once more to America their worth through the myth of the meritocracy. Once the battlefield, then the scoreboard, still the body over the mind.

The third act was the money story. As final acts go, it was the least heroic but the most American of the three, a cynical finish in a land that craved happy endings, but most of all was built on the allures and resentments of capitalism. The third act wasn't just about free agent money. It was about the effects of the money on a player, deliberate in the fabulous wealth they would now enjoy and unintended in the distance created between the player and public, the effects on his worldview, his universe. It was about the growing power and influence of corporations, as team owners, as image manipulators for players, emerging as the true powers behind every team. The game itself would be devoured, swallowed whole by a corporatocracy that would transform sports into its own industrial complex. The third act belonged to the corporations fronted by icons, a formula perfected by the Chicago Bulls superstar Michael Jordan and Nike, each creating the other. O. J. Simpson may have embodied the initial assault, but the power of Michael Jordan and Nike presided intentionally and deliberately over the death of the Heritage. It was bad for business.

MORNING IN AMERICA

There is no question that the factors that shaped sports in the 1980s—the conservative political climate and the third act of corporate super wealth that redefined the industry—were transformative, but so too were the personalities involved. To have a Heritage, you had to have the best players in the game leading it. The Heritage was formed because the leaders on the field led the sensibility of the game. They made being outspoken safer for the players committed to the ideals but less insulated from the inevitable public backlash. For the next forty years, the opposite occurred. Embodied first by OJ and then by Jordan but followed by generations of other legendary black superstars, the game's great players moved away from the Heritage and into the arms of the cash register. The third act was a fight against the dollar, and in America, money never lost.

Dissent was never popular, but during the Reagan 1980s, Americans grew hostile to unions and identified more closely with management. The prevailing attitude suggested that union protections existed only for the untalented. If wealth and celebrity combined to create a class of super-wealthy athletes and entertainers (not to mention corporate executives who distanced themselves financially from average Americans at a rate even faster than ballplayers), it also was accompanied by the strengthening of the *shut up and play* code: If you had the money, you should be grateful for it. If you did not, you just weren't working hard enough. Everything was fair.

If resentment was simmering, it was in the 1980s, when it became acceptable to suggest that the poor actually had it better than the rest. And it wasn't just any poor people; it was the black and brown poor who were constantly and publicly accused of gaming the system, turning poverty into an advantage. The ghettoes, isolated from the mainstream were, according to a rising wave of Americans, inundated with "welfare queens," who used public assistance to live in a sort of opulent poverty, at the expense of hardworking, white Americans.

When Michael Jordan entered the NBA, in 1984, the census reported the mean income for a white male as $20,259; for a white female, it was $9,682. Black males earned slightly more than half as white men, at $12,119; black females earned $8,622, much closer to white women and black men but roughly only 45 percent of what white men earned. The Bureau of Labor Statistics reported that in the prime earning years, ages twenty-five to fifty-four, blacks earned 76.2 cents on the dollar to white workers. Yet the attitude that American opportunity lay in the hands of the industrious was adopted not only by whites weary of black grievances, tired of being seen as the bad guy, but also by a new generation of conservative black intellectuals who, despite the data detailing the great disparity in education and income, saw balancing remedies as patronizing, even detrimental to black economic and social progress. A rising Yale-educated lawyer named Clarence Thomas, who would one day become a Supreme Court justice, said he took a 15-cent price sticker from a box of cigars and affixed it to his Ivy League degree to, in his words, "remind him of the mistake I'd made by going to Yale." Thomas felt disdain for racial considerations in admissions and hiring, even when he owed his career, in part, to the educational and professional opportunities created by affirmative action.

By calling affirmative action as egregious a historical crime as slavery, and by blaming it more than the firms that he said would not hire him, Thomas fell for the fiction that white was not a color, criticizing what he termed "social engineering" on behalf of blacks, while conspicuously failing to acknowledge that the United States was socially engineered to create an exclusive white (and male) society. It was an orthodoxy that defined the decade of the 1980s, fostered by a wave of powerful opinion shapers such as William F. Buckley, Charles Krauthammer, and George Will, and aided by black conservatives such as Glenn Loury, Shelby Steele, and Thomas Sowell, who viewed affirmative action programs that compelled institutions to consider race as a component in the hiring or admissions process as harmful to blacks. They acknowledged the existence of systemic structures such as redlining and discriminatory hiring practices but rejected them as fatal or even major impediments to improving the black condition.

Whites in the 1980s took a new position: being white was an impediment to success. It was an attitude that had most minorities laughing to keep from crying but nevertheless, despite virtually every statistical metric to the contrary, gained national traction. In 1988, at Temple University in Philadelphia, a white student named Michael Spletzer made national headlines by forming a "white student union" on the school's campus in response to the existence of the African American student union, even though the white enrollment on campus was more than four times that of black students. Other campuses followed, as did a new argument: historically black colleges and universities (HBCUs), created because African Americans were barred from mainstream universities, were unconstitutional, discriminatory against whites. It is an argument Donald Trump revived in 2017 to suggest that HBCUs should not qualify for federal funding.

The white American majority was on the attack, and terms such as "reverse discrimination" and "reverse racism," which had existed on the periphery in the 1960s and early 1970s, became bedrocks of the common discourse. During the 1980s, the same white conservative politicians, who just two decades earlier had ridiculed Martin Luther King Jr. as a Communist, had, with help from conservative black intellectuals, co-opted King's message of equal opportunity to undermine the very people King gave his life to uplift. This was the culture at the dawn of the Age of Jordan.

NOT A BUSINESSMAN BUT A BUSINESS, MAN

The athlete response to the corporatizing culture was largely to avoid it. *Stick to sports* quickly became the default. The fates of Curt Flood, the Black 14, and the Syracuse 8 served as a warning. Ali was gone, hammered into retirement by Larry Holmes and Trevor Berbick. "Activism" was a hostile word. O. J. Simpson did not hide his belief that being African American was the central impediment to his success in America. Whether by negotiated compromise or natural disposition, Simpson decided that in order to enjoy the riches America had to offer, he needed to discard race as a component of his identity. Simpson wanted to be greenwashed. The Heritage should have been brought into the 1970s and 1980s by Kareem Abdul-Jabbar, but Abdul-Jabbar turned inward, perhaps tired of fighting alone and disillusioned that he was the only one who had actually gone through with the 1968 Olympic boycott, became a distant voice of a fading movement. Los Angeles was Magic Johnson's town. The money was big. The backlash was strong. The Heritage was at best quaint; at worst, toxic.

Michael Jordan was the newest electrifying black body to dominate sports. He did not engage politically, but he was no Simpson. He came from Wilmington, North Carolina, the site of one of the highest-profile assaults on a black city by whites as Reconstruction was violently dismantled, the Wilmington insurrection of 1898, where white supremacist Democrats stormed the city, burned down the local newspaper, killed fourteen people, and retook power. Jordan did not privately disengage from his black roots, but publicly, he was a businessman.

Jordan accepted his image as a racially disarming corporate super-salesman, an irresistible, no-risk victory for all. Through Nike, Jordan was armed with America's favorite mythology of redress: that money, via the elevation of a few into the super-rich, ubiquitous celebrity class, could eliminate the necessity of the Heritage. Instead of athletes using their celebrity to advocate for black people, as the old guard had, elite black players now opted for big salaries to sell sports and products, to help white America believe that all the messy history—and the nagging realities of the present—was gone. It was high fantasy.

Even the best thinkers fell for the seduction. In his Jordan biography, *Playing for Keeps*, author David Halberstam, one of the greatest journalists of the twentieth century, detailed an early meeting between Jordan and Nike executive Peter Moore, describing the bargain and all of its presuppositions:

> As Jordan smiled, race simply fell away. Michael was no longer a black man, he was just someone you wanted to be with, someone you wanted as your friend. The smile was truly charismatic, Moore reflected in later years: It belonged to a man completely comfortable with himself and therefore comfortable with others. It seemed to say that only good things would now happen. More, it had a lift to it, a lift that carried ordinary people past their own normal prejudices. If Michael Jordan, he of the brilliant smile, was not burdened by the idea of race, why should you be burdened by it either?

As Jordan smiled, race simply fell away. . . .

As gifted a chronicler of the American century as Halberstam was, as groundbreaking was his civil rights reporting, he was unable to escape writing through the lens that belonged almost exclusively to the eyes of the white executive, the white writer, the white consumer, without considering the unique and bitter insult to the black player. The seduction of erasing the black identity, which seemed so necessary to the mainstream, rarely was confronted with the simple cross-examination: Why was it so necessary for the black athlete's skin to be erased? Why was it that the only way he could be enjoyed by the white public was for him to not be seen for what he was at all, in full dimension? Why was the public asking him to make this deal? And what were the future effects constant erasure might have on the black player himself charged with the responsibility of making race irrelevant, on his wife, his children, and his life beyond the zeroes on his paycheck? Instead, Halberstam accepted this narrative of black-identity amputation as a welcome given. Take, for example, his description of the first Nike Spike Lee-Jordan ad collaborations and the reasons for their success:

> The commercials worked for a number of reasons, [Jim] Riswold [the commercials' director] thought. The first was that both he and Lee were demented fans, and they brought to their work the same wonder that any fan would have. Race, he thought, did not factor in. He did not think of Jordan as black. He had always loved the game, and the game was black, and he had the assumption, like many young men of his generation, that if others could only see what he saw in the game—the artistry and the beauty—they would love it as much or more than other sports then seemingly more popular. And of course, the more they enjoyed it, the less they would see race as a factor.

He did not think of Jordan as black. . . .

It wasn't just the athletes; the writers and reporters succumbed to it as well, deciding the willful surrender of their blackness was the magic formula to put an end to the Race Thing and finally be left alone. The great European writers? You knew them. Oscar Wilde could not be separated from his Irishness any more than Jimmy Cannon could. Hemingway wrote through an indomitable lens of alpha manhood, the Great White Hunter. They used their roots to shape their world, make them better, let the world see and accept and want to emulate their blood. But for a lot of black writers, especially in the 1980s and into the 1990s, the weight was too great, and as a white flag, they issued a common refrain of self-amputation: "I don't want to be a *black* writer. I just want to be a writer."

Of course, the question of what to do with black people, whether it was called the Negro Question or the Race Problem or "erasure" or the White Man's Burden, whether it was navigating slavery and integration or something as ephemeral as selling soda and Raisinets to consumers during a basketball game—was nothing new. Black people knew that outside of being a class of controlled laborers, America never wanted them and had been trying to retrofit the society with varying degrees of success since

1863. The unfiltered recognition that they were unwanted and relied upon each other was one of the reasons the Heritage was so strong for so long in baseball. Black players would not say on the record to reporters but acknowledged to one another that the last thing baseball wanted was more black people. There was a saying in baseball—"no blacks on the bench"—which meant that if you were black, chances were you were an above-average player. The spots on the bench for borderline players went to the white players, who invariably would one day become managers.

Greenwashing was simply an updated form of erasure, a more humane sort—the same trade of an identity but this time at premium prices, to silence the black identity while idolizing their talent. The truth was that no one quite knew what to do with a people who had no home and were unwelcome in America but, after 220 years in bondage, were unfamiliar with Africa. In her book *White Trash: The 400-Year Untold History of Class in America*, Nancy Isenberg described both Thomas Jefferson's belief that Africans were so naturally and intellectually inferior to whites and his solution to black rehabilitation, a solution Jefferson employed by fathering children with his slave Sally Hemings: "It is understood in Natural history that a 4th cross of one race of animals gives an issue of equivalent for all sensible purposes to the original bloods." Jefferson's remedy was the scourge of whites and the baseline for rigid segregation: miscegenation. If generations of white men systemically fathered children with black slave women, by the fourth cross, the black race would eventually be erased. They would become white.

According to Lincoln biographer David Herbert Donald, Lincoln had long preferred the repatriation of blacks to Africa as early as twenty years before the Civil War. As war began and the Emancipation Proclamation grew closer to reality, Lincoln still favored repatriation or colonization and drafted proposals to deport freedmen and newly freed slaves to a new settlement in Central or South America. In her book *Team of Rivals*, Doris Kearns Goodwin, another Lincoln biographer, softened Lincoln's stance on colonization, positing that Lincoln favored "voluntary" deportation out of the country while other members of his cabinet believed colonization, to Africa or South America, should be mandatory. In either case, the rationale for colonization was clear: whites and blacks could not coexist, nor should they. The legacy of the slave trade, and by extension the existence of black people in the United States, could not be reconciled with the constitutional ideal of a free American society for all. Black people would never quite fit.

Weary of being part of the despised class, unwilling to be "reconstituted," and convinced American whites would never accept them without some method of erasure, black intellectuals weren't adverse to the idea of a new start in a new land. They could do the math, and the good math concluded that only by being a majority could black people hope to attain freedom. In 1854, as slavery became a more intractable issue, Lincoln proposed sending American blacks to Liberia.

That same year, perhaps in response to Lincoln's public proclamation, there were blacks who agreed. "In the United States, among the whites, their color is made, by law and custom, the mark of distinction and superiority, while the color of the blacks is a badge of degradation, acknowledged by statute, organic law, and the common consent of the people," wrote Martin Delany, one of the early black nationalists of the nineteenth century, adding, "But we have fully discovered and comprehended the great political disease with which we are affected. . . . We propose for this disease a remedy. That remedy is Emigration." Marcus Garvey believed in emigration in the twentieth century, and his views inspired Malcolm X. Whites would often use the phrase *Go back to Africa* as a way to undermine black citizenship—completely unaware just how many black people thought getting away from them was a pretty good idea.

What was left was a grudging coexistence. Jefferson's science project never quite took hold. Lincoln did not force colonization. African Americans did not receive reparations, nor did they accept segregation. Whether it was the Great Society or "empowerment zones," desegregation or greenwashing the professional athlete, the African American remained not quite a citizen and not quite at home. The concept of home was a clear subtext in one of the greatest modern sporting events in American history: Muhammad Ali's 1974 knockout of George Foreman in Zaire (now the Democratic Republic of the Congo) to regain his title after having it stripped by the federal government seven years earlier. That fight, in which Ali connected so deeply with the people, solidified his Pan-African kinship to Paul Robeson and his status as an international legend to the black peoples of the world—but it was also an indictment of America. "In Zaire, *everything* was black—from the train drivers and hotel owners to the teachers in the schools and the pictures on the money," Ali said. "It was just like any other society, except that it was all black, and because I'm black oriented and a Muslim, I was *home* there. I'm not home *here*. I'm trying to make it home, but it's not. Black people will never be free so long as they're on the white man's land."

Without exporting blacks back to Africa or erasing black skin through the extreme measures of systematic breeding with Europeans, the question of what to do with the black grievance of American history remained. In the modern world, the answer for the really talented was to give them money. Commodifying black celebrity to the mainstream replaced "reconstitution." Making the black athlete "colorless" smoothed the perceived jagged edge of racial identification that made whites uncomfortable. With enough money, race would *simply fade away*.

THE JORDAN MANDATE

Jordan became the athlete as CEO, taking to the golf course, that haven of white business leadership and deal-making. He looked legitimate. Jordan privately gave money to social justice causes but made sure he was never visually associated with any political cause or issue, nothing polarizing, real or imagined, that might damage Nike or Jumpman, the personal Jordan brand Nike would one day create for him.

"I met Michael a couple of times, and Michael was just, 'I'm an athlete.' I never asked him for anything, but it was almost like he was putting it out there even before we talked: 'I'm an athlete,'" Al Sharpton recalled. "And I don't think I've ever seen him do anything for Jesse [Jackson], and I'm talking about in Jesse's heyday. And Michael was the biggest in that whole generation."

Jordan was a hero to millions, not just to people in the United States but also to the world, thanks to the globalization of the NBA, culminating in Jordan's appearance as part of the Dream Team in the 1992 Barcelona Olympics. His public identification, however, was not aligned to black or white, Republican or Democrat, rich or poor, but to an elite corporate sensibility, at a considerable remove from the real world. And what was Jordan supposed to "do" for Jesse Jackson, anyway? Jordan was not hostile to the Heritage, but he did not feel a personal connection or commitment to it.

"MJ's reality was not just that he might have been disinclined to stand up and speak up re critical black issues, but MJ never had a politically 'forted' [as in frontier fort] position that he could take," Harry Edwards said. "I believe that his real concern was more that he would be left out there alone, turning in the wind, lacking an established black ideological context and directive. MJ likely didn't know what to say. Even those who did have an idea of what to say lacked the immediate ideological/movement framing and context. They found themselves essentially alone and to a substantial degree eventually forgotten."

There were serious high-profile moments when the Heritage waited for Jordan to take a stand, like the time when it was revealed that Nike employed laborers, many underage, in Asian sweatshops to manufacture its hundred-dollar shoes with Jordan's name on them. The greatest athlete in the world, essentially profiting off of child labor, sidestepped the controversy as he would a defender on the fast break.

Craig Hodges, the Chicago Bulls' three-point marksman and players' union representative, saw in Jordan an extraordinary chance to begin to wrest economic control from the owners and the corporations who did not easily offer players, especially black players, a seat in the boardroom. In his memoir, Hodges recalled his memories of a Jesse Jackson-Nike conflict:

> The summer of 1990, I also had other issues on my mind. Jesse Jackson's organization, Operation PUSH, had organized a boycott of Nike. Nike did huge business in the Black community yet had no Black vice presidents, few Black employees, and almost no connection to Black-owned companies. I had been encouraging Jordan to break from Nike and go into the sneaker business for himself, with the aim of creating jobs in the Black communities whose residents were buying his product—Air Jordans, of course—in large numbers.
>
> I'd brought this up with Michael on more than one occasion. "We need to start thinking about more meaningful ways to empower and raise our community up. Nike is paying some poor child in Vietnam or China slave wages to make your shoes. Does that sit well with you? Why shouldn't Black families reap the financial windfall that you are handing over to Nike? Nike would be nothing if it wasn't for you, General."
>
> "I hear you, Hodge, I'm just not in a position to do that," Jordan would dismissively reply.

Then there was the story that would become a second skin to Jordan, when he refused to engage in the infamous, racially charged 1990 North Carolina senate race between Republican Jesse Helms and Democrat Harvey Gantt, who was African American, because "Republicans buy shoes too." It was the single sentence that for more than three decades labeled Jordan as a willing soldier in the corporatocracy, allegiant to Nike and not the Heritage, black people, or anyone besides himself. Helms-Gantt was highlighted by a Helms attack ad showing just a pair of white hands crumpling up a rejection letter accompanied by the voice-over, "You needed that job. You were the best qualified, but they had to give it to a minority." Though no explanation Jordan gave would ever change the perception of the player, author Sam Smith tells a different story about the anecdote's origin:

> Michael was unusually image conscious, and I probably got him in trouble in my second book, *Second Coming*, when he returned [to the NBA] in 1995, as I told the story of how I was urging him to get involved in Democratic politics in North Carolina (I was the Rockefeller/ Jacob Javits Republican, an extinct species now). Michael was always quick and clever, first to win a word race, and he joked to me that "Republicans buy shoes, too." It wasn't the political statement many have made it out to be, and I've felt badly I hung it on him.

Except that it *was* precisely the political statement Jordan would come to embody. Had he over the years contradicted the statement, repudiated it through his actions, it wouldn't have been so defining, but *Republicans buy shoes, too* became a part of Michael Jordan because his public reaction to the political world around him would almost always embody what he said to Smith that day.

Despite Jordan's indomitable championship will and his signature moments and achievements on the court—that spectacular first-right-hand-then-left-hand layup in Game 1 of the 1991 NBA Finals against the Lakers, the record sixty-three points against the Celtics in the 1986 playoffs, the numerous dunk-and-staredowns of Patrick Ewing, the nailing of the winning shot to beat Utah in the 1998 Finals—his ambivalent social and political positions also became a large part of his legacy.

By the time Jordan left the game, in 2003, he was the winningest player of his time, having won six titles and never lost in the Finals. (Even Bill Russell, though injured, lost once, in the 1958 Finals, against St. Louis.) Jordan made the most money in the game and built a corporate empire— for Nike. Thanks to endorsements, he would become America's first black billionaire athlete; in fact, the first billionaire athlete of any race. Because of Jordan, top players would now earn more money in endorsements than from their multimillion-dollar salaries. Tiger Woods would sign a $40 million endorsement deal with Nike in 1996 as a twenty-year-old. The Jordan model culminated in 2003 when Nike signed the next phenom, LeBron James, to a $90 million shoe deal before he had played his first NBA game. By following in precedent established by O. J. Simpson, Jordan had perfected the position of the detached athlete.

But for the money and opportunities assimilation afforded athletes of the Jordan era, there were two issues that rendered greenwashing tenuous at best, illegitimate at worst: The first was that, whether acknowledged or not, the issues that created the Heritage in the first place still remained. The second was that for all the money, the players were still black, and the minute any one of them ran afoul of the white mainstream public, either by decline in play or by specifically taking a political stand that advocated for African Americans, that same public would be quick to turn on him.

INVISIBLE MEN

On October 29, 1984, three days after Jordan made his NBA debut scoring sixteen points in a win over the Washington Bullets, New York police responded to a complaint to evict Eleanor Bumpurs, a woman with a history of mental illness, from her apartment in a Bronx public-housing complex for being three months behind on her rent of $98.05. The encounter, in which Bumpurs allegedly lunged at police with a 10-inch knife, ended with police shooting the sixty-six-year-old twice with a 12-gauge shotgun. The first shot struck her in the hand, the second in the chest, killing her.

Two years later, a week before Christmas, four black men whose car broke down were chased out of the Howard Beach section of Queens by a gang of whites wielding clubs, including baseball bats. One of the men was beaten badly with a tree limb, and Michael Griffith, a twenty-three-year-old Trinidadian immigrant, was killed on the Belt Parkway, hit by a motorist while attempting to flee.

In 1989, after being chased by a mob of whites brandishing baseball bats in the predominantly Italian Brooklyn neighborhood of Bensonhurst, Yusuf Hawkins was shot and killed. Leading a peace march through the streets of Bensonhurst, Reverend Al Sharpton was stabbed. The Hawkins killing was seen as a transformative moment in New York, and partially as a result, the city elected its first and only black mayor, David Dinkins.

New York in the 1980s resembled a flashpoint similar to more recent years, when the Trayvon Martin, Ferguson, and other high-profile incidents in a short amount of time activated athletes. But during those years, the players did nothing. Michael Jordan said nothing. Patrick Ewing, the superstar of the New York Knicks, in whose backyard national headlines were being made, said nothing. The best football players, Tony Dorsett and Jerry Rice and Lawrence Taylor, the last another superstar playing in New York, were as silent as the baseball players, Dave Winfield and Rickey Henderson, Darryl Strawberry and Dwight Gooden, playing for the New York Yankees and New York Mets, respectively. Yankees all-star second baseman Willie Randolph, who grew up in the Brownsville section of Brooklyn, not far from Howard Beach, said nothing.

"In the 1980s and '90s, when we started, with Howard Beach in '86, all the way through Bensonhurst and Yusuf Hawkins, all the way through Abner Louima in the '90s, there was no support either publicly or privately from the athletes," Sharpton recalled. "And the irony was because we were doing this in the Northeast and urban centers, that clearly they were familiar with it. I led the marches and the mobilizations, including Rodney King in LA, and [athletes] were not there, not even privately."

Shawon Dunston arrived in Chicago in 1985 as the Cubs shortstop of the future. Being a black player, selected with the first overall pick in the 1982 draft, taking over the position once held by the legendary Ernie Banks, the greatest player in the franchise's history, was heady stuff. Dunston grew up in East New York, the Brooklyn neighborhood bordered by Howard Beach and the Belt Parkway, the freeway where Michael Griffith was killed, on one side and the heavily Italian Canarsie section to the west, where the racial boundaries between neighborhoods, and the potential dangers of crossing each, were clear. "We went all over the place,"

Dunston recalled. "Canarsie and Brownsville were fine, but it was up to you if you wanted to go to Howard Beach."

When Dunston arrived in the big leagues, Dallas Green, the Cubs general manager, told him he was going to be the team's starting short-stop for the next ten years. "I lasted twelve," Dunston said. The two most influential voices in the Cubs organization for him were white men, Don Zimmer and John Vukovich. Dunston was aware of the opportunity to be a big leaguer, a potentially great one, and also cognizant of the larger world around him. Though not making a conscious, direct repudiation of the Heritage, he knew the job was too hard to anoint himself a political leader as well. His recollection of those early days with the Cubs was put simply: "Gotta concentrate on that slider."

If at first Dunston's refusal to engage politically appeared to be a dismissal of what was happening in the streets, it also underscored the conflict of the player. The level of talent and concentration, excellence and results, required to play professional sports is enormous, and Shawon Dunston had a day job, and it was to play baseball at the highest level. The constant competition, for some ninth-grade hotshot on a sandlot might become the next Barry Bonds and take your job, was pressure enough. The game itself was hard enough, and now the pressure to perform was compounded by the pressure to also be a leader on child labor or police brutality in the community, never mind most likely having more wealth than every member of your family combined. It wasn't an easy or fair burden. White players wore Nikes, too, but they weren't being asked to picket the sweatshops. Sharpton was nevertheless unmoved. You owed because you received.

"I knew and saw Jackie Robinson and Kareem, and got very close with Ali, and [singer] James Brown took me in under his wing as his son," Sharpton said. "Jim Brown used to come around Operation Breadbasket. So I'm a kid watching these legends [who] would be in the movement, but by the time my time came, none of the legendary figures of my generation came. I never saw the athletes get involved until Trayvon. But the gap between the '80s and 2012? [Athletes] were absent. They were missing in action. When they were confronting racists in the South, it was permitted to fight Archie Bunker. That's dumb, down-South rednecks. But when we started fighting Howard Beach, the Northeastern crowd, now you're attacking the cousins of the guys who own [the teams]. Big difference."

WHO ARE YOU?

Tiger Woods won the 1997 Masters Tournament as a twenty-one-year-old by a record twelve strokes, and alongside Michael Jordan, he would quickly become the most famous athlete in the world. For a country that craved post-racialism, Woods was too good to be true. If O. J. Simpson and Jordan had distanced the black athlete from the Heritage in favor of a race-neutral, greenwashed corporate image, one that superstars from Derek Jeter and Alex Rodriguez to Shaquille O'Neal and Kobe Bryant would emulate, Woods added an even more attractive dimension. He was born to an African American father and a Thai mother, and he played golf, the sport most closely identified with white elitism. Woods's father, Earl, predicted his son would not only become the greatest golfer who ever lived but would also be an heir to the Heritage, not just an athlete but an important world figure in the mold of Jackie and Ali. Earl Woods would call his son a "prophet" who, through golf, would "move mountains," obvious nods to both a biblical power and Muhammad Ali's ability to spiritually lift the poor as he rose to fame. For his son, Earl Woods was forecasting a cultural transformation. Through Tiger, golf, with its all-male clubs and white-man winks and nods and racial slurs when the drinks were flowing in the clubhouse, its financial and cultural snobbery, would finally become a sport of the people, its class barriers lifted, its racial legacy rewritten.

When Woods won his record-setting Masters title, forty-four million viewers watched that final Sunday on television. At his best, Woods attacked the record books with a singular, unstoppable ferocity that resembled the focus and fire of Michael Jordan. And Nike, following its Jordan template of creating a style icon as much as an athletic one, made sure he looked the part with unforgettable touches. Only on Sundays, the final round that determined a champion, did Woods wear a red shirt and black trousers. It sent a message to the world that Sundays were closing days, and closing days required a different garb, because the fans (and his opponents) would be seeing a different, more focused, hungrier Tiger. On golf courses around the country, duffers were now wearing red on Sundays, just to be like Tiger. The clothing added to the mystique, and Woods's popularity soared so much, both for his golf and for what he represented to different people, it was clear that viewers were watching him not just for his athletic prowess.

For a time, Woods would embrace the destiny his father had forecast for him, paying homage to the history of the sport, to the lonely pioneers such as Lee Elder and Charlie Sifford, black pros who endured the insults and indignities of playing a game in a white world that could not have been more metaphoric of the impediments to the American dream for black people. As with Jordan, the seasoned Nike ad machine was there, choreographing the legend that was being built on the course, the ads voiced over by the father (even after Earl Woods died, in 2006) reinforcing his specialness, packaging his destiny.

And when it came time for the prophet to spiritually lift the poor and the weak and the despised black people and give them dignity through his talent, as he was destined to, he sat down with Oprah Winfrey, the wealthiest black American in the world, and told her and the world that he was not black. He was a composite. He was Caucasian, black, and Asian. He told Winfrey that, growing up, he had coined a term for his multiethnicity. He told Winfrey he was "Cablinasian."

Woods did not say, "I'm not black. I'm OJ," but he gave the equivalent for a multicultural world. The end result was the same: a reinforcement of the O. J. Simpson model but on an even more public stage—there was no advantage to identifying with being black. That came with responsibility. Take, for example, the time when Woods was hitting supernova status, the most talked-about athlete in America. He had just won the Masters, and now, as his father predicted, he would "move mountains." It was an unsubtle comparison to Ali, a wish to join the Heritage. It was all coming together.

It was also 1997, the fiftieth anniversary of Jackie Robinson entering the majors. The Jackie Robinson Foundation contacted Woods, asking him to participate in the celebration at a Mets game, side by side with Rachel Robinson. Woods demurred. He said he was busy. He said he had an overwhelming number of commitments to his sponsor, Nike.

Tiger Woods stiffed Rachel Robinson.

Frustrated but undeterred, the foundation looked down the lineup card, went to the bullpen, skipped the eighth-inning setup guy, and went straight to the closer. Not Michael Jordan or Arnold Palmer or Jack Nicklaus but the most powerful man in the free world: President Bill Clinton. The president personally called Tiger Woods, and Woods told him the same thing: Thanks for the call, Mr. President, but I'm swamped.

"Tiger," Bill Clinton said, "what commitments? I'm the President of the United States. Who do I have to call? I think I can get you out of them."

Tiger held firm, giving President Clinton the stiff-arm as well. The president offered to send an Air Force jet to deliver him to Shea Stadium. Instead, Woods was in Mexico partying on the beach with friends.

Tiger said no, not just to the president but to the Heritage. Now he wasn't even black. He was Cablinasian. Even Nike, his risk-averse corporate sponsor, was horrified. Cablinasian? What in the hell was Cablinasian? Nike sold products but did so through storytelling, and here was Tiger Woods telling America that its favorite bedtime story—the black athlete breaking barriers to entry, and those old white institutions bending to a new day, each meeting in the middle to mutually overcome racism and fulfill the promise that America could overcome its deepest scar after all—wasn't the story at all. Nike saw the lucrative and eminently sellable narrative of the African American who conquered the exclusive, white sport of golf go up in flames.

"I thought that this was a new form of denial," Al Sharpton said, "and the subtlety that was disturbing to me was it was a subliminal message that our children should feel almost ashamed of being black and we have to find a way to not be that. The message was, 'He's all of this, but doesn't want to be *that*. Therefore, I shouldn't want to be that.'"

"Cablinasian" was an all-around disaster, but it wasn't exactly inaccurate. Woods was biracial, black and Asian, and the rapidly changing world of mixed marriages and biracial children created a collision with the American historical edict of one drop of black blood made a person African American, and thus less than a full citizen. The year before Woods won the Masters, another biracial player, Derek Jeter, won the World Series with the Yankees and was on his way to becoming a superstar.

"It makes sense and it doesn't make sense. My guess is that Tiger, like me, got asked, 'What are you?' A lot. Most mixed people say 'mixed but black,'" said Grand Valley State associate professor of history Louis Moore. "By the time you get asked this, you know you're black. Tiger, I think, tried to run away from that a bit. From my experience, people from our generation who are mixed but go out of their way to not say they're black, do it intentionally."

Whether intended, unintended, or both depending on the expediency of the moment, "Cablinasian" represented the ultimate consequence of greenwashing, of decades of selling the idea that identifying with the black identity was the worst thing a person could do. What an irony it was, that after the learned behavior of avoiding pride in being African American, the one time America wanted finally someone to be black, when the corporations actually encouraged it and were hungry to profit from it instead of running for fear of offending the white mainstream, Tiger Woods did not cooperate.

"I was troubled by it," Harry Edwards recalled, "not so much because [Woods] seemed to be disassociating himself from African American roots [and therefore any perceived obligation to "represent"—think OJ] but because, as a man who has from the outset been perceived and defined by society under the rubric of the 'one-drop rule' as black/African American [remember Fuzzy Zoeller's "fried chicken" and "collard greens" slur], given the inevitability of trials and tribulations ahead, he undercut his support base, left himself no place to turn—no struggle heritage, no survival heritage to lean on, no identity, no refuge."

At least for the mainstream fan and skittish team management who didn't want their players getting involved in race and social issues, the messy stuff of raised black fists and boycotts, greenwashing solved the issue. By the end of the twentieth century, it had been nearly thirty years since a top-shelf, in-his-prime athlete had embraced the Heritage. Jackie Robinson had been dead nearly thirty years. Muhammad Ali had been ravaged by the effects of Parkinson's disease, and he and the country had reconciled. Ali was embraced as a courageous warrior of yesterday's fights, not a living, activist threat. Kareem, by rights, should have been the standard bearer, but he was not. The trinity of OJ, Michael, and Tiger, and the wealth they tapped, had created a new template for a new generation, which had no personal memory of when athletes took principled stands on issues. The Nike-led machine of commercials and star-making followed—Derek Jeter, the Williams sisters, Ken Griffey Jr. Players scored touchdowns and sold sneakers, using the fear of offending a potential consumer as a justification for their silence. The greenwashing of the players signaled they had made it, that they identified more with their corporate sponsors and their celebrity neighbors than with the black communities that bought their sneakers. In 2000, Alex Rodriguez signed a ten-year $252 million contract with the Texas Rangers, the richest in the history of the four major professional sports in the US. By 2001, the average annual salary in baseball and basketball was well over $2 million, and Shaquille O'Neal signed the biggest NBA contract ever. And the greatest players made more money in endorsements than in salaries.

The Heritage was dead. The paying customer never wanted it, and now the players believed that being a political athlete was either no longer their responsibility or too costly for the wallet. In a sense, the players had won. The black body remained a multimillion-dollar commodity to America, but this time they got to keep the money. They were rich beyond the imagination, and their wealth provided them access to the best Western culture could provide: housing, schools, business opportunities, luxuries. Racism still existed, but the players were considered, because of their money, beyond it. Players not only avoided racial subjects in talking to the press, but as long as they didn't talk about it, they could avoid being black altogether. There was even a phrase for it: athletes now *transcended race*. If there was a need for players to make a social statement, it was not done by standing in the streets, physically arm-in-arm with their people, but by privately sending a few bucks along a back channel, with a slickly produced ad campaign that also showed the shoe company on the right side of a social issue. Sports would now be in balance: abundantly commercial, lucrative for all, and without the polarizing sociopolitical component. Sports was now like the music or movie industry, just another form of entertainment.

And then the Twin Towers fell.

PART TWO

WAR GAMES

5

"OUR WAY OF LIFE"

Eventually, in Life on Earth, people will try to tell you that sports is the toy shop, a mindless entertainment that exists basically to hold down or delude or opiate people, an inferior concept to business, because business is pure. And you might buy into all that for a while—up until some hurt or pain you know you aren't strong enough to handle alone comes down on you. Then you put in that emergency call. And it ain't to no bond trader. To the Home Team. *"What's the score? C'mon, guys . . ."*

—RALPH WILEY, September 11, 2001

THE WRITER AND HISTORIAN David Halberstam conceptualized book projects by identifying what he called *intersections*, those crucial pivots where decisions or indecisions made by a handful of key people at key times altered the arc of history. Halberstam reasoned that history could not be understood without deep examination of those intersections. As sports fractured along the lines of the protest and politics, race and patriotism, 9/11 was that intersection. Referring to it as such even felt like an understatement, for nothing about the current state of the sports world can be explained *without* the context of September 11, 2001. It wasn't an intersection of American life. It was a full freeway interchange.

The death toll was just under 3,000. Of the first responders, 343 firefighters were killed, as were 60 combined officers from the New York and New Jersey Police Departments and the Port Authority. The media showed chilling, heartbreaking images of the doomed inhabitants of the World Trade Center towers, holding hands and leaping into the air to their deaths before the skyscrapers imploded.

The trading firm Cantor Fitzgerald lost nearly two-thirds of its workforce, as 658 of 960 employees were killed. Howard Lutnick, the Cantor CEO, only survived because that morning he had taken his son to his first day of kindergarten. According to the Centers for Disease Control, 1,361 bodies, or nearly half of the total death toll, were never recovered. For months following the attacks, when the Manhattan winds would shift north, they carried a daily reminder of death: visible flakes of debris from what was once the World Trade Center flew biliously into the air.

America had fought many a foreign war, but it had little experience with fighting on its soil, trying to enjoy life while its streets, subways, buildings, and civilians were under threat. September 11 forced a certain, though by no means complete, reattachment to the world. "I went back to thinking about watching war movies, as all kids did, and realizing that all of those things happened in someone else's country," recalled the baseball Hall of Famer Joe Torre, who was the manager of the New York Yankees at the time of 9/11. "And now you're attacked in downtown Manhattan, in my hometown."

What would America do as it reattached to a dangerous world? Would it rethink its enormous role and influence and image in the world, understanding that its power was also responsible for conflict and might one day invite deadly challenge? Would it seek blind revenge? Would it descend into religious war? Would it turn inward?

The attacks changed who could speak and who could not, and on what issues. Out of respect for the victims, the men and women killed in the line of duty, and in the interest of unifying of the country, the attacks tempered much criticism. Police and military were elevated for their sacrifice and bravery and the coming two-front war.

Of all American social institutions, 9/11 most radically altered sports, from the place where fans escaped the world and its problems to the definitive staging ground for the nation's war effort, the restoration of its wounded spirit, of taking back everything Osama bin Laden took from it. Sports would embody the way the United States would view itself and its institutions. If the opportunity for the riches of the good life destroyed the political foundations of the Heritage, September 11 both killed *stick to sports* and became a patriotic war cry, even if the people who most used that term didn't know it at the time. What was thought to be a period of grieving and a temporary display of militarism became a permanent, cultural transformation, now going on nearly twenty years.

America had been there before, when the 1991 Super Bowl between the New York Giants and Buffalo Bills was played during Operation Desert Storm. The touches would soon become familiar: yellow ribbons signifying support for the Gulf War soldiers were affixed to flagpoles, ribbon magnets attached to cars. On game day, a giant American flag covered much of the field, and F-16 fighter jets roared over the stadium.

The national anthem that year was performed famously by the pop star Whitney Houston. Sports had recognized wartime in the past but never with such fervor, with seventy thousand fans waving tiny American flags. Houston's performance was so iconic that two weeks after her performance, Arista Records released it as a single. But once the war ended, a month after the Super Bowl, virtually all daily traces of patriotism on the field, on the court, or at the ballpark disappeared. Neither the subsequent 1993 World Trade Center bombing nor the 1995 Oklahoma City bombing elicited the same cultural response. The Whitney Houston moment was over.

September 11 was different. The 1991 Super Bowl was a pep rally. The resumption of sports following the attacks were a combination of wake, defiance, hero worship, and a deeply rooted, dormant nationalism as a response to having home soil attacked. Between September 11 and 14, Walmart sold more than five hundred thousand American flags, and Samy Yousef, a forty-five-year-old immigrant from Egypt who worked for the nation's oldest American flag manufacturer, assembled 200 flags per hour and received seventy orders per hour. "Some 2.3 million American flags were imported last year, almost all of them from China and Taiwan," the *Times* reported. "But many retailers will sell only flags made in America, and many Americans will pay more for a flag with a 'Made in the U.S.A.' label." National Public Radio reported that 98 percent of all American flags, however, were made in China.

By the first week of October 2001, the United States began its bombing campaign of Afghanistan. Everyone had a job to do. President George W. Bush urged the public not toward introspection or service but to spend money, to shop and to travel. Sports had a role, too, and a new word was added to our vocabulary right alongside *winning* and *losing*; the new word to describe sports' mission was *healing*. Teams and their leagues felt an obligation to be involved in the patriotic rush. They had to show their colors and show their faces. At first, Joe Torre was unconvinced. He was not sure that sports had any business being thrust into the center of America's geopolitics. "Baseball was the last thing any of us were thinking about at that moment," he recalled. On the morning of the attacks, Torre was at home with his five-year-old daughter, trying to shield her from the horrific television images of the Towers burning before their collapse. "I was trying to get her to look at something else while I was paying attention to what was going on," he said. "When we got back on the field and they'd play 'God Bless America,' and the camera would pan to little kids in the crowd, I just started crying. You couldn't help it."

Part of the healing was rebuilding confidence in American resolve. Jerry Laveroni, head of security for the New York Yankees, handed out tiny American flag lapel pins to everyone in the Yankee clubhouse, a little item that would soon become a mandatory accessory for politicians. Wearing the pin may have seemed optional to staff, coaches, players, and the writers as a show of respect for, solidarity with, and loyalty to America, but it angered Laveroni tremendously whenever he noticed anyone connected with the Yankees without one.

In Queens, the city had used Shea Stadium as a relief center for victims. New York Mets manager Bobby Valentine and pitcher John Franco, a Brooklyn native, joined volunteers in the parking lot, handing out food and clothing to people, packing supplies, serving coffee to weary first responders, connecting eye to eye with New Yorkers. Privately, George Steinbrenner simmered that the Mets were being perceived as more patriotic than the Yankees. However anecdotally, the Mets were being identified as the city's most visible sports face of the recovery. (That some of the star Yankees weren't even in New York on 9/11 didn't help. Within hours of the disaster, Andy Pettitte and Roger Clemens got in a car and drove to Texas.)

The weekend following the attacks, Yankees manager Torre, his coaches, and players made a goodwill mission to visit with victims, and his belief that their presence was inappropriate in the aftermath of the disaster began to change. "We had a workout on Saturday for whoever who was in town: Bernie Williams, Derek [Jeter], [Don] Zimmer, Willie [Randolph]. Just going down to the staging area at the Javits Center and seeing all those sleeping bags on the floor, people appreciative that we were there. . . . Meanwhile, at the same time, I'm thinking, 'These people have work to do. Why are we down here getting in the way?' That was exactly how I felt: what right do we have to be here when people are dealing with all this tragedy in their lives? We play a game."

Then, the Yankees went to the Armory, on Lexington Avenue and Twenty-Fifth Street, where the city had set up DNA staging areas to identify the missing.

"Clergy members, councilors were there, and we just walked around the outside," recalled Torre. "One family recognized us. Bernie Williams walked up to this woman and said, 'I don't know what to say, but you look like you need a hug.' So, he hugged her, and with that, we were like magnets. . . . People were sort of looking to us, showing us pictures of family members in their Yankee jackets and jerseys. And it struck me that day [that I needed] to go back to work. It felt like we had a job to do."

On September 21, the first sporting event was played in New York after the attacks: the Mets against the Atlanta Braves. The Mets handed out miniature American flags to the sellout crowd. The Mets (and football's New York Giants, whose season was also under way in the aftermath of 9/11) wore New York Police Department and Fire Department of New York caps to honor the survivors and those killed in the line of duty.

At Major League Baseball headquarters in midtown Manhattan, a minor eruption occurred when some league officials considered fining the Mets for a violation of the team uniform code by wearing FDNY hats in-game instead of the team's official cap. Patrick Courtney, then the number-two communications man at MLB, sensed disaster. He recalled his boss, Rich Levin, lambasting the decision. "Are you fucking kidding me?" Levin said. "After everything that city has been through you're going to threaten them with fines for supporting organizations that risked their lives?" Baseball wisely backed off.

Police officers at Yankee or Shea Stadium would then be honored on a nightly basis, to throw out the first pitch or sing the national anthem. American flags were stitched to the back of every major-league jersey, just below the collar, and on the side of every major-league hat. Daniel Rodriguez, a member of the NYPD, became such a fixture performing the anthem at sporting events that he became known as "the singing cop."

The Mets played at home first. Eighth inning, one on, one out, Braves up 2–1, Mike Piazza, New York star faced Steve Karsay, Queens kid, born and raised in Flushing, attended Christ the King High. Karsay delivered. Piazza swung. A mammoth two-run homer to center, and a week's worth of contained emotion erupted. "I remember that being the moment where you were allowed to cheer again," recalled Sweeny Murti, who covered the Yankees for the all-sports radio station WFAN. "People treated it like it was an escape, but was it really when everyone is wearing the flag and people are bringing their own flags during the seventh-inning stretch and they're holding up signs? Was it really an escape? Because it sure didn't feel like one, but Piazza's home run made sports feel normal again. It was an outburst. Before that, you weren't sure. That moment sort of told everyone it was okay to let it out, that we could start going forward."

In Chicago, where the Yankees resumed play after 9/11, old animosities were tabled. "We Love You, New York" signs were prominent throughout US Cellular Field, the corporate takeover of New Comiskey Park. Once a sworn enemy of all things Yankee, the White Sox held a moment of silence for victims and, as in New York, Chicago police and fire officers were on the field during the pregame ceremonies. The Yankees then traveled to Baltimore, where the two teams just five years earlier had been involved in a bitter pennant race and at least one brawl. This time, the Yankees were received not as the hated overlords of baseball but as the sentimental representatives of a wounded city and country.

When the Yankees returned home, George Steinbrenner made certain there was no ambiguity about the team's commitment to the city's healing and its defiance. The Yankees took batting practice wearing NYPD, FDNY, and Port Authority caps, and added the great Irish tenor Ronan Tynan to the payroll to sing at home games. During the seventh-inning stretch, Tynan, with his beautiful voice, full of pride and pain, the old country weeping in solidarity with the new, would not just sing "God Bless America" but the *long version*, Irving Berlin's 1938 full-length original, the one with the "solemn prayer" preamble. Bob Sheppard, the legendary and eloquent voice of the Yankees over the public-address system began every home game with a reminder of a city's pain—and an unsubtle message to the world showing just who was boss.

"Ladies and gentlemen . . . would you please rise," Sheppard would begin. "And now, please offer a moment of silent prayer for the servicemen and -women who are stationed around the globe. And especially remember those who have lost their lives defending our freedom—and *our* way of life."

But it was the 2001 World Series between the Yankees and the Arizona Diamondbacks that encapsulated what post-9/11 sports would become. In many ways, the Yankees served as a larger metaphor for America at the moment: the superpower as sentimental favorite. The game did not provide any escape from wartime signifiers: from the police, fire, military, and first responders honored at Game 1 at Bank One Ballpark in Phoenix to the Game 7 appearance of the military's futuristic new weapon, the Northrop B-2 Spirit, better known as the Stealth Bomber.

When the series shifted back to New York, cleanup crews from Ground Zero were invited to Yankee Stadium, as were some families who had lost loved ones in the Towers. A tattered American flag recovered from the rubble stood above the scoreboard at the stadium. Word buzzed through the clubhouses and stands that President Bush might be on hand to throw out the first pitch. As game time neared, the umpires gathered for their pregame meeting. One of the umpires, Jim Joyce, recognized each member of the crew except one, who turned out to be a member of the Secret Service. The president would be on hand.

The legendary baseball played in the middle games in New York was unforgettable not so much for the Yankees' championship fight, with comebacks in Games 3, 4, and 5, as it was for President Bush, fitted with a bulletproof vest while snipers manned the Yankee Stadium roof, throwing out the first pitch of Game 3 at Yankee Stadium. Right before the game started, the president walked up to Yankees manager Joe Torre and said, "Kick their asses." This time, New York, the team that had won the last three World Series, four of the last five, and twenty-six overall, was in the minds of many, the underdog. The moments were memorable, the graying Yankee dynasty fighting to win one more championship, this one maybe the most important. Though the Yankees didn't win that year, the series was a catharsis, and they stood as the symbol of a rebuilding of spirit. Figure that: the New York Yankees, America's Team.

During the postseason, the Yankees' pre-game ceremony included Challenger, an American bald eagle, flying to the pitcher's mound while the stadium was awash in American flags, pictures of the Twin Towers, and fans wearing NYPD baseball caps. "We were really representing, for that brief moment, America," Torre recalled. "And it was a rare thing for the Yankees to walk into a visiting ballpark and receive anything but boos, but I think that was indicative of how much people were hurting for what happened to the country and to the people of New York. I told my players they were representing everything that New York was all about."

―――――――

FROM THE MOMENT THE GAMES resumed across all sports after the attacks, sports sold the idea of healing, of everyone coming together at the ballpark in a combined show of force. It also sold another product: conformity and obedience cloaked in an ostensibly benign patriotism. It was an easy sell because who *wasn't* against terrorism? The fervor was too seductive to challenge.

The post-9/11 template carried into the following years. Following the Yankees' lead, the rest of baseball added the playing of "God Bless America" to the seventh-inning stretch. The Montreal Expos and Toronto Blue Jays, of course, were exempt. (So were the Cubs, incidentally, because of their long-standing tradition of singing "Take Me Out to the Ball Game.") Then, caught in the wave, the Commissioner's Office got into the act, and commissioner Bud Selig made the playing of "God Bless America" *mandatory* at every ballpark in the country, with all uniformed personnel required to be on the field or top step of the dugout, or face discipline.

Meanwhile, the NFL stitched American flags onto the black-and-white-striped referee uniforms. And the American flag decal from the 1991 Super Bowl returned to the back of players' helmets.

The San Diego Padres wore camouflage uniforms for every Sunday home game, but this was the nation's preeminent US Navy town, so the mood, the touches, had to be perfect. The Padres' television broadcaster, former ballplayer Jerry Coleman, had left the Yankees in 1943 to serve in World War II, flying fifty-seven missions in the Philippines and Solomon Islands. The city's greatest baseball player, Red Sox star Ted Williams, had been a war hero not once but twice, having served in the navy during World War II and the marines during the Korean War. In the weeks following 9/11, the Padres organized a day to honor the soldiers. Coleman, of course, was there. He worked for the team. The Padres, however, were having difficulty securing Ted Williams. Williams was in ill health and, though no one knew it at the time, had less than a year to live. The Padres begged, to no avail. MLB got involved, offering to send a private plane for Williams with full accommodations, but Ted's son John Henry refused to commit the Splendid Splinter to the event. Ultimately, the son turned down the request, and the ceremony commenced without the Greatest Hitter Who Ever Lived. Days later, baseball public relations man Patrick Courtney was sitting at his desk in New York when his phone rang. Before he could speak, the voice on the other end did all the talking, at top decibel: "HELLO? THIS IS TED WILLIAMS. WHY THE FUCK WASN'T I IN SAN DIEGO LAST WEEK?!"

———

ON THE ORDER OF THE NFL, teams handed out American flags and "United We Stand" placards to every fan entering the stadium. "It was to show that as a nation we were unified and resilient and determined and not cowed," NFL commissioner Paul Tagliabue told NFL Films. After beating the Kansas City Chiefs in their first game back in New York, the Giants took a team photo with every player wearing an NYPD cap.

Over in the NBA, for the Washington Wizards' home opener, commissioner David Stern took the microphone to applause at half-court at the MCI Center in DC. "Tonight, as we have done at every opening night, and as we will do all season long, we honor our heroes: the armed services, our fire departments, our police departments, our emergency services, our relief services," he told the crowd. Stern was followed by Washington mayor Anthony Williams, who also honored the heroes by alluding to the NBA return of a legend, Michael Jordan, who had joined the Wizards after a two-year retirement.

Months later, in February 2002, the underdog New England Patriots met the heavily favored St. Louis Rams in the New Orleans Superdome in Super Bowl XXXVI. The TV production of the game was virtually themed after the military and in honor of the war effort, down to the Fox broadcast creating a video graphic with a marine or navy member introducing the starters once the game began. The background behind each graphic was an American flag. When the game began, the broadcast frequently cut away to video feeds of American troops in Kandahar, Afghanistan, watching the game. The Super Bowl XXXVI logo was the shape of the United States covered by an American flag. When the

Patriots completed the 20–17 upset win, team owner Robert Kraft took the microphone amid the confetti cannons and told the crowd, "Today, we are all Patriots."

Army Lieutenant Colonel Mark Zinno saw the tragedy of 9/11 and the subsequent eruption of patriotism at ballparks and in New York as exactly the reminder he needed to rededicate himself to the purpose of serving his country. "Ever since 9/11, everything in my military career has had impact," he said. "And maybe that held true beforehand, but I just couldn't see it. Most people enlisted because they were bad kids. They were trying to stay out of trouble. You used to hear it all the time, 'Why don't you get a real job?' Well, my job got real, *real* quick. And it gave me an anchor for my life."

In many ways, Zinno reflected the attitude that made sports celebrating the military so powerful. Not a fervent flag-waver in spirit or ideology, he had entered the army not with patriotism in mind but pragmatism: serving was the best way to pay for college. While energized by its potential in theory, he had not found the daily experience of military life particularly rewarding in practice. "I was a cocky son of a bitch who thought he knew better than the military what it would provide me. In the pre-9/11 world, I wanted to do something impactful, but I didn't feel that I was. I was living in places I didn't want to live, [like] Fort Hood, Texas, doing a job I didn't want to do," Zinno recalled. "I was a maintenance officer. It was very *Groundhog Day*: Get up, fix vehicles, wash, rinse, repeat. I wasn't even turning wrenches. I was handing out orders for other people to do the work. Couldn't see what my role was and why it was important. With a couple of exceptions, in the military, you are literally as far away from any place you'd want to be. The thought of being stationed at Fort Riley, Kansas, was like taking a baseball bat to my own skull."

Zinno grew up in the Roman Catholic hamlet of Franklin Square, a part of Hempstead on Long Island, New York. His stepfather, Joseph, was a police officer, a sergeant with the county police department. His sports teams were all New York-based: the Yankees, Giants, Knicks, and Islanders. He received early release from active duty in June 2001 and joined the Maryland National Guard. Searching for purpose, he had also requested a deployment to Honduras on an overseas mission that contained some familiarity, as part of his unit would be there. Around the same time, through an army recruiter, Zinno found a job in sales with the uniform company Cintas. He was twenty-three, living in Baltimore as a part-time civilian, part-time soldier.

"I remember we were at a hotel in a training conference. People from all over the company had come in. We were on a break, and a guy from Boston, in his Boston accent, said, 'A plane just hit the World Trade Center.' I said, 'Get the fuck outta here.' We all found a TV and gathered around it.

"Me, being a native New Yorker, once the second plane hit, I picked up the phone. I had a half-dozen friends working on Wall Street. I remember somehow getting hold of my mother. I remember asking about my brother. He worked in the city, but I wasn't sure where. My good family friend, her brother was in the [one of the] Towers. Another friend worked on the 104th floor for Cantor Fitzgerald, and we all know what happened there. Right after it happened, I remember going to the [Baltimore] armory and asking what I could do. To me, it was personal. That was my city. I grew up in the shadows of the Towers. It was my America, and I was going to do my part."

"OUR WAY OF LIFE"

There was something in the way Bob Sheppard, whose first day on the job was April 17, 1951—Mickey Mantle's debut—emphasized, with his trademark dramatic pauses and intonation, the word *our* that telegraphed the emerging American attitude—and it wasn't exactly a compliment to everyone. The country's view would not be complicated: America was attacked without reason. Innocents were killed. America was not part of a global community collectively wounded by terrorism, nor did its foreign policy invite conflict. America didn't start the fight, but be damned sure she planned on finishing it. And too bad for the peaceniks who felt uncomfortable with the new reality.

"Well, the reason we don't have peace is because we got a bunch people that are trying to fucking kill us," Lieutenant General Russel Honoré said. "We didn't start 9/11. They came over here and bombed our shit, and after that we had to go over there and open up a big old can of whup ass. . . . So, if people didn't bomb our people and kill them, we wouldn't be doing this. Come over here, wreck three airplanes, and attack our citizens around the world?"

The ballpark was the place of defiance and the introduction of a new, post-9/11 character: *heroes*. On the field, the players had always been the ones celebrated as heroes. Now sports would recognize the off-field citizen in uniform as heroes too: police, fire, military, sometimes emergency services. The ballpark atmosphere made sports the perfect venue for that form of tribute, but it was also the perfect place to bring out the worst elements of our cultural instincts. Political confrontation was never supposed to be the plan. For years, sports was the country's province of political neutrality, of fun and games, of root, root, rooting for the home team.

And when the Heritage got involved, when a player wanted to make a political statement, the business of sports backed away, assuaging the public by clarifying that a player's act of political protest was an *individual* one, not endorsed by the team. Teams knew politics were polarizing, and no way were teams going to risk alienating half the people who bought tickets.

September 11 posed no such risk. Not only did America seem to be in lockstep in honoring the military, but the cultural pressure against dissent was so strong, opponents didn't dare speak out against fifty thousand flag-wavers, still waiting to get its collective mitts on Osama bin Laden—and that was the danger. After the initial pain, when fans needed to look fellow Americans in the eye and feel safe, the ballpark brought out the dangerous side. Sports was rooted in conflict, confrontation already in place. Two sides wore different colors, *Us* against *Them*, home versus road, good guy versus bad, winners and losers and no backing down. It was the province of machismo and competition, of imposing will, and every other sports cliché the broadcasters had ginned up over the past fifty years. The line was delicate, but in the moment, the country felt itself in the fight of its life and those not on board, even if they were Americans, were not particularly welcome. Fans expected every other fan in the ballpark to go along with the spectacle, to *act right*. Hand on heart. Sing along, or *you* were the problem.

"I remember everybody showing up [at games] with an American flag. And they supported the NYPD. They were at the game, but they were still thinking about everything that's important. I loved seeing that," Mark Zinno recalled of those first months and years after the attacks. "Nothing was better than watching people celebrate the anthem for the first time in my life. It wasn't a matter of routine. It mattered for the first time. I remember the anthem giving me chills, actually striking a chord in my heart. The minute it stops giving me chills, it's time to hang up the uniform."

To anyone at the ballpark not joining in, there seemed a collective, tacit threat to the flag-waving. *Defiance* and *healing* were not competing emotions but complementary to a people who were emotionally wounded by the attacks—yet hungry to kick some ass. "I admit it," Zinno said. "I wanted to do my part, but I was angry. I wanted to get back at them for what they did. I couldn't wait for the chance to hit back."

There would be no dissent or neutrality at the ballpark. Underneath the inspiring sentiments of *resilience* and *unity*, however, was fear. And anger. "The United States is really good at investing in violence. We're interested in solutions that come through violence," said Toni Smith-Thompson, a former Division III basketball player for Manhattanville College in Purchase, New York, who would go on to work in education policy at the New York Civil Liberties Union.

"The way we feel we best solve problems is through vengeance, revenge, or punishment. It's power. It's dominance. Even these displays of unity were not unity. It was a temporary rallying of people to take up arms to kill other people. That's not unity. That's nationalism and, in essence, white nationalism. This country has never reckoned with that."

During the 2001 American League Championship Series between the Yankees and the Seattle Mariners, hell rained on two Seattle sportswriters, John Hickey and Larry LaRue, for not standing during the singing of "God Bless America" during the seventh inning. Yankee writers, many lifelong New Yorkers still processing 9/11, seethed at the perceived disrespect. One New York writer looked at Hickey sitting while Tynan's voice broke hearts across the stadium and muttered under his breath, "Look at that fat fuck."

"I remember it," Hickey recalled of his decision not to stand. "Maybe it was a statement, I don't know. I remember all of it just being over the top. Sometimes I got up. Sometimes I didn't, and at that moment, I really didn't feel like standing up."

The hero narrative rose, as did identifying the bad guy. This was channeled through sports and the popular culture, where Muslims would become the new screen villains du jour, like the Nazis, the blacks and hippies, the Soviets, and the South Africans before them.

"I'm living proof. You don't need to wear a turban to have people looking at you cross-eyed," said Sweeny Murti, a sports journalist who grew up in central Pennsylvania. He isn't Muslim, but his Indian descent made him a target for post-9/11 racism. "The end of the [baseball] regular season, we were in Tampa. I had to piss like crazy, but security being what it was, you couldn't get out of line; you had to wait to get on the plane. First thing I do, I get on the plane, I put my bag down on my seat, and I go straight to the back of the plane. I'm not even thinking about what it looked like. I've got to pee. The bag goes down. I go to the back of the plane. [then *New York Times* Yankees writer] Buster Olney was seated a few rows by me and told me later he saw people's heads turn, and they were all thinking, 'Where's that guy going? What's he doing?' He kind of laughed to himself, and I'm thinking, 'Yeah, whatever.' But as the next month continued and we were on one cross-country flight after another, I was getting agitated having to go through all those layers. And I understand people wanted to be safe, but a lot of it was for show. The most popular place in line was right in front of me or right after me, because they weren't taking two people in a row for the 'random' security check."

During his time as a Yankee, David Justice was a favorite with many of the Yankee beat writers. A perennial all-star, he'd appeared in the World Series with two teams before joining the Yankees in 2000 and was one of many accomplished great players on a great team. His home run in the clinching Game 6 of the 1995 World Series won the Braves their only title since moving to Atlanta in 1966. He had been married to the actress Halle Berry, and unlike many players who could never get comfortable with the crush of people and expectations to win, he was generally unfazed by the aura of New York City. Justice and Sweeny Murti had forged a good relationship, and a key to success as a reporter in a major-league clubhouse is the ability to talk with players about anything other than the game. Players quickly ostracized media members who only talked to players when they messed up a ballgame.

"Go back a few months. Locker-room humor is what it is. David Justice and I got to be pretty tight. One day we were talking about world politics, and a couple of reporters came over," Murti recalled. "Justice put his arm around me and said, 'You know who this is? This is Bin *lay*-den. That's who that is.' Everyone laughed. You didn't know who he was. You could tell by the way Justice pronounced the name. Bin *lay*-den. He wasn't a household name. It was before the attacks.

"So that first night in Chicago, the locker room is quiet. Justice's locker is the first one in. I walk up to him and say, 'Hey, you've been throwing around that Bin Laden stuff. Might want to cool it.' And he looks at me and says, 'Look, the day you wanna bring your bomb to the ballpark, tell your boy, and I won't show up to work that day.'

"I can't say I was offended then or now, really," Murti recalled. "I laughed and repeated the joke many times. It was between friends."

It went unarticulated at the time, for there was no historical precedent for its scope, but 9/11 was the ultimate of one of David Halberstam's intersections. The games would never again be neutral. The people who thought they were experiencing a temporary condition to get America back on her feet found post-9/11 sports to be nothing like how it was at the 1991 Super Bowl, when everyone carried tiny American flags but the ceremony ended when the war did. *Stick to sports* was dead. More importantly, sporting events were now *political*, selling touchdowns and beer, three-pointers and home runs, but also fidelity to police and military and to a point of view that accepted the American government's war on terror.

You didn't have to be a genius to guess that the encroaching jingoism would crush the broader critiques of the wars in Afghanistan and, later, Iraq or to raise an eyebrow at the agents of authority with sometimes infamous histories, now being universally beloved. Nor did you have to be particularly astute to recognize that a big part of the ceremony was designed for that very purpose: to make anyone who was considering getting too loud about opposing it to think again.

Toni Smith-Thompson was offended by the loudening scene around her. She did not approve of the violence of war, the ease in which it was waged, and America's inability to consider the effects of its policies in real time on the people—not the governments—of other countries. As a biracial black woman whose eyes were opening about the realities and hypocrisies of the world, as happens to many during college, learning the history did not square with the myth that America was always the good guy, especially with so much evidence to the contrary. The response to the attacks did not help. In many ways, they provided a dual effect: the drumbeat of 9/11 emboldened her fellow citizens to increase the *us against them* mentality, which intensified the aggressive instincts of American culture that made her the most uncomfortable.

It was during a basketball game in December, at New York University—December 7, 2002, the sixty-first anniversary of the Japanese attack on Pearl Harbor, coincidentally—when Smith-Thompson joined the Heritage. She was twenty-one-year-old Toni Smith back then and had talked with her boyfriend at the time about doing something to challenge the climate. When the national anthem played, Smith turned her back to the court. No one noticed.

She never told anyone, not friends, not teammates, what she planned to do. She didn't even tell her parents because they always arrived late when the anthem had already played. After the game, her teammates did not say anything. The next game, Smith turned her back again, but fans didn't notice for the rest of the month or in January or most of February as the Valiants compiled their third-best record in school history. After a few games, the school president, Richard Berman, gave her words of support. "If anyone gives you a problem," he said, "come to me." No one gave her problems—until they did.

On February 25, 2003, at home against Merchant Marine, Smith became a national story—a black woman protesting her country not living up to its flag's ideals. The *New York Times* and all the cameras and the television shows descended. The school received demands to have her removed, but Berman supported her right of expression. The hate rained down in letters and boos—as did heartwarming support. A St. Joseph's player yelled at her at the end of one game. There were the teammates who held her hands during the anthem and the home game when a random fan charged the court to berate her while another player was shooting free throws. He tried to hand her an American flag.

Today, working on education policy at the New York Civil Liberties Union, Smith-Thompson recalls the parallels between her action and what Colin Kaepernick faced nearly fourteen years later. She did not do interviews out of the conviction that the media filter would distort her protest into an attack on soldiers. She said nothing, and the media distorted anyway.

"People remember it as an antiwar protest, but it really wasn't. It was a statement about the way people of color have been treated over the history of this country, and we've perpetuated it around the world," she said. "You're sitting here with a broken people and a broken country. And racism breaks white people the way it breaks black people. And you have to sit with that. One of the things I wanted to say during my protest was, 'I don't want to play this game anymore.' We haven't handled any of this, we haven't handled slavery. We haven't handled the Constitution never being an equal document. We've never handled that it was all a lie. Maybe it would do a whole lot of good for us to be able to say it out loud."

Around the same time, just as the ground war in Iraq began, MSNBC (a joint venture between the NBC parent company General Electric and the tech giant Microsoft) fired the legendary talk-show host Phil Donahue from his primetime show for criticizing the decision to invade Iraq. "They were terrified of the antiwar voice," Donahue said. In an internal memo, MSNBC—the supposedly "liberal" voice of cable television—said that Donahue was a "difficult public face for NBC in a time of war" and that MSNBC becoming "a home for the liberal antiwar agenda at the same time that our competitors are waving the flag at every opportunity" would be nothing less than a disaster.

September 11 defined the career of Ashleigh Banfield. It was Banfield, also from MSNBC, who stood in front of the North Tower as it collapsed behind her, live on the air. It was a star-making moment. At a 2003 talk at Kansas State University, Banfield offered her thoughts of what she saw as scrubbed, dubious coverage of the Iraq war. "What didn't you see?" she said. "You didn't see where those bullets landed. You didn't see what happened when the mortar landed. A puff of smoke is not what a mortar looks like when it explodes, believe me. There are horrors that were completely left out of this war. So was this journalism or was this coverage?" For that mild critique, Banfield was banned from any significant role at MSNBC.

Most famously during that period of smothering opposing views in the mid-2000s was the public and corporate silencing of the country music group the Dixie Chicks. During a March 2003 concert in England, the trio told the crowd they were against the coming war in Iraq and ashamed that the president, George W. Bush, was from Texas.

The criticism of an initially very popular war destroyed them. No one wanted to hear a word of dissent, not from a Texas country band or from Phil Donahue or Ashleigh Banfield. And no one, not liberal MSNBC or media mega-giant Cumulus Radio, which owned hundreds of radio stations, had the courage to go against the tide by defending the musicians' right to protest. The Dixie Chicks were now considered un-American, unpatriotic. Radio stations dropped the band within days of the remarks. They were now toxic. Their single "Landslide" fell from number ten in the Billboard chart to forty-fourth in one week. Their sponsor, Lipton, dumped them. Death threats to the band followed. The Cumulus-owned radio station KRMD ("All American Listening Family"), in Bossier City, Louisiana, fielded calls from angry listeners and presented a stunt protest: if the Dixie Chicks were metaphorically being run into the ground, KRMD decided to physically do the same and crush the group's CDs. "I said, 'Yeah, I'll jump on that in a heartbeat,'" recalled Darrell Robertson, the general manager of Goldman Lawn and Tractor, which provided the 33,000-pound tractor to run over a pile of discs.

Even money couldn't save the Dixie Chicks. The band attempted to make a million-dollar donation to the American Red Cross, which, too scared to challenge the perceived public sentiment or find itself at the center of a possible boycott, rejected the money. One sentence about a war that would soon be historically discredited ruined the Dixie Chicks' careers.

The old guard of the Heritage, the ones such as Muhammad Ali and Jackie Robinson, who would one day end up on a stamp or light the Olympic torch to weepy, national admiration—but who in their time were the subjects of widespread hatred—knew this response well. There was always going to be a price to pay, and in post-9/11 America, everybody—pop stars, reporters, *everybody*—was expected to stay in line. This was the real reason for the ballpark ceremony night after night. It was to ingrain a mind-set. "These people may think they are patriotic, but I think they are irresponsible," Natalie Maines of the Dixie Chicks said in a 2006 interview. "And this whole episode has fundamentally changed my definition of patriotism. Do I have a flag on my car? No. Do I stand up for my rights as an American? Yes."

There was a name for what was happening: nationalism. But Americans were too cool, too comfortable to believe not only that it was happening to them, but they were willful participants in it. Nationalism was for the Nazis or the fascists in Italy—the World War II stuff. Couldn't happen here. It was much easier to laugh off anyone who took the signs seriously as paranoid—or to produce enough pressure to shut them up.

Two weeks after the Towers fell, Arista re-released Whitney Houston's rendition of "The Star-Spangled Banner" from the 1991 Super Bowl. A month later, the same week the Stealth Bomber flew over Bank One Ballpark in Phoenix before Game 1 of the 2001 World Series, the single peaked at number six on the Billboard Hot 100, sandwiched between Jagged Edge and Nelly's "Where the Party At" and "It's Been Awhile" by Staind. It went on to sell one million copies. Nothing better illustrated the new mood of patriotism that swept the country than this: for the first time in history, *the national anthem went platinum.*

6

THE SANITATION DEPARTMENT

Colored men are being clubbed for the slightest provocation. If the magistrates don't look into the clubbing business, the police as a body will commit more murders than any other class, and will go unpunished because they wear blue coats and brass buttons.

—*THE NEW YORK FREEMAN*, 1886

THE DUAL COMBINATION OF threat and grief changed the look, feel, and purpose of sports following September 11. It also changed the actors in the drama. There were still the players, but the police and the military and the flag across the expanse of the field had become permanent additions to the game-day roster. The military was fighting two wars in two countries, but no institution in American society would be more rehabilitated in the years following 9/11 than law enforcement.

It was the fear talking, fear that the sleepy-looking dude on the subway, or the expressionless woman next to him, or especially that guy in the turban, that any of them might be carrying explosives under their winter coats. Fear drove people toward police, toward safety, seeking a guarantee in an America that suddenly didn't feel so guaranteed. There, too, was the natural sadness, sympathy, and newfound respect for the people who risked their lives in jobs that were always dangerous, but in a safe world still felt kind of cushy. Before 9/11, there were cop-donut jokes, funny paintings of firemen and their Dalmatians. Afterward, the jokes weren't so funny anymore. There was nothing cushy about the job, not when the numeral 343—the number of New York City firefighters killed on 9/11— remained fresh in the minds of New Yorkers.

The enduring images of firefighters charging into the Towers to save civilians at the cost of their certain death resonated with an American public that seemed to suffer from a moral inadequacy from insufficient sacrifice—and an embarrassing, paunchy comfort on the part of national defense agencies that probably contributed to it having its guard down just enough for 9/11 to happen. Now the people were scared, and a scared people needed to rely on their institutions.

For the white middle class, police officers had always contained a community element. The "Officer Friendly" archetype went back to when cops visited schools, told kids to stay off drugs and do their homework. The aftermath of the terrorist attacks only strengthened people's fidelity to police. The police-as-hero narrative appeared, stuck, remained, persisted, and spread. Police suddenly were everywhere. Tourists would roam Times Square and take more selfies with the cops than the Naked Cowboy, one of New York's more notable street artists. They were a presence, especially at sporting events. Daniel Rodriguez, the singing cop who captivated New York with his rendition of the national anthem at ballgames and "God Bless America" at events, spawned an industry of singing police at every ballpark in every sport across the country. A respected but often divisive occupation became an institution at the ballpark, an extension of patriotism, a symbol of the goodness of sports. Rodriguez became so famous as the singing cop, in fact, that he eventually quit the force and embarked on an opera career. Once the Yankees and the Mets wore Port Authority, NYPD, and FDNY baseball caps pregame to show their support and gratitude, the fans did too. No matter the seats—bleachers, loge, or even the tony box seats—or whether the venue was Yankee Stadium, Lincoln Center, or the Gramercy Tavern, the caps became the hottest fashion accessory in town. Men wearing a $1,200 Hugo Boss suit topped it off with an NYPD ball cap. Women who dropped a paycheck on Jimmy Choo and Gucci wore a $25 Port Authority cap on top of their $175 haircut.

A cultural shift was occurring, but Americans were too comfortable to speak up or even think about it. Support grew not just for the cops, firefighters, and Port Authority workers but also for more shadowy authoritarian gestures, not only from Congress in the form of the invasiveness of the Patriot Act but through tacit approval shown by the public's fashion statements. Americans and tourists alike now wore baseball caps and

T-shirts that read "FBI," "DEA," "CIA," and it wasn't with irreverence or irony but in *solidarity. With the state.*

In post-9/11 America, ordinary citizens were advertising the government agencies of spies, assassinations, and foreign coups, of information files on prominent citizens and wiretappings of anonymous ones, as *cool.* When fear spoke the loudest, the FBI, bearing the legacy of J. Edgar Hoover, became both trendy and disturbingly benign—even though, in truth, it and other government agencies were spying heavily on their own citizens. Encroaching on basic privacy was now justified under the guise of fighting terrorism—and America, scared to death of the Muslim guy minding his own business reading the *Daily News* on the D train, bought it.

"America is a strange place. America believes in the Constitution up until the point where it is scared," said Eric Adams, Brooklyn borough president and former NYPD officer for twenty-two years. "When she becomes afraid, the Constitution means nothing. All those words about life, liberty, and justice, the freedom to do this and that, all that shit goes out the window."

In this spirit, as an extended thank-you, the people gave the police greater dispensation. It meant salutes at the ballpark. It meant cops ringing the bell at the New York Stock Exchange. The addition of police in the shadow of the Towers represented another unassailable piece of America's strength and rehabilitation. The sports teams, the leagues, and their broadcast partners, eager to be supportive of any 9/11-themed element, not only did not complain about the police presence but increased it, elevating the influence of officers in the dugouts and the bullpens. In the pre-9/11 days at Yankee Stadium, team security guards would ring the field in between innings or during pitching changes. Post-9/11, eight NYPD officers would stand around the empty baseball diamond, as if the pitcher's mound were a crime scene. As it did with soldiers overseas, the broadcasting network partners would cut away to any shot of police, either in uniform working the game or in the seats watching it, followed by the broadcasters saying a few nice words about police keeping everyone safe. Everyone was in agreement. The police were not just heroes but a vital optic element of selling sports to America.

There was one big problem with all the hero worship: everyone *didn't* agree. The runaway 9/11 narrative of police pageantry did not square with the daily experience of how law enforcement dealt with black people.

In fact, two Americas could be seen through the lens of law enforcement, seen increasingly in sports, where the highest-paid black employees in America worked.

"After 9/11, there was a desire to renew our patriotism. People appreciated and took notice of the role of the police, the large number of firefighters who died, the number of police who died," Adams said. "Black and brown people took notice of their roles also. It's just that their roles were different. Police did not stop serving and protecting. They also didn't stop serving summonses and serving stop-and-frisk and locking folks up. So both groups took notice of what [police] were doing, and those in the inner city who wanted to take notice of the serving and protecting aspect were too busy being hit with overaggressive policing."

INFILTRATION SYSTEM

Eric Adams was born in Brooklyn, in Brownsville, and he never wanted to be a cop. His dream was to live amongst the binary, surrounded in the world of ones and zeroes that composed the realm of computer programming. As a self-described nerd, working with computers was his goal, but in Brooklyn, the issue of policing was omnipresent, and the elders in the black community, notably the activist minister Herbert Daughtry, tapped Adams and several other promising black men for a special mission: to join the police force with the intention of creating a group of officers who could be trusted to be ethical with the black community. Daughtry envisioned Adams as the first of a generation of black police officers as noble double agents: upholding the law and keeping communities safe while undermining and dismantling the police culture that so often included black people getting their heads bashed in. Essentially, Daughtry saw Adams as the first piece of a heritage of black cops.

Even more so than the military, where so many unskilled white veterans entered the middle class through a GI Bill whose benefits were largely unavailable to African Americans, in most major cities, the blue-collar union professions of roofers, firefighters, and policemen belonged for decades almost exclusively to the Irish and Italians. So intertwined was ethnicity to the culture of the job that even when African Americans slowly began to increase their numbers on the police force, beginning in the mid-1970s, they recognized that the force, for all its union benefits, opportunities for overtime, and entry into the middle class, wasn't a welcome place. Eric Adams in Brooklyn and De Lacy Davis in East Orange, New Jersey, were two African American officers in the 1980s and 1990s who realized that joining the force meant confronting its culture—and trying to change it.

Adams joined the NYPD in 1984, during the years of Eleanor Bumpurs, the racist vigilante Bernie Goetz, and Howard Beach. Surrounded by resistance, Adams straddled the hard lines, untrusted by the white officers who believed that, as a black officer, Adams would be less willing to enforce laws many African Americans believed were purposely tilted against them.

"I'm very conservative when it comes to public safety," Adams said. "If you commit a rape, a homicide, or commit bodily injury to another person, you're going to jail. And if someone wants to give you that 'Hey brotha' stuff, I'd say, 'Hey brotha, get your life together.' No innocent person deserves to have their life threatened by anyone else, whether they wear the uniform or whether they don't."

In 1995, Adams started 100 Blacks in Law Enforcement Who Care, an organization designed to connect African Americans officers to community grassroots initiatives. With the country especially polarized during and following the O. J. Simpson double-murder trial, Adams's effort was an attempt to bridge what had long been considered an intractable tension among African Americans: you could either be on the police's side or on the community's side, but not both. Immediately, Adams found that when he did his job, he was seen as the enemy of the community or, worse, aligned with the white power structure he'd vowed to reform. When he pledged to listen to the concerns of citizens, especially in African American communities, he was considered disloyal to the codes of police. When he communicated with advocacy groups such as Al Sharpton's National Action Network, his fellow cops trusted him even less. You didn't huddle with the enemy.

Adams, however, had joined the police for his own reasons, to serve and protect—but also to eliminate police brutality. It was a goal that ran directly counter to the institutional attitude of the NYPD, which during Adams's tenure had viewed minority communities with an "Us against Them" mentality, making any encounter between police and citizen a potentially deadly one.

In 1984, police officer Peter Marsala was sentenced to twenty-eight months in prison for assaulting multiple citizens in his custody. Marsala was a star in his department. Supposedly, he had joined the force for the right reasons. Some officers even reserved that special word for him— *hero*—before it would be tossed around so casually it would lose its meaning. In Marsala's file were twelve commendations, including the day he raced into a burning building and saved twelve women and children. As a transit cop, Marsala had nearly twenty times saved riders who had fallen beneath subway cars.

Marsala was an example of good police. He was also nearing a mental breakdown from the pressures and realities of the job. The public didn't respect him or the police, and his superiors within the force weren't doing enough about it. The public thought it could do whatever it wanted to cops, like the guy Marsala tried to go easy on after listening to a sob story about starting a new job and the stress, only to have the guy punch him in the face. Marsala's worldview was evolving into dark, Dirty Harry territory, except this was no movie: in his eyes, the system protected lawbreakers more than it did law enforcers.

He decided to fight back, and suddenly he was no longer the rising star who rescued kids from burning buildings but the cop the black and the poor knew existed behind the Officer Friendly posters, the cop who would handcuff you—and probably fuck you up when nobody was looking. During a 1981 traffic stop, Marsala took the motorist to the subway, handcuffed him, and beat him with a nightstick, an incident similar to another three years earlier, when Marsala received a thirty-day suspension for taking a nightstick to two handcuffed suspects in a locked room. Then there was the guy Marsala stopped for a minor infraction, who ended up with permanent brain damage. "I considered myself the law," Marsala said in 1997. "Instead of giving a summons, they got cracked a little bit and then they got a summons and sent on their way. People don't respect the law. They fear the law."

When Marsala's story ended, it was with a sentence at the Midstate Correctional Facility in Marcy, New York, and the New York City Transit Police being admonished by judges for failing to appropriately discipline officers. Marsala was fired from the Transit Police and by being convicted, lost his pension.

During the 1970s and '80s, the percentage of Americans who said they had a "great deal" of respect for police dropped, according to Gallup pollsters. In 1968, the figure was 77 percent. By the end of the 1980s, it had fallen to roughly 63 percent. At that point, the police had abandoned the pretense of being members of or even allies of the lower-class and minority communities they patrolled. Sgt. Friday had left town. Officer Friendly was dead.

"When you sit a guy down for an interview and you ask him why he wants to join the force, almost to a man the first thing they say is, 'I want to help people,'" said one Massachusetts police officer. "Then you say, 'Okay, how many people in your life have you actually helped? Have you ever done volunteer work? Were you in the Peace Corps? What have you done to help people?' Virtually every time, they had no answers. The real reason most times was the action, the adrenaline, being able to put your siren on and blast through a red light."

THIRD VERSE, SAME AS THE FIRST

Peter Marsala went to jail believing the cops were under siege by a public that didn't respect the law, and as it had when Richard Nixon promised law and order back in the late 1960s and early '70s, Hollywood came to the rescue, normalizing the increasingly rough edges of policing that were dropping their favorability ratings. Thus, in 1989, Fox premiered *Cops*, an early reality-TV show that featured *en verite* camera techniques following local police departments on patrol and filming their encounters with citizens—citizens who needed to get cracked on the head. *Cops* aided with the dual tasks of manufacturing the heroic image of police and standardizing tactics that public policy advocates saw as abhorrent. "You could count the constitutional violations in every show," said John Burton, a Los Angeles defense attorney. The show glamorized approaches that just a few years earlier got Pete Marsala sharing time in the prison chow line with pedophiles.

Cops was a slick production and an instant success, dominating television ratings consistently from almost the beginning. By concentrating on the poor, and dramatizing low-level drug busts and domestic disturbances, the show reinforced the stereotypes that many mainstream middle-class

Americans held about the lower classes, while romanticizing the police who braved the streets and entered unstable situations. To Fox, it made all the right people look terrible.

"It is absolutely a very powerful show," said Randy Sutton, a retired Las Vegas sergeant who appeared on *Cops*. "I've had no less than 50 police officers tell me that the reason they became a cop was because they saw me on the show and they said, 'That's what I want to do.' It's the best recruiting tool for policing ever."

The show was also dishonest. Three-quarters of interactions between the police and community resulted in an arrest, clearly not the case in the real world, where the number was under 20 percent. The formula of the show and its successors was in showing black and brown suspects muscled by white police, which activated the segments of the viewership who believed blacks needed to be put in their place. One study of police-based reality TV found it complicit in reinforcing negative attitudes that could contribute to the real-life increase of force that minority communities experienced:

> Crime-based reality TV misrepresents actual crime in society, principally by exaggerating the scope of violent crime. . . . Whites were overrepresented as police officers and African Americans were underrepresented in that role, but . . . African Americans and Hispanic citizen-suspects were to a substantial degree more apt to be physically attacked by police. So, even as violent crime rates decline, these programs may encourage fear by over-representing violent crime. By promoting a fear of crime and the image that minorities are responsible for most crime, these reality programs may serve as justification for harsher penalties and even police aggression toward citizen-suspects.

The show yielded editing control of the episodes to the police, allowing them to omit any negative, embarrassing, or illegal actions, while the camera zoomed in on the "bad guys"—the white and black poor, black inner city—sitting on the sidewalk handcuffed. Another study concluded that *Cops* led viewers to see crime as a "battle between white officers and nonwhite violent offender[s]. Such messages should not be too surprising if one considers that these reality TV programs are products, at least partly, of a cooperative effort by media and law enforcement."

So, the fix was in, and pop culture, just as it did with *Dirty Harry* and *Rocky*, used *Cops* to show the heartland that black America needed to be "kept in line" and that the white mainstream needed protection from it. While *Cops* became one of the top television shows in the country, the goalposts moved closer toward authoritarianism and contributed to the lack of support white communities expressed for black communities complaining of police mistreatment. Tactics that once got Peter Marsala locked up were being glamorized in prime time—and instead of being horrified, the public loved it. Even fellow cops knew it.

"I watch these 'Cops' shows and they show officers violating the Fourth Amendment routinely, manhandling people, not employing the escalation-de-escalation concepts of the use of force," said Stephen Downing, a retired Los Angeles deputy police chief. "The public is conditioned to believe that it is okay for our police to behave in this manner—they see it in fictional movies and television and they see it on 'Cops,' so it must be okay—until they are on the receiving end and personally experience what it is like to be the victim of police misconduct."

A year after 9/11, the Center on Media and Child Health published "Race and Attitudes Toward the Police: Assessing the Effects of Watching 'Reality' Police Programs," a study in the *Journal of Criminal Justice* that concluded: "Watching reality police shows increased confidence in police among Whites, but not Blacks; watching television news programs increased confidence in the police among both black and white viewers. Overall, watching reality police shows improved attitudes toward police among Whites, males, and those with no college education."

POWER BLOWS

For years, black communities had waited for that moment of truth when white America could see just how they were treated by police. Treatment by law enforcement was one of the great divides between the races. The March 3, 1991, beating of Rodney King by four Los Angeles Police Department officers was finally the proof for horrified whites, who always said they'd believe police misconduct *if only they could see it, if only there was evidence*. Now here it was, and a new day of understanding would surely begin. Vindicated black America had an ally with an outraged white public, right? Wrong.

George Holliday, a local resident, filmed the beating for several minutes. Holliday's belief in police was so firm that he first offered the video to the LAPD, which rejected it. (Had they accepted it, the world would have never seen it.) What happened was unambiguous: King, an unarmed man, was stopped after a high-speed chase, pulled out of the car, thrown to the ground, and kicked and beaten with nightsticks. On the order of the sergeant in command, Stacey Koon, he and his three officers repeatedly beat King. Additional officers arrived on the scene and, on Koon's order, were instructed not to intervene. In all, nineteen officers witnessed the beating. Koon ordered his men to deliver "power strokes" on King, and then he himself delivered two Taser shots, each carrying fifty thousand volts of electricity. The officers delivered fifty-six baton blows and six kicks.

The beating spurred international outrage and professional legwork in the form of an independent commission's report, authored by Warren Christopher, later Bill Clinton's secretary of state. The report concluded that the LAPD had systematic problems, from implicit bias to the refusal of officers to hold one another accountable, and no mechanism or desire to fix them. "Perhaps the greatest single barrier to the effective investigation and adjudication of complaints is the officers' unwritten code of silence: an officer does not provide adverse information against a fellow officer," the report read. "While loyalty and support are necessary qualities, they cannot justify the violation of an officer's public responsibilities. . . . A major overhaul of the disciplinary system is necessary to correct these problems."

The video was bad enough. The report was worse. It put words and motive to the beating and published examples of LAPD officers referring to aggressive patrols in the black community as "monkey slapping time"; one officer is quoted as saying that he regretted a missed opportunity to kill a Latino man ("I almost got me a Mexican last nite but he dropped the dam gun to [*sic*] quick"). The report noted that more than 25 percent of citizen complaints against police were for excessive force, and that a quarter of the 650 officers surveyed in the LAPD believed "an officer's prejudice towards the suspect's race may lead to the use of excessive force." The Christopher Commission reported 63 LAPD officers had 20 or more public complaints of their use of force, and that the LAPD did very little to discipline fellow police. Between 1986 and 1990, the LAPD averaged more than one excessive force complaint against it *per day*.

To black and brown Angelenos, the report said very clearly: *This is what they think of you.* The officers were arrested but none was internally disciplined, not the officers who administered the beating and none of the nineteen who watched. Public confidence in the police bottomed out, but when it came to policing, "bottoming out" meant overwhelming support, just less of it. Any other institution would have faced crisis. For police, even a quarter-century low, highlighted by police beating a citizen captured on film and broadcast around the world, only meant more than half the public still maintained a *great deal* of respect for law enforcement. And yet, despite the video, the report, and the outrage, change did not easily or convincingly come to police departments or the courts.

Three weeks after the King beating, Latasha Harlins, a fifteen-year-old girl was shot in the back of the head and killed by grocery-store owner Soon Ja Du after a confrontation over a $1.79 bottle of soda. Security cameras captured the killing. Du was indicted, and jurors in the case found her guilty of voluntary manslaughter, which carried a maximum sixteen-year prison sentence. The judge, Joyce Karlin, intervened, rescinding the juried verdict and, for killing a fifteen-year-old girl, sentencing Du to probation and community service.

––––––––

ON MARCH 2, 1991, the day before Rodney King was beaten, the Indiana Pacers wiped the floor with the Chicago Bulls, 135–114, one of the Bulls' worst losses of the season. After hearing about and watching Holliday's video, enough was enough for Craig Hodges. The King attack was an issue with which virtually all of the black athletes had personal experience, Hodges believed. As the most visible and powerful black employees in America, Hodges concluded, black athletes didn't just have to do something. They were *required* to.

There was just one major roadblock: Michael Jordan, king of the world, on his way to a dynasty, wanted nothing to do with it. Magic Johnson, king of Los Angeles, was silent. NBA bad boy Charles Barkley, silent. All the stars, quiet.

Months earlier, when the Bulls were playing in Atlanta against the Hawks, Coretta Scott King invited Jordan to attend a wreath-laying ceremony at the gravesite of Martin Luther King Jr. in commemoration of what would have been his sixty-third birthday. Jordan agreed, but hours before the event, he wanted out. He called Craig Hodges, who recalled, in his 2017 autobiography *Long Shot*, that Jordan asked, "Hey Hodge, do you want to fill in for me at this wreath ceremony? This is your thing, not mine." When the Finals against the Los Angeles Lakers began, Jim Brown, charter member of the Heritage and living in LA, invited the Bulls to his house to discuss Brown's initiatives, primarily keeping kids from joining gangs. Only Hodges accepted. Incurious about Brown's movement, Jordan said, "I want to stay focused on the series," but added, to Hodges, "But ask Jim how he made all his money."

Hodges and Jordan embodied the Heritage in repose. Hodges believed in the traditions of the black political athlete, but he wasn't famous enough to garner major, sustained attention for activist activities. Jordan was the superstar who had abandoned that inheritance. Hodges reminded his fellow players of what had come before them, in history and sacrifice, telling them about the 1964 player boycott of the All-Star Game. Hodges reminded other players that they were wasting an inheritance without putting any resources back into it. Hodges wanted to educate players, but Jordan was the king, the guy the others followed. "What do I need an education for?" Scottie Pippen said to Hodges one day. "I make six figures."

On April 29, 1992, the defending champion Bulls swept the Miami Heat in the first round of the playoffs. That same day, the four officers charged with beating Rodney King were acquitted by a Simi Valley, California, jury. Los Angeles had already been on edge from the outcome of Latasha Harlins's case months earlier. The verdict in Simi Valley pushed the city until, finally, it burst.

Six days of riots broke out in Los Angeles, the worst civil disturbance in American history. Michael Jordan said nothing. Well, he said *something*, but it might as well have been nothing. Jordan's response was weaker than a Coors Light: "I need to know more about it."

Like O. J. Simpson before him and Tiger Woods after, this was Jordan's Halberstam moment of intersection, and he used it, Al Sharpton thought, to kill the Heritage. "History will make them have to answer 'Where were they?' just like somebody's grandchild will ask where were y'all when Dr. King was marching and Malcolm was doing this," Sharpton said. "Someone's going to ask them, 'You were the biggest guy in basketball or tennis or football from Howard Beach to Trayvon. What were you doing?' What are you going to tell them, 'Look at my trophy?' *Who cares?*"

The end came quickly for Craig Hodges, whose contract was up after the Bulls won the 1992 title. He was only thirty-one, but the phone didn't ring. No one called—not teams that were a shooter away from a chance at winning a championship, not teams that couldn't shoot at all, ones he could have helped. He received no return calls from sports agents. His career was over, killed by the two defining forces of his time: a responsibility to the Heritage and Michael Jordan.

Hodges had exposed the players. That made him toxic. He proposed a boycott of the 1992 Finals after the four officers were acquitted, correctly predicting how powerful a united front of black players unwilling to perform in response to injustice in the legal system would have been, an idea that angered both Jordan and Magic Johnson. *That* made him toxic, especially after he famously showed up to the title celebration wearing a dashiki and handing President Bush a list of concerns of the black community, and called out Jordan for not sufficiently using his power to help black people. That *really* made him toxic. Soon, as the days without an invitation to play in 1993 turned into weeks, Hodges knew he was being punished, as so many others who bled the traditions of the Heritage had been.

> I knew [Bulls] management thought I was corrupting the minds of the players and compromising relationships with corporate sponsors. Certainly Michael wanted me gone. And my controversial visit to the White House the previous fall hadn't helped my cause. . . . I personally called each of the most respected agents in the NBA. No one would return my calls. It was a tight community and I had committed many cardinal sins. I wasn't playing the game the way Jordan thought it should be played. No, I wasn't playing the corporate game.

Michael Jordan was not only *not* part of the Heritage but had supplanted O. J. Simpson as its greatest threat. Maybe Jordan's exceptional gifts weren't limited to basketball genius. Maybe he understood the American racial-power dynamic best, that as romantic as it seemed, black people would never have real power, just as Robinson and King understanding that the romance of armed revolution could never be the answer came not from cowardice but from the bad math: 12 percent of the population couldn't overtake any majority by force. Jordan never renounced his racial identity. Jordan steered away from controversies where an affirmation of his blackness was required. By allowing himself to be positioned as elite and wealthy but race-neutral, he made greenwashing an essential component of his public persona. Maybe Michael Jordan simply realized that in America, African Americans were never going to get a majority of seats at the table, so getting as much money as possible was as good as it was going to get.

"Maybe," Al Sharpton countered. "But that still makes you a coward."

A HARD ROAD TO GLORY

On February 6, 1993, Arthur Ashe died, and another voice of the Heritage was prematurely silenced. Ashe was only forty-nine years old when he died from complications of AIDS, which he contracted five years earlier from a blood transfusion. In many ways, he represented the complexities of the civil rights movement, both in style and tactics. For years, Ashe was underestimated. Harry Edwards thought Ashe was an "Uncle Tom" because he didn't join the boycott movement in the 1960s or speak out at the accepted decibel level. He played tennis, often seen as the sport for wimps and one that was almost entirely white. When the Kerner Commission report was released, in 1968, Ashe responded that black people had to work harder. Playing a white sport, joining the army, and telling black people to get off of their asses made those in the movement wonder if he was one of them.

But when it came time to count all the chips on the table, Arthur Ashe was a frontline member of the Heritage. By connecting his vision of racial justice to apartheid South Africa, Ashe was like Robeson and Muhammad Ali, a Pan-Africanist who saw racial struggle in global, not national, terms. Like Ali's, Ashe's upbringing in a segregated city (Richmond, Virginia, in Ashe's case) created the tough outer covering of a fighter who, because he didn't expect cooperation from hostile whites, demanded more of himself and his people. Even though millions of African Americans lived it, Arthur Ashe articulated a position few people would accept in a world that viewed nuance and complexity as confusion: he demanded self-help *and* American acknowledgement of its institutional racism, which left the people on the bottom of the economic scale with a harder fight. "Having grown up in a segregated environment, in the South," Ashe said after winning Wimbledon in 1975, "I know what it's like to be stepped on. So I know what it's like also to see some black hero do well in the face of adversity."

When he was a young boy, Ashe told his brother that he wanted to be the "Jackie Robinson of tennis." Like Jackie, Ashe attended UCLA, and like Jackie, he was a veteran. Also like Jackie, it was Arthur Ashe who stood alone, apart from the rest of his sport, the first and only African American male player to win the US Open, Wimbledon, and the Australian Open; to represent the United States in and win the Davis Cup; and to be ranked number one in the world. And like Jackie, he stayed so committed to the fight even when his own people—including some of the leaders of the civil rights movement—questioned his authenticity, his commitment, and essentially his blackness. This was especially so during Ashe's missteps, such as playing in South Africa during apartheid twice in the early 1970s, even after the country denied him a visa on two previous occasions. Playing in South Africa was important for him, Ashe said, so black South Africans could see black success occur in their own country—and to illustrate the illegitimacy of the government-imposed apartheid. His moderate and soft-spoken approach may have fooled some, but segregation had made Arthur Ashe, and he knew better than most that no one gave you anything, and certainly no one gave you anything if you were black. You had to be willing to stand for it, fight for it, and die for the principle of what was right. And like Jackie, the closer Ashe stayed to the front lines, as he did the math and saw that the odds were always with the house, the more he saw the accumulation of fame and riches for the disaster it was. What Ashe did not do in terms of rhetoric, he compensated for on concrete. Until the Williams sisters arrived, Venus and Serena, Ashe was the dominant African American name in tennis, and he built tennis centers, created tennis programs, and forced the sport's powerful white leaders to invest resources in black communities.

In the years before he died, Arthur Ashe reached the similar, disillusioned conclusion as Jackie Robinson: the Heritage never should have existed in the first place. The black mind should have never been secondary to the black body. It was a formula that elevated the winners of the athletic gene pool and abandoned the rest. "What's my advice for black parents?" he once said. "Take your kid out of the gym and into the library."

PROPHETS OF RAGE

The superstars may have abandoned their visible social responsibility, but some non-stars kept the Heritage flickering. In 1993, Detroit Pistons center Olden Polynice led a three-week hunger strike in support of 230 Haitian refugees infected by HIV detained at the notorious US military installation at Guantanamo Bay, Cuba, and against the Clinton administration's refusal to address American immigration policy.

"I just feel like something has to be done," he said. "We're talking about the Bosnians and the Somalians and everybody else, but nothing is being said about the situation in Guantanamo or in Miami or the Haitian plight, period." But no protest would achieve maximum impact without the players at the very top of the game, the ones whose talent made everybody follow and made other players less vulnerable to retribution from the league or the public.

For the riches of their shoe contracts, the players relinquished their voice, but in its place was the music, rap music in particular, which stepped in the arena. On police brutality, the rappers Chuck D and KRS-One (as well as the younger, more confrontational emerging West Coast band N.W.A.) accepted the challenge the athletes abandoned. Chuck D and Public Enemy hit national prominence in 1987 with an unprecedented sound for hip-hop and a political presence that followed in the tradition of Gil Scott-Heron, Curtis Mayfield, and Stevie Wonder. There was the revolutionary sound, the noisy beats, chaotic and ferocious, but it was Public Enemy's subject matter, lyrics, and powerful delivery that made it a messenger of the Heritage that sports built but athletes discarded.

"In my home, there was culture. There was music, always music," said Chris Webber, former NBA All-Star and NBA broadcaster. Through the music, Public Enemy articulated the mission of the Heritage, what Harry Edwards referred to as the "sustained ideology." The concerns of African Americans were rarely going to be the concerns of the mainstream, and thus Public Enemy provided through rap the modern mission of the Heritage: mass incarceration, anti-capitalism, capitalism-as-racism, slavery, police brutality, corporate exploitation of poor communities, the refusal by the state of Arizona to recognize Martin Luther King Jr.'s birthday as a federal holiday, and alcoholism in the black community but also the redlining and physical segregation that isolated the ghettoes. KRS-One confronted the conundrum of the black police officers, men like Eric

Adams and De Lacy Davis, often caught in conflicting forces. While the Nike dollars bought silence, conscientious rap groups like Public Enemy did the work of the Heritage.

Public Enemy did something else: the rap group provided an alternative to the greenwashed black athlete. Chuck D did not create a corporate image to shield himself from blackness or appear palatable to whites. He did not refer to himself as "Cablinasian," and as the group's fame increased, he did not make his message more mainstream. It was actually the opposite: Public Enemy was the only group in America that required a minor in black history, its music an indictment of an educational system that did not teach black history to black children, or to any American children. Public Enemy referenced Huey Newton, Bobby Seale, Marcus Garvey, Gabriel Prosser, Denmark Vesey, Nat Turner, and Nelson Mandela (still in prison when Public Enemy's first two albums were released), making listeners scurry to the encyclopedia—or the African American studies department—but emerged armed with information no school would ever teach.

Public Enemy, along with the other emerging groups at the time represented a contemporary rebirth of the "black is beautiful" movement of the 1960s but with greater defiance, one rooted in history, not identity. While the athletes were too busy tripping over themselves to make the white consumer comfortable, the currency of Chuck D and KRS-One came precisely from being black. Unlike players willing to trade blackness for green, a new generation of hip-hop artists was not willing to make that deal.

"That silence was real, and it was definitely deliberate," Webber said about his fellow athletes. "You had a lot of people in your ear telling you cultural currency meant nothing in the end. Look at Joe Louis. The same government he boxed for and fought for and they wouldn't help him. As an athlete, all you hear is all those guys losing money, and you're saying to yourself, 'If Joe Louis was the best of America and they didn't love him, what are they going to do to me?'"

As the leader of the legendary Michigan Fab Five, Webber was already famous when he was taken first overall by the Golden State Warriors in the 1993 draft, and following Michael Jordan, and like most athletes of that era, he joined the Nike stable. Webber received his own shoe line, the Nike Air Unlimited CW, and won Rookie of the Year. Then Webber followed his own path. Upon entering the league, he made it a point to hire black agents to represent him, Fallasha Ervin and Bill Strickland.

"I specifically wanted that, and I remember black players telling me not to have a black agent. Just having a black representative was looked at as being confrontational," Webber said. "It was like owners took it as challenging the system. And it was black players who were the ones who told me not to do it. It wasn't about being anti-anything. It was about giving qualified people an opportunity."

Webber was already sensitive to the increasing violence in the city and a new danger: kids being jumped for their shoes. When he signed his Nike deal, he wanted to make a statement that recognized the issue.

"We were in negotiations with Nike. There was a story of a young man who was robbed and killed over a pair of shoes, one of my shoes," Webber recalled. "We could not verify it completely, but I believed it to be true. And my shoe the next year was going to be the biggest shoe in Nike's line because Michael had just retired. It just wasn't cool to me. My mother was big on value systems, and I didn't want to be part of that value system. All my friends had Jordans, and having those sneakers was the biggest value in their lives, bigger than school, bigger than college, bigger than everything, and I didn't want to muddy the waters any more than they already were."

Webber wanted Nike to lower the price of his signature shoe. Nike refused. The two sides hardened, and in 1996 neither Webber nor Nike sought to renew their shoe agreement. Webber negotiated first with Converse but wound up joining Fila.

"I told them they didn't have to be that expensive. You can make them $20 less. It wasn't like they were $200," he said. "At that time I was a rookie. That's the thing about finding your voice: you want to express yourself, but you're still young and dumb in other places. I felt like it wasn't going to be the biggest deal. Then when word got out, it turned out to be a big deal."

For the next decade, Webber felt the cost of his independence, of challenging Nike. "I know I paid the price because companies in the future wanted to know about me before they would agree to work with me. They wanted to know what I was about. They used the term 'angry' with me, because I had a black history collection. They were already calling me angry for being part of the Fab Five, for having a black agent. Let's just say there were a lot of working parts at that time. I had to rebuild everything to convince business that they could work with me."

If Chuck D maintained the Heritage during portions of its dormancy, it was the Heritage that in some ways created him. A native of Long Island, he was not immediately a fan of the Mets or the Yankees but rather the Pittsburgh Pirates and the magnetism of its superstar, Roberto Clemente. The year before Clemente died, Chuck D remembered doing a book report on Jackie Robinson for school. That was 1971, the year Clemente hit .414 in the World Series and the Pirates won in seven. Chuck D's attraction to Clemente was not simply a reflection of the player's kinetic gifts but also the off-field manner in which Clemente carried himself. He never forgot the people of Puerto Rico, his home country, no matter how high he climbed athletically. Like Ali, Clemente's lifeblood was drawn from the soil of his native land and from the blood of his people. Celebrity, a World Series championship, and batting titles never changed that.

"It's a full circle," Chuck D said. "Beyond my parents, watching Ali, Kareem, Jim Brown, and key sportswriters and broadcasters showed me the path to follow, Ralph Wiley, Art Rust, Earl Caldwell, Les Payne, Melba Tolliver, Carol Jenkins, and Gil Noble, especially."

Though Craig Hodges could not convince Michael Jordan to use his considerable influence to engage in social issues germane to the black community, he did strike up a friendship with Chuck D, who also formed a friendship with Mahmoud Abdul-Rauf, the former NBA guard who, like Hodges, found himself blacklisted, out of the league for refusing to salute the flag before games—as Toni Smith-Thompson would also do nearly a decade later. Chuck D supported both men more than many of their old NBA teammates did, and, in the 1990s, he worked with Hodges on several youth initiatives in the Chicago area. Around the same time, Jesse Jackson and Craig Hodges implored Michael Jordan to use his power to act with Nike, Public Enemy in 1991 released "Shut 'Em Down," a track about the corporate exploitation of black consumers that mentions Nike by name and threatens a boycott. With no contemporary heritage, a new generation of athletes drew inspiration from musicians.

"Chuck D I consider a close friend. I was raised by Chuck D," Chris Webber said. "Chuck D is why I didn't care. You wanna put that thug label on me? Fine. We were fed by that generation. From them, we could say 'We're aware of all the things that you did to us. You can say whatever you want.' Chuck said, 'I got a letter from the government the other day. I opened and read it, it said they were suckers.' I mean, come on! The athletes were silent then, but those men weren't. Players were silent, but it wasn't like there was no sound."

THE BYGONE ERA

If *stick to sports* would later become the reactionary response designed to put players on the defensive, in the 1990s, it was a place players weren't only comfortable with but proud of. In 1997, Michael Jordan had won his fifth NBA title and solidified his public image as the master pitchman and buzzer beater. Charles Barkley neared retirement, but his signature statement had been a 1993 Nike spot where he declared he was not a role model. "Just because I can dunk a basketball," he says to end the ad, "doesn't mean I should raise your kids." It was the perfect anti-Heritage counterprogramming for Nike, balancing Jordan's smooth apolitical "Be Like Mike" persona with Barkley's smoldering repudiation. Both Barkley and Jordan took different approaches to reach the same place: don't ask anything of me.

On the morning of August 9, 1997, four years before the World Trade Center attacks, NYPD officers responded to a call at the Rendez-Vous night club in Queens after the patrons spilled on to the street after the club closed. Police arrived to control the crowd and arrested Abner Louima, a thirty-year-old Haitian immigrant and another man, Patrick Antoine. The arresting officer, Justin Volpe, claimed Louima had punched him. Louima and Antoine were taken into custody. On the drive to the precinct, police beat both of them with fists and nightsticks. Upon arrival, Volpe and another officer, Charles Schwarz, took Louima into the public men's room, which was filthy, with walls covered in hardened feces. According to one report:

> What allegedly happened to Abner Louima represented an almost un-
> imaginable display of psychosexual criminality. . . . If the allegations are
> correct, there was an indication that [Volpe] entered the bathroom with
> specific intent. . . . Inside the bathroom, according to the source, Volpe
> seized a wooden handle, screamed "Fucking Haitian" at Louima, and
> slammed him up against the wall. According to Louima, "They threw

me to the ground and start beating me up. And then one of them—
there was two of them—one pick up something on the floor. I don't
know what it is, but it looked like a plunger to me, and just, you know,
push it on my ass, and then it came out with shit and blood. . . . They
put it in my mouth. He said that's my shit."

"He was rubbing shit all over Louima's ass, and he had his head shoved
up against the wall," the investigator said. . . . It was at that moment that
Volpe is alleged to have shoved the handle into Louima's mouth.

Volpe bragged to his fellow officers about beating Louima. After,
he even offered to show other cops the broken broomstick he had first
shoved into Louima's rectum and later into his mouth. Louima was
charged with disorderly conduct, obstructing government administration,
and resisting arrest.

In the days that followed, officers came forward denying that they'd
beaten Louima and Antoine in the car, and said that the injuries Louima
sustained in the beating in the Seventieth Precinct bathroom stemmed from
"extreme homosexual activity" at the Rendez-Vous club. Four officers—
Volpe, Schwarz, Thomas Bruder, and Thomas Wiese—were arrested in
the beating, and a fifth officer, Sgt. Michael Bellomo, was charged with
attempting to cover it up.

The Louima case represented the proof that African Americans had
insisted was the basis of their historical claim against police, and it fed two
hopes in minority communities. The first was that a reexamination of police tactics was inevitable, and the second was a recognition on the part of
the white mainstream—who one day might serve on juries—that just six
years removed from Rodney King and occurring on two different coasts,
police *were* capable of treating citizens with such subhuman contempt.
Even cops who were Little League coaches and trusted neighbors, who
lived in their community as important, respected members of the social
fabric, could do this to people who weren't their neighbors.

As in the 1980s, when New York was struggling through racial strife
with the police, its athletes ran for cover. New York teams were prominent, and their players counted their money. The Yankees, emerging as
a dynasty with an African American captain, Derek Jeter, said nothing. It
wasn't much of a surprise, for Jeter had been raised at the foot of Nike
and Michael Jordan, and businessmen didn't get their hands dirty. Jeter

was beloved also because behind the scenes he did the right thing. For years, Jeter was the only active player in Major League Baseball to financially support the Jackie Robinson Foundation, and it was a really big check, six figures. And it came every year, so no one could say Jeter didn't know his roots. But no one showed his face for Abner Louima, not New York Knicks player Allan Houston or any star athlete or especially those in a Yankee organization connected to the administration of the pro-cop mayor, Rudy Giuliani.

The Knicks, who in 1999 would reach the NBA Finals, also said nothing. The Mets and Giants, who would reach the World Series and Super Bowl in 2000 and 2001, respectively, stuck to sports. Justin Volpe was sentenced to thirty years in prison on December 13, 1999, so there was nothing controversial about voicing disgust about him. Charles Schwarz was sentenced to fifteen years, eight months. Three other officers were sentenced to the maximum for their part in covering up the assault. Louima was awarded $8.75 million in civil damages. Louima had been brutalized, and with the sentencing, the jury did its part. Justice, in the sense that it could be achieved, had been done. The system worked, or so it seemed.

"Some of the finest people I know are police officers. After Officers Wenjian Liu and Rafael Ramos were killed [in a horrific December 2014 ambush], everyone was grieving. The officers were slated to deliver Christmas presents to the kids in the community," Brooklyn Borough president Eric Adams said. "Everyone would have understood if they didn't under those circumstances, if they postponed. Their colleagues, friends, were just murdered in the most terrible fashion imaginable, ambushed with no chance to defend themselves. And, to a person, every one of those officers went out that night and delivered toys to the kids because they didn't think the children should have been deprived of their happiness on Christmas.

"At the same time, some of the most fucked-up and sadistic people I know are also police officers, people who have nothing inside and fill it by making life difficult and miserable for other people. There are cops who will stop you for nothing and make you suffer. You could tell them 'I can't take this arrest' or 'I'm starting a new job tomorrow,' and they won't care. They'll say 'Too bad,' just for the satisfaction of hurting you."

Six weeks after the Louima verdict, in an Albany, New York, courtroom, four white police officers were acquitted of all charges in the infamous 1999 killing of Amadou Diallo, a twenty-three-year-old Guinean immigrant whom police mistook for a serial rapist. They fired forty-one shots, hitting Diallo nineteen times. Diallo was part of the American immigrant story, just a guy selling merchandise on the sidewalk in that New York tradition. He had been approached aggressively by the officers, who were undercover, and had panicked and retreated into the vestibule of his apartment building. Upon further command, Diallo reached for his wallet, which police believed was a gun, and they proceeded to unload their clips into him. Diallo's family was awarded $3 million by the city. Police admitted no wrongdoing, and a jury set the officers free.

One newspaper columnist, Steve Dunleavy of the *New York Post*, illustrated the power of media-as-advocate for police by writing more than fifty columns in support of Charles Schwarz, whose conviction in the Louima case was being reviewed on appeal.

"Dunleavy generally ignores the details of the case, writing instead as if Schwarz's status as 'the most innocent man in America' were a given," Jeffrey Toobin wrote in the *New Yorker*. "Most of Dunleavy's pieces concern such things as the toll on Schwarz's family. . . . By Dunleavy's own admission, he has a reflexive sympathy for police officers, and in the Louima case that sentiment initially extended to Justin Volpe. 'I'm the first to admit that I didn't even believe that Volpe was involved. I didn't believe it happened at all.'"

Less than a year after 9/11, an appeals court overturned Schwarz's fifteen-year sentence; the convictions of Bruder, Wiese, and Bomello were also overturned. Schwarz was later convicted for perjury and received a five-year sentence. Where Peter Marsala once did time for assaulting New York City citizens, the sanitizing power of 9/11 was strong enough to overturn convictions.

"The story of Charles Schwarz belongs to a suddenly distant era, when the public image of New York police officers was largely shaped by their fraught relations with the city's racial minorities rather than by their heroics on September 11," Toobin wrote. "In part, Schwarz had the good fortune to be caught up in the slipstream of the city's renewed appreciation for its police force, but, more important, he was the beneficiary of the indefatigable, and largely unrefuted, efforts of a pro-bono attorney, a newspaper columnist, and a steadfast wife. Through their work, Schwarz's incarceration seemed to reflect the sensibilities of a bygone era."

It was a bygone era whose demise was heavily aided by post-9/11 hero worship of police officers and reinforced, at least optically, through sports, even if the reality was wholly different in the black community—and no amount of protest or video evidence would convince the public otherwise.

"There was an empowerment of those who were abusive," Eric Adams said. "When you did the shootings and the unethical behavior, even when caught on tape, you had twelve men and women of the jury who took notice of how much we appreciate our police saying, 'We're going to give the benefit of the doubt to our police. We don't believe they could have done anything wrong.' It made it very difficult for those who were trying to seek any kind of reform and justice."

7

PROPS

The new patriotism boosting America's waning new war often proved to be little more than vicarious patriotism reminiscent of the pre 9/11 fetishism of the greatest generation. While Americans applauded the selfless men and women in uniform, whether at Ground Zero or in battle, we could rest assured that the all-volunteer army would take care of everything. We didn't have to do our part, whatever that was. . . . Supporting the war by plastering flags on a gas guzzling foreign car, Bill Maher observed, was "literally the least you can do." And we leapt at that option.

—FRANK RICH, *The Greatest Story Ever Sold*

IT WAS AT THE 2013 Super Bowl, the San Francisco 49ers versus the Baltimore Ravens—San Francisco quarterbacked by one Colin Kaepernick—when the sports-industrial complex reached its apex. After a dozen years of repetition, all the pieces were locked into place: the white-gloved servicemen, the flags, the flyovers, the remote feeds of young, homesick Americans in desert camo watching the Big Game from Kandahar or Iraq or some other military base tens of thousands of miles away from home, the cutaway to a serious-faced law enforcement officer. Marine corporal Cecilia Evans remembered seven years earlier, on the last day of her tour in Iraq, watching her hometown Pittsburgh Steelers beat Seattle in the 2006 Super Bowl. She recorded one of those messages from overseas for Steelers fans back home. "Until I had kids, it was the happiest day of my life," she recalled. "I survived Iraq, the Steelers won the Super Bowl, and I was going home."

Once unique and touching following the Twin Towers collapsing, the images were now daily touchstones of a skillfully packaged, post-9/11 American sports product sold to the public. That year, the great bellwether of the American mood, the Super Bowl commercial, reflected the emotions these decade-long machinations wanted to coax from consumers. And what Madison Avenue wanted was an even bigger dose of what the public was already getting by the bushel at sporting events across the country: patriotism.

GOOD HOUSEKEEPING

Super Bowl ads are as much a reason casual fans flock to the Super Bowl as the Big Game itself, and amid commercials for the Puppy Bowl and Cool Ranch Doritos, one image dominated the rest that year: being an American. From gasoline and cars to fast food and salty snacks, loyalty Rorschach tests were in play: an American flag, a soldier walking in slow motion toward a house, presumably coming home after deployment, a shot of a first responder from the police or fire department. One ad, for Dodge Ram trucks, particularly illustrated the theme. Using the late radio host Paul Harvey's 1978 speech "So God Made a Farmer," Dodge sold cars and the nostalgia of a stiffer, more resolute America through evoking the most noble and unselfish of professions. In an age of special effects and pyrotechnics, the ad used two simple devices: Harvey's authoritative voice and the powerful still photography of up-close, weather-beaten American faces, toughened by life but held together by core values, with images of the family at dinner (and a brand-new, $30,000 truck in the driveway) and of the lone farmer, surrounded by acres of responsibility that could only be met by work, by putting tired hands into the soil.

The ad sold something as basic as a truck, but it also answered a yearning for a mythological place that could not be disputed even during the most polarized of times: the American heartland as the epicenter of loyalty, patriotism, and hard work. One photograph spoke loudest for the theme: a haunting shot of a winter-whipped barn with a lone American flag pressed against a frost-covered window. Harvey's voice gave the imprimatur of unmistakable strength, honesty, and political impartiality in a bitterly divided time—the stern corrective for just how far off track we'd really gone. The ad, created by the Dallas-based Rogers Group, was lauded by the punditry for how it "resonated with blue and red states alike," pulling at the nostalgia of yesterday, demanding something better of ourselves and for tomorrow.

The Ravens beat the 49ers on the last play of the game, and the takeaway from the Super Bowl that year was that patriotism delivered the Good Housekeeping seal of advertising.

The Rogers Group received accolades for a triumphant Super Bowl commercial, but selling patriotism in post-9/11 America was a universal blueprint. Marathon, the gasoline company, was "Fueling the American Spirit." To a twangy country music jingle touting a "full tank of freedom," one Marathon spot in thirty seconds hit all the red, white, and blue notes, showing a car passing a sign for the town of "Independence," the American colors visible throughout the commercial, and a fatigues-clad soldier embracing his sweetheart in the front yard—in slow motion, of course. The bank USAA, positioning itself as the financial institution of veterans and, thus, of patriotism, ran spots about how it took special care with military families and had been for decades, except that Navy Federal Credit Union was doing the same damned thing. The voice of Paul Harvey echoing over everything well and good about America wasn't just a stylistic touch by Dodge; now the military got all the special treatments, too. The company offered a $500 military discount to prospective Dodge-buying veterans, a special offer for "those who risked their lives for us." Ford offered the same $500, "Saluting those who serve." The Japanese manufacturer Nissan's Military Program brought the money and the snappy slogan, "You Serve, You Save," offering up to $1,000 in discounts for buyers. Military was being sent to the front of the line.

The rest was a race to be the most patriotic. Well, actually, that wasn't exactly true. The rest was a race to *look* the most patriotic. The NFL promoted its "Salute to Service," a slate of games that ostensibly paid tribute to the armed forces, with players and coaches wearing camouflage uniforms and caps—all of which were for sale. Even the audio headsets the coaches used contained a camouflage pattern. Major League Baseball did the same. The pink hats once sold for Breast Cancer Awareness Month every October now featured camouflage (with the pink team logo for the ladies). Each team sold them. Nothing said "USA" like rocking the camo gear on a Philadelphia Phillies hat. Once, it was just the Padres, playing in their navy town, who wore military-themed uniforms for Sunday home games. Now, the Mets, Pirates, and Reds also donned alternate uniforms entirely of desert camouflage. Baseball issued special, patriotic-themed uniforms for Memorial Day, Armed Services Day, and Independence Day, while adding "Military Appreciation Days" and "Law Enforcement Appreciation Days" for discounts and giveaways across the calendar.

In college football, the Eagle Bank Bowl in Annapolis, Maryland, was renamed the Military Bowl (sponsored, naturally, by the defense contractor Northrup Grumman). In college basketball, ESPN created the "Armed Forces Classic," a preseason tournament played on a military base or sometimes even on an aircraft carrier. In 2017, the Boston Red Sox created a replica of the Vietnam Veteran's Memorial in Washington, DC, to be displayed at Fenway Park.

All four major professional American sports, as well as soccer and NASCAR, brought the military to the ballpark, hosting surprise homecomings for soldiers, holding induction swearing-in ceremonies before games or at halftime, having a serviceman sing the national anthem or, in the seventh inning, "God Bless America." The charities dedicated to supporting veterans followed suit. Major League Baseball even partnered to start its own, Welcome Back Veterans. The Boston Red Sox still had the famous cancer-research fund-raiser, the Jimmy Fund, but now the team partnered with the Home Base Foundation, and there were also the Wounded Warrior Foundation and a host of other charity organizations. Embedding military and law enforcement into sports was a radical departure from the way sports once did its business. But in post-9/11 America, patriotism was good for business, and an entire business model shifted.

John Skipper, the former president of ESPN, believed the shift was harmless. The country needed to bond, and sports was as good a place as any. When the first tower was struck on 9/11, Skipper had been in the air, on a regional jet from Birmingham to Atlanta, and when the flight landed, he saw dozens of people staring at the television sets in the terminal. "We were watching when the second plane hit within minutes after we got there, and at that moment you had a collective understanding that this was not some random thing, that some pilot fucked up and flew into the WTC. This was a deliberate act," Skipper said.

As the most powerful sports-media force in the US, ESPN was central to the shift in the game-day images the public saw. Much of the effectiveness of the Great Camo Takeover was due to the power of television:

ESPN partnered with the Department of Defense on various features and sponsored military-themed programming such as the Warrior Games. Halftime and pregame features were not short of content that tied the game or a player to the armed forces. The network's stated mission was to serve sports fans anywhere, anytime, and the public had shown a considerable appetite for patriotic images at the ballpark—especially because it did not view patriotism as politics.

"We did that little film about George Bush throwing out the first pitch, and it was actually a great moment. And you felt proud that the president was there," Skipper said of the iconic moment at Yankee Stadium before Game 3 of the 2001 World Series. "I think most people felt proud. Most people were not immune or cynical about that Yankees game and what it meant. People did use sports to bring themselves back together, to rally around, and I remember thinking that was okay. That was appropriate."

———

THERE WAS ONE IRREFUTABLE rationale for ramping up patriotism: it sold. It sold *big*. And, with little to no opposition regarding the appropriateness of wrapping everything from baseball to gasoline to your checking account in the flag, there was no reason to stop. The public embraced this bold, chest-puffing landscape as ticket-buying enlistees in the rebuilding of American pride. This was a way to do their part in fighting the war on terror.

As was the case with *Dirty Harry*, *Rocky*, and *Cops*, pop culture was doing its part to embed the narrative—especially with Hollywood blockbusters, like *Godzilla*, *The Avengers*, and *Kong: Skull Island*, for instance. Moviegoers expecting mindless pyrotechnics and giant reptiles demolishing major cities received, in addition, gratuitous nods to the heroism of cops and the military or, in the case of *Kong*, a giant monkey had to share screen time with an entire subplot of *service* in the film.

In public life, a new ritual was introduced: thanking veterans for their service. It showed everybody was all in it together, even if they weren't exactly sure what *it* was. Like the police, veterans were heroes and no longer shunned as they had been during the Vietnam War, at least in public. In private—where reality lived without smiles and cameras but with the unglamorous, unmarketable effects of ongoing war, the prosthetics, the debilitating mental and physical ailments without sufficient services to accommodate re-entry into civilian life, which left generations of veterans self-medicating at the VFW—that was another story. The thanking of veterans could also be distorting, because it suggested their reasons for joining the armed forces were primarily patriotic and not practical.

"The whole 'thanking you for your service' made me uncomfortable," Cecilia Evans recalled. She served in the Marine Corps from 2004 to 2011, including a tour in Iraq from 2005 to 2006. "I got paid. I wasn't drafted. I got a paycheck every two weeks. You paid my salary, so thank *you* for paying your taxes."

The Pittsburgh-area native joined the marines after graduating from Allegheny College, but she never imagined herself as a member of the military. "I was way, way left. I'm the person who voted for Ralph Nader and screwed Al Gore out of the presidency," she said. Evans enlisted for economic reasons after she found herself competing for waitressing jobs with people who had master's degrees. In her words, she did not enlist because of a "9/11 epiphany." The GI Bill and improving her financial situation was the attraction, but she always sensed a feeling of inadequacy from people who wanted to honor her.

"I didn't get the treatment for being a marine that the men got. I wasn't Johnny Patriot with blond hair, blue eyes, and the chiseled jaw. A million times, because I was a woman, I was asked if I really served and . . . I got accused of 'stolen valor,' you know, people who say they served but there's no record of it," she said. "But there was a blind hero worship to it, the whole thanking thing. Maybe people felt like they hadn't done enough in their lives. Whenever I met a guy and he found out I was a marine, eight times out of ten they *always* had to come up with excuses, to tell me the reason why they didn't serve. Automatically. It was like a compulsion. 'Well, I was going to, but I went to college,' or 'I was gonna join, but I got hurt.' Maybe they felt emasculated because I'm a marine, and that's the toughest one. I'm like, 'Chill. Relax.' It's not for everyone."

Whether at the mall, the train station, the airport, or the ballpark, the public turned real life into a commercial, thanking veterans for their service, a gesture central to the new patriotism. Guilt may have underlined the motive, but veterans—who in every branch would reference the spat-upon treatment Vietnam War veterans received—now got the star treatment, reserved, in Bob Sheppard's majestic voice, for those fighting for our freedom and *our* way of life.

"When I came home from Iraq on mid-tour leave in November 2005, a friend of mine who worked for the [New York] Islanders got me, my brother, and a few friends tickets to a game. My friend told me that they were going to put my face up on the big scoreboard during one of the breaks. When they did—a picture of me in uniform on the big screen and then a live shot to me in the stands—the entire [Nassau] Coliseum went ape shit," Mark Zinno recalled. "I mean, people were going nuts. It was a warm feeling. It wasn't embarrassing, but I was a little caught off guard. People next to me were standing up, cheering. A guy behind me gave me $100. I said, 'I'm not taking your money. I have a job.' He insisted. I told him I wouldn't take it. He wasn't taking it back, so I used it to buy beers for him and his friends, me and my friends. When that happened, I felt overwhelmed. It was a humbling experience but also gratifying to know that people gave a shit. When you're that far away over there, people care but they don't care. Then, when the entire world stops for you for thirty seconds, it was pretty cool."

THIS IS NOT THAT (OR IS IT?)

To the public, cops and military were interchangeable, even though the two occupations were markedly different. One did very little business on domestic soil, the other no business on foreign land, where America's two wars were being fought, and the people the latter interacted with were not foreigners but American citizens. None of those distinctions mattered at the ballpark. They were all the same, no matter how different. In the new world of fighting terror, police and military fell under one giant 9/11 umbrella: heroes.

It was all one big, dangerous thank-you. And who could possibly have a problem with that? Except that the conflation wasn't harmless, nor was it merely semantics. With law enforcement, conflation made it easier for police departments across the country to continue militarizing its local police forces, which had been happening since the early 1980s with Ronald Reagan's war on drugs and the federal government easing or, in many cases, eliminating laws restricting military-police cooperation. If in the minds of the public, police and military served the same function in a time of terror, it only stood to reason they should be able to use the same equipment, employ the same tactics, wear the same gear. But was that what America really wanted, cops dressed in fatigues and military uniforms, Officer Friendly turned Robocop? Was a militarized force how local police wanted to interact with the people they were supposed to be serving and protecting? For all the hand-wringing, the answer seemed to be yes. As early as 1983, California had begun using U-2 spy planes to search for large-scale marijuana growers in the northern part of the state. As aggressive police tactics grew more accepted during the 1980s and 1990s, police departments began accepting an increasing amount of military equipment, vehicles, and weapons from the Department of Defense, culminating in the post-9/11 exploitation of the notorious 1033 program, through which local police acquired military gear. And who was going to bear the brunt of this new look, which was accompanied by the attitude of occupation? It would be the poor, the black and brown. The high-powered weaponry the American military was using on other countries was now being used on its own people.

"As the police raised the bar, standing at games with automatic weapons with high-capacity vests and helmets and police presence, with that presence also came a larger crackdown and more power," Eric Adams said. "And then when you raise your voice and criticize, you had the beneficiaries—the prosecutors and judges, newspaper editors and writers—who were like, 'You cannot criticize our police because they were there during 9/11.' It was a very difficult scenario for people who were saying, 'What we've complained about is still here and has even increased.'

The conflation did not stop with tactics and clothing and a smudging of the rules, but with the actual servicemen and -women themselves. If fans at ballparks treated the police with the same deference as the military members, the police looked directly to the military for its next generation of officers. When a soldier's term ended, he or she was required to take a weeklong course on transitioning back to civilian life. At military bases across the country, state police would recruit potential officers, offering them state-trooper exams on the spot, and another pipeline between police and military formed. Soldiers could become cops before the ink was dry on their discharge papers.

———

WHILE THE COPS RECEIVED standing ovations at the ballpark, and the fans expected unquestioned deference to them, the black community found itself shattered once more. During the early hours of November 25, 2006, twenty-three-year-old Sean Bell, due to be married later that day, left a strip club in New York City with friends following his bachelor party at Club Kalua. An undercover unit that was performing a prostitution sting of the club believed Bell and two friends were heading back to their car to retrieve a gun to settle an argument. As the car started, the lead officer, Detective Gerald Isnora, engaged Bell and his companions. Two other officers, Detectives Michael Oliver and Marc Cooper, joined and fired fifty shots into the gray Nissan Altima, killing Bell, wounding the two other men in the car, and sending stray bullets and glass throughout the area. Each of the men was unarmed.

Isnora and Oliver were charged with first- and second-degree manslaughter, as well as first- and second-degree assault and a count each of second-degree reckless endangerment. Both faced five to twenty-five years in prison. Cooper was charged with second-degree reckless endangerment. Eighteen months later, each of the three detectives was acquitted by a jury. Isnora avoided jail, but his career was over after an internal review found him not to have acted in a manner consistent with department policy. He was fired in 2012 and also forfeited his city pension. Cooper and Oliver were forced to resign.

These two Americas persisted, locked in their separate realities, exacerbated by conflation at the ballpark and confusion away from it. The Bell verdict and its aftermath were emblematic of just how complicated "justice" could be. Isnora, Oliver, and Cooper would not go to prison, but they would lose their careers. The city would pay Sean Bell's family a $7 million judgment—while admitting no wrongdoing.

With the death of Sean Bell in the background, the black players played. No one spoke out. No one spoke up for Sean Bell. Three years later, in 2009, Oscar Grant was shot and killed by police at the Fruitvale Station mass transit stop in Oakland, California, setting off protests. But the great black players—Kobe Bryant, LeBron James, Dwyane Wade, Barry Bonds, Shaquille O'Neal, and Randy Moss, not to speak of Tiger Woods—said nothing.

They couldn't be blamed, really, for outside of textbooks and grainy television footage, the Heritage was not a part of the modern player's life. LeBron James was born in 1984, Michael Jordan's rookie year in the NBA. He was six years old when Rodney King was beaten, twelve when police sodomized Abner Louima and the big stars of his sport said and did nothing. James was sixteen on September 11. His entire road to adulthood was devoid of the athlete's voice taking the lead on an issue. His was a generation that had been detached from the Heritage for nearly forty years, a generation weaned on Michael and Tiger and, to a lesser extent, OJ, without real-time, contemporary examples that told them activism was part of their bloodline and responsibility. During the third act, the black body existed to earn, not lead.

The players of the millennium were not the children of 1968 but of 9/11. Kobe Bryant was twenty-three years old when the Towers fell, playing the majority of his professional career in a time when the military and police were viewed as heroes to be treated with deference not only by the public but also by his employers. Standing for Sean Bell or Oscar Grant meant standing up against the police-hero narrative and the league that paid him.

"Those happy Negroes were afraid of their blackness. The average athlete was not going to get involved. They weren't going to risk anything," said De Lacy Davis, a twenty-year police veteran who worked in East Orange, New Jersey, and, in 1991, after an incident of brutality against a black police officer around the time of the King beating, founded Black Cops Against Police Brutality. Davis's organization, like Eric Adams's, was an attempt to create a tradition of black police officers holding police departments accountable for their actions. "It's an oxymoron. Rodney King is hit fifty-six times, and white folks said, 'We didn't see what happened *before* the filming of the video.' The black community said, 'This has been our experience all along,'" he said. "White people essentially said, 'We don't believe our lying eyes, and now we elevate police to hero status.' The night unit that killed [Amadou] Diallo, their motto was 'We own the night.' The Rampart division in LA used to say, 'We eat our dead.' The contradiction is, you have these people being held up as heroes while simultaneously this information is being reported."

The country was in no mood for dissent, however, and the construction of the sports machine—white owners, white coaches, white season-ticket holders, white media, black players—amounted to bad math for black players; the deck was stacked against them. It was bad enough for players to speak out when fans wanted them to stick to sports, but it was even worse when the large numbers of fans, media, coaches, and owners fundamentally disbelieved and politically opposed their world-views. The paying customer was not sympathetic to Sean Bell or Rodney King or Amadou Diallo. But nor was the paying customer sympathetic to Medgar Evers in 1963. It identified with law enforcement. Unless they were planning on exercising a courage that had been absent for years, the owners were not going to openly support players if it meant angering the people who paid for the tickets, jerseys, and foam fingers. Only backlash awaited the player who spoke his mind. Black players saw those odds and concluded that outspokenness was a privilege they did not believe they could freely enjoy.

THE SEVENTH-INNING KVETCH

August 26, 2008, a dreary day in the middle of an uncharacteristically dreary season at Yankee Stadium. The Yankees had started the baseball tradition of playing "God Bless America" during the seventh-inning stretch. In the early days, when the pain from 9/11 was fresh, the Yankees would feature a live singer, sometimes the Irish tenor Ronan Tynan, other times Daniel Rodriguez, the singing cop. But after seven years, the ritual grew tired and the public seemingly responded to it more out of obligation than for healing. Even the Yankees treated it like something of an obligation, now using a 1976 recording of Kate Smith. The 2008 season at Yankee Stadium was known for two things: It was the last year the Yankees would play on their famous site, where the stadium had stood since 1923. A new $1.2 billion stadium being built across the street would be completed for the 2009 season. The second was the Yankees' nondescript play. They wouldn't make the playoffs as they had every season since 1995.

The Red Sox were hammering the Yankees, 7–3, when Bradford Campeau-Laurion, a thirty-year-old from Queens, decided to use the restroom in the middle of the seventh inning. As he rose from his seat and headed up the stairs, he was blocked by a uniformed NYPD officer, who told him he couldn't leave. In fact, Campeau-Laurion was told, fans were not allowed to leave their seats during the playing of "God Bless America." Campeau-Laurion told the officer he had to use the men's room and attempted to walk past when the officer forcibly restrained him and police ejected him from the ballpark.

The irony that in a free country the Yankees owned a policy of ejecting people for moving during a song espousing the virtues of American freedoms was not lost on Campeau-Laurion. He called the New York Civil Liberties Union, which promptly sued the Yankees and the city for religious and political discrimination. Eleven months later, the NYCLU won the case, the Yankees pledged to cease prohibiting freedom of movement during the playing of "God Bless America," and the city was ordered to pay Campeau-Laurion $10,000.

"This settlement ensures that the new Yankee Stadium will be a place for baseball, not compelled patriotism," said NYCLU executive director Donna Lieberman in a statement. "It's a victory for the freedom of expression—a core constitutional principle." Campeau-Laurion added: "It's a proud day for freedom to know that people can enjoy America's pastime at Yankee Stadium without being forced into acts of patriotism."

When the *New York Times* arrived at the new Yankees Stadium for the first game after Campeau-Laurion's successful lawsuit, it found support for him but also a number of fans who did not see forcing people to accept a patriotic ritual at an entertainment venue as a sign of authoritarianism. In fact, some saw Campeau-Laurion as the problem. "God Bless America" was being played. It wouldn't kill him to wait a minute, would it? "If they tried to do that in my aisle, I would have stuck out my leg," Sue Coster, from Waterbury, Connecticut, told the newspaper.

The picture formed; the post-9/11 displays of patriotism became increasingly less authentic and more rooted in enforcing obedience. Seriously, who really gave a shit? In ballparks across America, fans waited in line at concessions during the anthem. They chatted with their friends and stared at their phones. *Nobody in the concourse* stopped what they were doing. Yet the cops, at the behest of the Yankees, could rough up and kick a guy out of a baseball game for trying to take a piss during a *recording* of "God Bless America"—*seven years* after 9/11? It looked authoritarian: big-time sports, corporate media, and the military selling the public on a perpetual war machine and using the troops to shut people up. If the public and media were too cowed to challenge the shifts taking place at the ballpark and why, there was one group whose critiques were difficult to dismiss: the veterans themselves.

FOR HIS ENTIRE ADULT LIFE, William Astore had been a soldier. His father fought in World War II. He came from a bare-knuckle city, Brockton, Massachusetts, home of Rocky Marciano and Marvin Hagler, and was born to a family of New England firefighters. Astore described his rise through the service in basic, self-deprecating terms, as that of "a guy who received the normal promotions typical of a military career." He started in the Air Force as an engineer, received his doctorate at Oxford University, rose to the rank of lieutenant colonel, and taught the History of Warfare and Technology at the Air Force Academy. By 2001, he had been on active duty for sixteen years. But he was starting to feel like a prop.

What began to turn him against the forced patriotism was the growing sense of manipulation—of people, of images, of situations, and, perhaps most profoundly, of language. Astore saw symbols without substance, heavy words with minimal depth. Mostly, he did not see actions commensurate with the values that supposedly mattered so much.

"The first thing that gave me pause was the anthrax scare. When did we become a place that responded in such an exaggerated, fearful way?" Astore recalled, referring to envelopes containing the spores that were sent to various media outlets and US senators in the immediate 9/11 aftermath. "Then there was Pat Tillman, and it gradually came out that we gave this soldier a Silver Star but that the military engaged in a cover-up. They tried to manipulate it and create a phony hero, but they didn't have to. If Pat Tillman wasn't a hero, he was a person who commanded respect because he put skin in the game. To see his sacrifice be exploited by the military was just disappointing. Integrity first. It is our highest core value."

The optics and feeling and sensibility about the war and the public selling were discomfiting, but Tillman's story put a face on the consequences of leadership cynicism. Tillman was the Arizona Cardinals safety who quit the NFL and the gilded life and the multimillion salary to join the army. Tillman soon grew disillusioned about the wars in Iraq and Afghanistan, and his transition mirrored the questions of many Americans. It was announced that Tillman had been killed by friendly fire in Afghanistan, but not before the army fabricated the details of his death, frustrating Tillman's family, who deserved to know the truth.

While fans would go to the ballpark uncaring about the images and messages being sent, the Tillman story was a real and chilling example of how the government manipulated the facts of an American life.

"For me, it was Pat Tillman's nobility, his idealism. He sacrificed millions of dollars and, ultimately, his life for his country," Astore said. "And then his country betrayed that sacrifice by lying about the circumstances of his death. That lie extended to the highest levels of the Bush/Cheney administration, revealing in high relief its cynicism and crassness and corruption."

The language of post-9/11, talk of *heroes* and *supporting our troops* made Astore uneasy. "The military propaganda phrase is 'our troops,' as in 'Support our troops.' This is critical. We are supposed to feel that the troops are ours, even if we have no family members or friends in the military," he said. "We are told not just to identify but [to] celebrate them, elevate them. . . . We are told our troops are the very best of us and therefore deserve universal praise. Anyone who 'dissents' is seen as ungenerous—at best—and un-American."

Words such as *militarism* and *authoritarianism* did not resonate with a polarized public. They were just part of the language of the paranoid, or the liberals, or the "social justice warriors," as the pundits called them, but even as the public rejected the idea of an intentional governmental and cultural imposition of authority through sporting events, the smothering frequency of images without any discussion of the real world—what was actually happening in Iraq and Afghanistan, how veterans were being treated—was nevertheless becoming the consequence of hero worship without also demanding accountability. There was nothing harmless in expecting the public to place blind faith in military, yet this was the very atmosphere being sold by the NFL and its fellow sports leagues under the benign guise of patriotism. Whether the public wanted to admit it or not, the end result signaled the elevation of military influence and the diminishment of citizens.

"When people throw that hero stuff at me. . . . You have to stop doing that. It's admirable, but we're not heroes. There's a lot of shitbags in the military too," army Lieutenant Colonel Mark Zinno said. "They're in all walks of life. The military has a sexual-assault issue. Those guys aren't heroes. Far from it. You just can't lump everyone in together."

Being a woman in the military undermined blind faith in the uniform. Cece Evans was proud of completing her training. She took personal satisfaction in proving to herself she could handle the challenge "You get caught up in it," she said. She remembered being proud of reaching beyond her physical limits. The marines were "the toughest," and by completing her regimen, she belonged. She also knew that a certain number of men and women, both inside and outside the service, did not respect her as a marine and did not consider her on the same level as the men. Unlike that of the other branches of the armed forces, marine training was segregated by gender. She knew there were fellow marines who only viewed women, in her words, "as sex objects." She saw through the hero narrative foisted onto the public. The armed forces suffered the same dynamics that left women humiliated and, sometimes, in danger. She recalled a friend who was assaulted in her barracks room. "Her roommate left the door unlocked and a guy snuck in. She punched the shit out of him and he ran out."

Evans had her own moments, including an especially disturbing one at New River Air Station in Jacksonville, North Carolina, with a superior who had been her officer in charge in Iraq. She had met his wife, his whole family. The two were on a twenty-four-hour shift when the superior made sexual advances toward her.

She knew the nicknames male soldiers had for women. 'WMs," they called them. It stood for "walking mattresses." That was an older term. The newer marines called the female soldiers "Wooks," as in "Wookiees," after Chewbacca, the *Star Wars* character ("To compare us," Evans figured, "to hairy, smelly, beasts, I guess."). During her time in the service, there would be other encounters like this one, in close quarters in an uncomfortable, compromising situation with a ranking officer. "He had his hand on my leg and asked me to take off my glasses so he could see my face, and I was thinking, 'I'm going to get raped in this tent, and you have to remember, all the while he has his hand on my leg, I have to call him 'Sir.'"

Ultimately, Evans escaped the night without further advance. She chose not to file a complaint against her superior, for nothing further occurred and a formal complaint carried its own set of concerns that could have affected her worse. "It would have been his word against mine. Would I want to deal with the fallout? Did I want to ruin this guy's career?

What if it ruined mine? Did I want to transfer to a different unit and deal with whatever my reputation was going to be because word travels? I figured, if I could put it down there, it would be done with. If it continued, then it would be out of my hands. It stopped there."

Yet, at the ballpark, the uniform made the cops all heroes, even those who could shoot Amadou Diallo nineteen times. No questions asked—unless you wanted to feel the full weight of your country on your back and be accused of being un-American. The small images, the supposedly innocuous ones, bothered Astore most. They felt like little signs of fascism. "When did every politician start wearing miniature American flag pins?" The NFL broadcast teams and pre- and postgame analysts wore them as well, and team helmets and jerseys had American flags stickered or stitched on them. For years everybody would play along, even though very little of it made actual sense. Each of the four major North American pro leagues would sell its gear—alternative J. J. Watt, Sidney Crosby, or Steph Curry uniforms—with camo patterns and offer first-responder and military discounts. The NFL offered a 10 percent discount on gear to veterans, first responders, active duty and inactive reserves, police, sheriffs, and state troopers. The NBA, MLB, and NHL discount was 15 percent. The leagues also partnered with GovX, a mysterious company that rejects press inquiries and which even the teams seem to have only passing knowledge of. GovX offered discounted tickets to military and police but with a catch—tickets were available in exchange for veterans agreeing to be added to their mailing list to be solicited for military products.

Mark Zinno was not a dissenter. He leaned conservative by disposition and Republican by politics, and yet the commercializing of the veterans made him uncomfortable. Like Bill Astore, Zinno was a lieutenant colonel, albeit in the army, and, like Astore, he could sense the gap between good intentions and naked commercialism at the expense of the soldiers.

"I do get a little bit angry at the events that go on. It is always self-serving," Zinno said. "You're not doing it for us. You're doing it for you. If you really want to help anybody, give [veterans] a job. Get them back on their feet. Don't bring any cameras. You're currying favor to the people who buy your tickets. Salute to Service is bullshit. The worst thing you can do is pretend to be something you're not. You're going to fool the average fan, but you're not going to fool anyone who wears the uniform."

The celebrators couldn't even get their symbols or actors right. ESPN would broadcast baseball on Memorial Day and would dutifully cut away to the military but also to law enforcement, even though Memorial Day has nothing to do with police. But post-9/11 conflation of the two had now become customary. Police and soldiers were the same thing. Even the language was conflated. When a group of Massachusetts police officers went to Puerto Rico to join the relief effort following Hurricane Maria, in the fall of 2017, one local newspaper referred to the group as having been *deployed*. When MLB issued its special Memorial Day uniforms, players would be clad in stars, stripes, and camouflage, even though, ostensibly, Memorial Day solemnly commemorates American soldiers who died in combat, not active duty, who are represented on Veterans' Day. One year, the special Memorial Day uniforms—which were, of course, for sale— even contained a patch of five stars across the short sleeve, an insult be- cause, if servicemen knew anything, they knew stars weren't decals, they were *earned*. "That is just dumb," three-star general Russel Honoré said, "a good idea gone bad."

Another year, the New York Yankees' Memorial Day uniform in- cluded not a black armband or some other in memoriam gesture to ac- knowledge the fallen but stars on its jersey numbers, as if the holiday were the Fourth of July. And on the Fourth of July, teams wore camouflage as if it were Veterans' Day. Baseball then turned to the next phase: the Inde- pendence Day uniform, where each team saw its uniform blended into a red-white-and-blue theme, replete with Stars and Stripes socks. Even the NFL cheerleaders were in the act: skin, tans, and camo bikini outfits— with matching pom-poms. Patriotism was for sale.

"While I appreciate the efforts to remember veterans and their sacri- fices, I cringe when it's connected to a crass commercialism," Astore said. "I also cringe when it's exaggerated and also when the military is used as props. For example, war planes are for war, not to generate cheers before a game. Keep sports and war separate. One is entertainment. The other is deadly."

Maybe if these disconnects had not been swallowed whole by the pub- lic through the forces of intimidation and jingoism, an actual dialogue could have taken place. The world *was* more dangerous, in that terrorist attacks were now affecting the West, especially in Europe. The airplane was the weapon on 9/11. Machine-gun attacks occurred at concerts. Now cars were being plowed into civilians. Two pressure-cooker bombs were detonated during the 2013 Boston Marathon.

"I have no reservations about us participating in a little flag-waving. In fact, if we don't do it, some of the kids would never see the flag get waved, because they go to these schools that don't do any of that," Honoré said. "And I think it's good when they go to a public event and learn they have to get up off their asses when the national anthem is playing. . . . Support of our traditions is not a law, but it's a part of our traditions and a lot of good things in America happen because of it."

Bill Astore retired from active duty in 2005. Two years later, he decided to write about the shift in sports toward the increased patriotic displays he was seeing and its implications. Freed from the potential conflicts of discussing the military while on active duty, he thought about and wrote regular columns for the blog *TomDispatch*, warning against the rising influence of the sports-military state that went not only unchallenged by the public but was encouraged by it. Astore lamented the emptiness and overuse of the word *hero*. He saw the Super Bowl being "militarism on steroids." In the post-9/11 world, Bill Astore was the rarest species once common: the veteran willing to question the militarism that was dominating the culture.

"My original purpose for writing was to highlight the undue deference being shown to our military by our civilian 'leaders.' They seem to have gotten their constitutional duties backwards: instead of leading the military, they allowed military to lead them," he said. "Slowly, inexorably, we're witnessing the rise of militarism in the USA. It's especially powerful because it's increasingly tied to popular culture, including TV shows, movies, and sports."

Astore found sports to be the fertile ground for deception, a place for large-scale deference to the armed forces, where it, the public, and the leagues benefited from the merger of sports and the military. The military remained in a publicly favorable light, which aided in recruiting soldiers. The public could act as though it was doing its part as a supportive nation and the leagues could appear on board as patriotic. What was really happening was professional sports was in the business of selling war.

"It's deliberate, and I'm not a conspiracy theorist," he said. "Basically, the message has been 'You don't have to worry about this. Let the experts handle this. You just have to live your normal life. We got this.' So there's been no national mobilization. The new American isolationism is that we are isolated from the effects of war. It is a deliberate effort to shield the American people from the effects of war. There's a vague sense of 'support the troops' but little sense why. There's nothing about the war other than, they're fighting for freedom. But what does that mean?"

The people who were paying attention knew the deal, and which political aisle they were on didn't matter. From more liberal thinkers like Bill Astore to loyal conservatives like Mark Zinno, the whole thing got the side-eye. Washington Nationals pitcher Sean Doolittle was another one. Doolittle came from a military family. One distant cousin wasn't just a veteran but a legend: the great Jimmy Doolittle. "Doolittle's Raid"—the daring April 18, 1942, response to Pearl Harbor that saw a dozen and a half American bombers buzz over Tokyo to let the Japanese know America was coming for them—was named after him. The problem was that, by now, the voices of the concerned were up against a financial machine.

"The main reason I don't like it is that the commodification of Memorial Day and events like NFL's Salute to Service month . . . capitalizes on a new strain of 'patriotism,'" Doolittle said. "In America today, we display patriotism through the lens of militarism and war and pass it off as support for the troops. It can smell a lot like nationalism. We'll buy a hat with a camo logo of our favorite team and wear it proudly, a way to show support for our team *and* our armed forces. There's more to patriotism than standing for the anthem and wearing red, white, and blue or camo-themed garb, but this new kind of American patriotism gets exploited in the name of capitalism, and days like Memorial Day lose some of their meaning."

What at first looked like well-meaning gestures had become chilling reminders of nationalism, but few people were watching, and the ones who were knew how delicate criticism had to be. But the veterans knew: If every symbol and gesture and holiday could be twisted into a sales gimmick, or if a citizen could be arrested for not standing during the playing of "God Bless America," and if no one was allowed to even voice a criticism of this camo-clad commercial machine, well, what was the fight really about?

"Gestures like standing for the anthem or wearing camo or putting a giant American flag sticker on your car can be hollow gestures," Doolittle said, "if we're not actively doing something to try and make this country a better place."

One day while watching the Red Sox, Bill Astore mused aloud to his wife that he felt an unease at yet another maimed veteran being brought on to the field to a standing ovation to throw out the first pitch. "I know this isn't a popular thing to say, but I really feel that when they bring out the guy who lost an arm and a leg in Iraq to throw out the first pitch to Dustin Pedroia, they're honoring him and that's terrific, but they're also sending another message. That message is that there is no cost to these wars. And people can say, 'Look at him. He's all right.' And he's not all right. He throws out the first pitch and then he goes home and has to deal with a lifetime of not having his limbs.

"And we never talk about peace. What is the purpose of bringing these guys out there if we're not going to discuss ending the reasons that put them in this condition? We never mention the killing involved or that you might be killed. Remember how during war you would hear people say, 'When the war is over . . . ' Remember how after the Cold War leaders talked about a 'peace dividend'? You never hear that anymore. And there is no end in sight."

PART THREE

THE AWAKENING

8

FERGUSON

Protest can be organized through social media, but nothing
is real that does not end in the streets. If tyrants feel no consequences for their actions in the three-dimensional world,
nothing will change.

—TIMOTHY SNYDER, *On Tyranny*

BILLY BEANE, the Oakland A's president, once tried to explain the ridiculous nature of massive, long-term baseball contracts, the ones that were
so back-loaded into the future that a team would wind up owing a player
much older and less valuable the most money when his best years were
behind him. "Most executives are like regular people," Beane said. "They
would rather put off the hard stuff for as long as they can. Does it make in-
tuitive sense to pay the most when the player is at his most productive? Yes,
but organizations don't look at it that way. They think short-term first. Besides, the way an executive sees it, they'll probably get fired before the big
money comes due. They're not going to be the ones paying for it, anyway."

The connection to that long-ago document wasn't immediately obvious, but anyone paying a little bit of attention could see that the warnings
of the Kerner Commission report, about police brutality, lack of jobs,
resources, and the continuing isolation of the ghettoes, were like one of
Beane's back-loaded baseball contracts. Reaching a half century old, the
bill was long overdue, the heavy lifting having been left to the next generation. By December 2017, ten of the eleven members of the Kerner
Commission were dead. Nearly fifty years had passed. It was time to let
somebody else pay for it.

THE BILL COMES DUE

Americans love confidence—having it, seeing it in their fellow citizens. They can talk about any subject with the passion and conviction of an expert, regardless of direct experience or personal history. Guy never played ball past the junior varsity? Put a beer and some hot wings in front of him, and he suddenly knows more than the pro coaches who've spent their lives at the major-league level. Television was a culprit, naturally, for Americans believed you didn't even have to be in the ballpark, the time zone, or even the country to know what was going on. People who didn't have passports spoke with authority on world affairs just because they watched CNN ("Let me tell you what's *really* happening over there . . ."). All you had to do was say it with conviction, and presumably louder than everyone else. It's the American way.

This confidence isn't always a virtue. It is, in fact, the worst possible trait a knowledge-deficient people can have when it comes to black communities in America. Many people talked, but few knew what they were talking about. Across the country, as the Kerner Commission report in 1968 and so many lesser-known attempts at redress predicted, ghettoes were isolated and bankrupted—by geography, from wealth, on purpose by government. And banks. And mortgage brokers. Those not from the ghetto never visit it, yet so many people feel license to speak about the place, the people who live there, and the circumstances under which they live.

Underneath this boldness, of course, is the misinformation of the decades, decades of textbooks and schools teaching students—by avoiding the sustained role of government in creating the architecture that formed the ghetto—that all one needed was harder work, or a serious jump shot.

"With very rare exceptions, textbook after textbook adopts the same mythology," Richard Rothstein wrote in *The Color of Law*. "If middle and high school students are being taught a false history, is it any wonder that they come to believe that African Americans are segregated only because they don't want to marry or because they prefer to live only among themselves? Is it any wonder that they grow up inclined to think that programs to ameliorate ghetto conditions are simply undeserved handouts?"

It's what anybody else, from any other country that lacked the luxury of living in the theoretical world of eternal *hope*, would call *fantasy*. It was through fantasy—and not the years of direct neglect and policy making that ensured its ruin—that so many people chose to see black communities. They *hoped* that schools would improve, even though insufficient resources were constantly under the assault of budget cuts and charter schools and privatization, the eternal siphoning of resources.

In 2016, Boston commemorated fifty years of the Metropolitan Council for Educational Opportunity (METCO) program, which bused minority students from the city to the nicer, wealthier suburban schools. There were documentaries and newspaper articles marking the occasion with celebration but little to no examination of the question of why, a half century later, black kids *still needed* to be bused an hour away from their communities just to go to school. Or take Chicago; with all the despair over its murder rates, the city, from 2004 through 2015, paid an estimated $662 million in police misconduct settlements while allowing its public schools to employ just two librarians for the entire school system.

That's why sports were so important. Sports reinforced the hope, for it was easy to fall in love with the magic bullets of talent, some can't-miss with the ability to sing or dunk or score touchdowns, make it big, ignore the rest and fall in love with the multimillion-dollar athlete *giving back*. It was easy to use sports as proof that it was permissible, even in a new millennium, to still continue to value the black body over the black mind—because Kevin Garnett, who came from one of the roughest Chicago neighborhoods in the country, earned $200 million in salary thanks to growing to be nearly seven feet tall and being really, really good at basketball. It was a delusion that allowed institutions public and private to point to Garnett's success while continuously failing its citizens. Looking beyond the individual, at the ghetto as a whole, wasn't nearly so attractive.

THE MONEY STORE

The US Department of Justice under Barack Obama looked beyond the individual following the August 2014 killing of Michael Brown by Ferguson, Missouri, police officer Darren Wilson. Obama didn't commission some soft, left-leaning, egghead think tank to investigate a city and its police department but turned to the Department of Justice, overseer of the FBI, the burly, seasoned Establishment vehicle the mainstream trusted. When federal investigators emerged, the scathing report they produced in 2015 was not about hope but about the reality of the blood from the cuts, what James Baldwin would call "the evidence" of the American situation.

The report read like a description of a protection racket. It found that the residents of Ferguson had been basically extorted by their local government and were essentially under occupation by their own police force through a byzantine system of fines and fees imposed on residents for minor infractions designed to raise revenue, which compounded due to the inability of many people to pay. The Justice Department message was clear: Ferguson and its cops preyed on its citizens.

Ferguson's law enforcement practices were at a safe distance to judge, the experts (of both the professional and armchair variety) could look down their noses at Ferguson, focusing on the fires and the tear gas and the hordes of people who took to the streets when the residents finally snapped. The experts could do this because in those good, safe communities they weren't reading the 105-page report that reiterated the *modus operandi* of Ferguson was to treat its residents alternatively as cash registers and punching bags, and to subject them to *a pattern of unconstitutional policing*. And the armchairs who said they loved the Constitution couldn't understand how people wound up in the streets because they couldn't conceive of such desperation, because it would be unthinkable for police to treat their white middle class so brutally, so humiliatingly. In Ferguson, 25 percent of residents lived in poverty, many more lived on the margin, and the city responded to its residents by preying on them—for money.

In one March 2012 email, the captain of the Patrol Division reported directly to the city manager that court collections in February 2012 had reached $235,000, and that this was the first month collections had ever exceeded $200,000. The captain noted that the "[court clerk] girls have been swamped all day with a line of people paying off fines today. Since 9:30 this morning there hasn't been less than 5 people waiting in line and for the last three hours 10 to 15 people at all times." The city manager enthusiastically reported the captain's email to the City Council and congratulated both police department and court staff on their "great work."

Police treated residents not as people who were part of a community to be protected and served but as "sources of revenue." That meant issuing relentless citations, especially for minor offenses. In the St. Louis County region, one town's "eyesore" fine—for instance, having tall grass on one's property—was five dollars. In Ferguson, the fine for the same infraction could range from $77 to $102. "These people were balancing their budgets on the backs of poor people trying to go back and forth to work and get kids to school," said Kareem Abdul-Jabbar, who had begun writing about social issues following Ferguson. Under the heading "Focus on Generating Revenue," the Justice Department's report noted that, in 2013, the Ferguson finance director wrote to the city manager: "Court fees are expected to rise about 7.5%. I did ask the Chief if he thought PD could deliver 10% increase. He indicated they could try."

City managers instructed police to issue citations to residents and the police complied. Over one two-year period, Ferguson police issued four or more citations to African Americans seventy-three times, but to non-blacks, Ferguson police only did so twice. To the black community, the Ferguson police operated as an occupying force. Over another period, black residents were the nearly exclusive target of certain types of offenses, such as "walking in roadway" or "failure to comply." The aggressiveness on the part of the Ferguson police was not only a source of harassment to black residents but also had serious financial consequences. The city extracted money from its residents and the police-community relationship was the vehicle:

> We spoke, for example, with an African-American woman who has a still-pending case stemming from 2007, when, on a single occasion, she parked her car illegally. She received two citations and a $151 fine, plus fees. . . . For each Failure to Appear, the court issued an arrest warrant and imposed new fines and fees. From 2007 to 2014, the woman was arrested twice, spent six days in jail, and paid $550 to the court for the events stemming from this single instance of illegal parking. . . . As of December 2014, over seven years later, despite initially owing a $151 fine and having already paid $550, she still owed $541.

The Justice Department concluded the FPD routinely violated the First and Fourth Amendments of the Constitution and used excessive force almost exclusively on African Americans. The report stated, "This culture within FPD influences officer activities in all areas of policing, beyond just ticketing. Officers expect and demand compliance even when they lack legal authority. They are inclined to interpret the exercise of free-speech rights as unlawful disobedience, innocent movements as physical threats, indications of mental or physical illness as belligerence. . . . In every canine bite incident for which racial information is available, the person bitten was African American." DOJ investigators found several examples where the Ferguson police attitude toward black people was inherently hostile:

> In June 2014, an African-American couple who had taken their children to play at the park allowed their small children to urinate in the bushes next to their parked car. An officer stopped them, threatened to cite them for allowing the children to "expose themselves," and checked the father for warrants. When the mother asked if the officer had to detain the father in front of the children, the officer turned to the father and said, "You're going to jail because your wife keeps running her mouth." The mother then began recording the officer on her cell phone. The officer became irate, declaring, "you don't videotape me!" As the officer drove away with the father in custody for "parental neglect," the mother drove after them, continuing to record. The officer then pulled over and arrested her for traffic violations. When the father asked the officer to show mercy, he responded, "No more mercy, since she wanted to videotape," and declared, "Nobody videotapes me." The officer then took the phone, which the couple's daughter was holding. After posting bond, the couple found that the video had been deleted.

HANDS UP

Ferguson provided the optics for the collusion between police and military that had been rising since the Reagan war on drugs. If the Justice Department's investigation of the FPD offered a glimpse of a city whose residents felt under occupation, the televised images of local police dressed in full military riot gear, commandeering military-grade, mine-resistant ambush-protected (MRAP) armored vehicles and staring down fellow Americans confirmed the conflation wasn't just in ballpark images but in attitude and dress. If mounting concern had existed in both the law enforcement and military communities about the increasing closeness between the two entities, which were long intended by law to be separate but had been brought together by the war on drugs, the sight of a fully militarized police patrolling the streets of Ferguson looking like an army, confirmed that too. That this authoritarianism was directed at poor black people underscored the unheeded messages of the Kerner Commission and exposed, too late, the surreptitious, forty-year militarization of the police. Adding to the tension for both black and white America was that Ferguson was occurring in the supposedly postracial, black-president America.

This time, the bill could not be passed to the next generation. To the white mainstream America already police-aligned and not being socked with $102 fines for failing to cut the grass, the remedy in Ferguson was for the residents to obey. They could not conceive of such treatment. Many also refused to accept that the intent behind those laws was to hurt residents. For them, there was always a good reason for law enforcement's actions; just buy a lawnmower or let your kid pee in a diaper. Ferguson was proof that people just needed to *obey*, an attitude that heightened in intensity when the "Hands Up, Don't Shoot!" anthem began to define the Ferguson protests.

Meanwhile, the Department of Justice report concluded that Michael Brown had reached into the police car during his struggle with Darren Wilson. The investigation said Brown's hands were not in the air when Wilson shot him and that he had not been running away. For the counter-protesters, they and the police were vindicated. The reason for Brown's death was unambiguous. "Hands Up, Don't Shoot!" was discredited. In Michael Brown's struggle with Wilson, he was killed, which is what could happen when a person struggles with police. Thus, in living rooms across America, Ferguson was not the story of a community breaking under the strain of illegal and extralegal behavior by its police and leadership but on bad information and bad behavior by an out-of-control teenager. The slogan was false. The outrage was misplaced. The protests were for nothing.

To black America—the black America that did not simply believe the stories of police harassment and debilitating fines and humiliation to be true but *knew* they were true because of personal experience—the "Hands Up, Don't Shoot" slogan couldn't have been more real, for the conclusion of the Justice Department in the Michael Brown case did not square with the *hands up* metaphor, for example, the number of times members of the black community were in a position of compliance or surrender and were harassed and humiliated by police anyway. The indignities were immediate. After Wilson shot Brown, the Ferguson Police Department left Brown's dead body in the street for hours, baking under the hot August sun. The forensic details of the Brown-Wilson struggle were secondary to the number of times these confrontations had occurred, the number of times hands were up, surrendering to the system and its ostensible fairness only to conclude with the same result: a black community overtaxed and underserved with a black male dead at the hands of the police—hands up or hands down—lying motionless in the street.

THE REBIRTH

It was the police who spurred the kids back into the streets, thanks to the viral nature of social media. It was one thing to isolate Rodney King, quite another to ignore the list of names and every viral video on Twitter and Facebook of African Americans that grew so fast that people couldn't remember every grisly incident—or the acquittals of the officers who did the killing and walked free, not only avoiding jail but often returning to their old jobs following suspensions. Adding to the anger were the staggering dollar amounts taxpayers had paid in police settlements across the country, in a time of massive cuts to social programs. In 2011, New York City paid $735 million in police misconduct settlements, and in 2015, Chicago paid $662 million in settlements. "The hope," said Donna Lieberman of the New York Civil Liberties Union, "is that these municipalities will see how much this reckless policing is costing them, in addition to the cost in human lives, and that will spur them to rein in their police departments."

A Gallup poll showed that between 2014 and 2016, 58 percent of whites reported a "great deal" of trust in police, double the 29 percent of blacks. Nearly 75 percent of African Americans polled felt they were treated unfairly by police compared to 34 percent of whites. Ferguson changed all of it. Twenty-three years after Rodney King was beaten, movements in support of holding police accountable brought activism back to the streets. The fault lines ran along two of three of the country's most intractable divisions: race and class, even when police were not involved. The third, gender, could never be separated from the other two. Weeks before Ferguson, Staten Island resident Eric Garner was killed by New York City police after being placed in a choke hold, which was infamously captured on video. Two years before Ferguson, in February 2012, Trayvon Martin was killed in Sanford, Florida, by George Zimmerman, who wasn't even a police officer but a "neighborhood watchman." Later that year, a seventeen-year-old named Jordan Davis was killed in Jacksonville, Florida, by a man at a gas station for apparently playing his car stereo too loudly.

All races of people protested and blocked streets—in Los Angeles, Minneapolis, Oakland, in Ferguson and New York City—expressing their frustration and grief but also their demand for justice. The Ferguson protests lasted sixteen days. Social media provided the kindling, spreading the word and quickly, *virally*. The new movement, formed by three black women following the death of Trayvon Martin, had a name: Black Lives Matter. Social media was key, but the real cord of wood that made the fire roar was video, along with the willingness of young people to physically occupy the streets. There had been video when Rodney King was beaten, too, but the combination of video and the speed in which each incident could be viewed around the world in an instant was something new altogether. The video of the asthmatic Garner being surrounded by cops, wheezing "I can't breathe" as NYPD officer Daniel Pantaleo continued pressing his nightstick into Garner's windpipe, was not theory. The NYPD caused Eric Garner's death, and the entire world saw it.

Then something happened. After forty years of OJ, Michael, and Tiger counting money and selling sneakers, at a physical remove from the people, aligning with the suits who made them millions, the players were paying attention. The videos of police shootings weren't grainy archival footage of a Newark cop stopping a car before shots were fired but real-time incidents that led to protests in the communities where so many of today's athletes were born.

CITIZENS

Fans had no issue with players being vocal. It was *dissent* from the black athlete the public didn't want. After the Boston Marathon bombings, in 2013, Red Sox superstar David Ortiz took the microphone at Fenway Park before Boston's first game back and said memorably, "This is our fucking city!" to the delirious applause of the grieving and the revenge-minded. Later that year, as the Red Sox were on their way to overcoming a dismal, last-place 2012 season with a World Series championship, one of the enduring photos of the playoffs was a police officer cheering in the bullpen after an Ortiz grand slam. The Red Sox, which adopted the citywide

"Boston Strong" motto as their mantra, would win the World Series. *Sports Illustrated* ran a cover photo of Ortiz standing with three members of the Boston Police Department with the cover headline "Boston's Finest Hour." Before the death of Freddie Gray spawned protests in Baltimore, Baltimore Orioles centerfielder Adam Jones agreed to an *ESPN the Magazine* cover shoot that showed him taking a selfie with a member of the Baltimore Police Department, and at the ballpark, everybody loved it.

On October 7, 2014, as the grand jury deliberated over whether to bring formal charges against Darren Wilson for killing Michael Brown, dozens of Black Lives Matter protesters returned to the streets, marching peacefully in St. Louis before Game 4 of the National League Division Series between the Cardinals and Los Angeles Dodgers. To a smattering of cheers from a few fans, the protest passed Busch Stadium. Demonstrators chanted "Justice for Mike Brown!" White fans, beers in hand, responded with a counter-chant in support of Darren Wilson. Inside the stadium, one fan taped "I Am Darren Wilson" over the name on the back of his home white Cardinals jersey. A protester, who was also a marine, captured the exchange between black protesters and white fans on video:

"Justice for Mike Brown!"
"Let's go, Darren!"

As the protesters passed, a white woman with blond hair and a red and white Cardinals jersey confronted the demonstration, shouting at the black protesters, "We're the ones who fuckin' gave all y'all the freedom you have!"

The next week, a few blocks away, Colin Kaepernick threw for 343 yards and three touchdowns in a 31–14 San Francisco 49ers Monday-night win over the home team St. Louis Rams. Inside Edward Jones Stadium, a banner unfurled in one of the nosebleed sections:

RAMS FANS KNOW THAT BLACK LIVES MATTER
ON AND OFF THE FIELD

The Ferguson grand jury continued to meet. Days before its decision, Missouri governor Jay Nixon preemptively declared a state of emergency. On November 22, 2014, 560 miles to the northeast in Cleveland, Ohio, twelve-year-old Tamir Rice played in a park near his house in Cudell Commons. Rice was playing by himself, carrying a toy gun that could be easily purchased at any toy store in the country. Periodically, Rice pointed the toy at people sitting in the park. A neighbor called 911, telling the dispatcher the boy was playing with a gun and that it was likely a toy. According to the official investigation conducted by the Cleveland Police Department, the 911 dispatcher did not tell the officers that the caller had specified the gun was likely fake. Nor were the officers told that Rice was a child but rather a "20 year-old male." Two officers, Frank Garmbeck and rookie Timothy Loehmann, rushed to the scene, drove up to Rice, and saw him standing in a gazebo in the park. In less than two seconds, they shot the boy in the stomach, hitting him from less than ten feet away.

Tamir Rice died the next day. Loehmann would be fired, not for killing Rice but for falsifying his job application. In St. Louis later that day, the grand jury declined to indict Darren Wilson. The Ferguson protestors returned to the streets as Nixon dispatched the Missouri National Guard, riot gear, MRAPs and all, to Ferguson. Days later, Darren Wilson resigned from the Ferguson Police Department. That weekend, before the Rams' home game against the Oakland Raiders, five St. Louis players—Stedman Bailey, Tavon Austin, Jared Cook, Chris Givens, and Kenny Britt—all African American, came out of the tunnel with their hands up in support of the "Hands up! Don't shoot!" protest of the Ferguson Police Department. Britt wrote the words "Hands up! Don't shoot!" on his receiving gloves. The Rams destroyed the Raiders, 52–0, but the big news story was the players supporting the protest. "I just think there has to be a change," Cook said after the game. "There has to be a change that starts with the people that are most influential around the world."

The Rams players coming out of the tunnel was a remarkable moment. It reconnected the chain, linking them to the Black 14 at Wyoming way back in 1969. Two years earlier, Dwyane Wade, LeBron James, and their Miami Heat teammates donned hoodies in response to the killing of Trayvon Martin, a galvanizing gesture that drew attention to the vulnerability of black people across the country. As much attention as the move received, it was nonetheless seen as an isolated one. Now, it wasn't.

A week after the Rams' demonstration, Chicago Bulls point guard Derrick Rose jogged on to court for pregame warm-ups against the Warriors wearing a pullover that read "I Can't Breathe" in support of Eric

Garner, killed earlier in the summer by the NYPD. LeBron James, now with the Cleveland Cavaliers, saw Rose's sweatshirt and wanted one. Brooklyn Nets guard Jarrett Jack, following James on social media, secured "I Can't Breathe" shirts for the Cavaliers and Nets players. A movement percolated. Days later, James and the Nets' Kevin Garnett wore the sweatshirts.

Kenny Britt and his St. Louis teammates challenged the police in a time of unbroken deference—at least by the white mainstream. The St. Louis Police Officers Association demanded that players be disciplined and apologize. NFL Players Association head DeMaurice Smith negotiated with NFL commissioner Roger Goodell, who concluded that the players would not be sanctioned. Inflamed, the police union's business manager, Jeff Roorda, responded not only with threats but with the kind of coded racial language that would be a staple of the response to the players asserting themselves: "I know that there are those that will say that these players are simply exercising their First Amendment rights. Well I've got news for people who think that way, cops have First Amendment rights too, and we plan to exercise ours. I'd remind the NFL and their players that it is not the violent thugs burning down buildings that buy their advertiser's products. It's cops and the good people of St. Louis and other NFL towns that do."

If Harry Edwards was convinced the Heritage failed beyond the 1970s due to a lack of a shared ideology, one had now been forged in 2014 around the misconduct and behaviors of the police. It was the protesters in the streets, blocking traffic and airports, combined with the viral nature of social media, videos being sent around the world in seconds, that had revived the athlete's voice. The players had gotten the message. The players had discovered that, apart from their own bank accounts, maybe nothing had changed since the days of their parents and grandparents, black president not withstanding, and that they were still some of the most visible people in the country. It was not lost on the players that the black bodies the mainstream cheered on Sunday were the same ones so much of the public seemed to fear Monday through Saturday. And though the murders represented a dynamic that had existed for decades, there was something fundamentally different about the Fergusons and Clevelands and Baltimores: they weren't supposed to be happening *today*. This generation was supposed to be past that. The belief that electing a black president not once, but twice, something black people thought impossible, had to be more than a seduction. A seat in the White House had to mean a seat at the table. Or maybe all that hope was all built on sand.

Ferguson was heartbreaking to the African Americans who believed a new day had arrived and that the past battles were not going to be theirs—only to be reduced, once more, to being on the business end of a service revolver or being told to be happy with your money and entertain the leisure class, only to be told to *shut up and play.* "The mistake," University of Southern California professor Todd Boyd said, "was in thinking you were different."

Even the money couldn't protect the athletes. There was that time in 2015 when former tennis star James Blake stood in front of the Grand Hyatt in New York during the US Open and an undercover cop mistook the Harvard-educated man for a criminal and, no questions asked, slammed him to the pavement and cuffed him in broad daylight. Or when Atlanta Hawks forward Thabo Sefolosha was on a New York street that same year and got roughed up by police who broke his leg. There was no escape. Nothing, not the gated communities or the tinted glass of their Escalades could protect them. Affected by the events in Ferguson, the incidents with Eric Garner and Tamir Rice, New Orleans Saints tight end Benjamin Watson took to Facebook: "I'M ANGRY because the stories of injustice that have been passed down for generations seem to be continuing before our very eyes." Watson added that he was frustrated by pop culture's glorification of confrontations between police and citizens. "I'M FEARFUL because in the back of my mind I know that although I'm a law abiding citizen I could still be looked upon as a 'threat' to those who don't know me. So I will continue to have to go the extra mile to earn the benefit of the doubt."

Collision was inevitable. The players were beginning to activate. There was more access to black voices and to the perspectives on conditions from a black point of view, which put white viewers on the defensive that the toy department was being devoured by the real world. Whether the source was an emerging young reporter like Wesley Lowery of the *Washington Post*, young activists such as DeRay Mckesson, or the works of towering writers like Claudia Rankine and Ta-Nehisi Coates, voices of a generation were forming. The election of (and vicious reaction to) Barack Obama, the conscience-expanding works of Rankine's masterpiece *Citizen* and Coates's writings in the *Atlantic*, culminating in his best seller *Between the World and Me*, sharply reminded a generation of African Americans who had believed they belonged, that maybe they didn't.

And it was here where sports no longer served as a unifier but instead reflected the great divide between the labor class (the players), the leisure class (the fans), and the ruling class (the owners). The dam had burst. For all the volumes of talk, no one would make it plain: the protests were racialized, because when it came to dealing with police, few experiences in American life were more racially disparate. As the black players spoke, the white ones stayed silent. History loved to hold up the 1960s Cardinals of Curt Flood, Lou Brock, Bob Gibson, Mike Shannon, and Tim McCarver as the model of players who fought through their cliques and regional biases and prejudices to become a powerful, championship team and better Americans. But that team was also the exception. Most then fumbled through racial discussion like they do now.

Take, for example, that moment in 2016 when on a team flight, some of the white New York Yankees couldn't understand why protests were occurring. "Why don't they just obey?" C. C. Sabathia, the star pitcher and elder statesman, recalled a teammate saying uncomprehendingly. Sabathia, who grew up black in the Bay Area in Vallejo, California, told the group gathering about the time he and his friends were in high school driving around when a cop stopped them at gunpoint, put them face down, unsure what they had done, unsure if they would be arrested or shot on the spot. Instead of shock or embarrassment or sympathy, the players, all of them young, white suburban kids, quickly concluded that *surely* he and his friends had done *something* to provoke such an extreme response. Cops, they told him, just don't act like that without a reason.

"I tried to tell them what it was like for us, and you could tell they weren't even listening," Sabathia recalled. "They were trying to tell *me* what *my* life was like. They heard nothing. They didn't want to hear anything, so I said fuck it. I don't even bother anymore."

The players were activated by different events that began to form a whole. Killings by police weren't isolated. They were personal. In July 2016, Alton Sterling, an unarmed black man selling music CDs on the sidewalk, was shot and killed at close range by two Baton Rouge police officers. Eric Reid, a safety for the San Francisco 49ers, lived in Baton Rouge as a kid. "When I look back on my life, I don't want it to be as a hypocrite," Reid said. "And when I raise my kids and tell them to do things the right way, I can say I did the same."

The players did not simply find themselves in solidarity with the marchers in the streets but also questioning their place in an industry that was selling an image of police that did not often square with their reality. Harry Edwards's vision of a sustained ideology began to organically take hold, for the competing images of black people being killed on dashcam footage and the dozens of the law enforcement appreciation nights across the sports calendar forced the players to confront the biggest fractures in their industry: the enormous gap between the business machinery of the game—the white owners, white coaches, white season-ticket base, and white media—and them, the majority-black workforces that played the games. The players played the game, but black people weren't exactly the target audience—despite the money they spent on sneakers and jerseys, and despite how, in the NBA's case, its slick ad campaigns used black culture to sell the sport. The players were recognizing that if they remained quiet, they had money but no power, money but no wealth, money but no greater belief that they were making a difference. They were being purchased. A collective light was going on. All the money and the commercials, the houses and the private jets and the fame had greenwashed them, and when so many players looked in the mirror after watching Eric Garner be choked to death by the state, they realized they had lost themselves.

The puzzle pieces began to interlock, but this time it wasn't the courageous and vulnerable showing their faces while the big boys wrote a check but steered clear of the spotlight. The Minnesota Lynx players, black and white women of the WNBA, came forward to speak about injustice. The Mount Everests of the game—LeBron James, Derrick Rose, Venus and Serena Williams, Kevin Garnett, and Dwyane Wade, are Most Valuable Players or NBA champions, the biggest gate attractions, merchandising leaders, the household names—put a face to their politics. The best player, James, being the loudest social voice advocating for black people had not happened since Muhammad Ali in the mid-1970s.

"I don't want the people in the community to feel like we turned a blind eye to it," Kenny Britt said. "What would I like to see happen? Change in America." After the final breaths of Eric Garner and Michael Brown and Tamir Rice, and after forty years of rejecting their inheritance, the players again believed they were part of the larger struggle.

Maybe there had always been a gauzy little lie to it all to make everybody feel better about the true depth of the country's divisions, the intractability of Monday through Friday, to give everyone a little hope that a cease-fire on third-and-inches every Sunday meant we really did speak a common language. Maybe the truth—resentments even in sports always simmered at low temperature, needing just a few degrees of heat to rip apart the calm—was too dark to face, and now there was no turning back.

"I'M GOING HOME"

What sports fans wanted most in the decade and a half that followed September 11 was proof that their eyes weren't deceiving them. The pageantry represented a shift in how the games were presented to the public and what messages the industry sent to consumers, in addition to the slam dunks and buzzer beaters, but it was also during this time that data—or that key word of the millennium, *analytics*—changed the way sports were watched, analyzed, interpreted. The eye test had to be backed up by the numbers, and in many cases, the numbers had to be backed up by more numbers inside the numbers. Experience was secondary to data. That was why it was suddenly permissible for people who only watched the game to laugh at people who once *played* the game, to pass them off as antiquated, and to hire, fire, and have more influence. Fans didn't want scouts, gut feelings, or emotion. They wanted research, facts, and numbers. They wanted Moneyball.

But when it came to the police, and the appropriateness of their being embedded in a sporting event where people of all stripes just wanted to crack a beer and have fun, fans didn't want numbers. They wanted emotion. They wanted *politics* by another name, dressed in ceremony. They wanted the racialized image of authority as America, the players to love America or leave it. They couldn't call it that explicitly, so they used another word: *patriotism.* Numbers would have created an entirely different narrative at the stadium. It would have forced the white mainstream to perhaps rethink the whole hero business, pump the brakes on the jingoism, and recognize that policing was difficult, complicated work, sometimes heroic, sometimes not and maybe didn't belong at the ballpark at all—especially when black players criticized law enforcement. No one doubted that police work was often dangerous and thankless. What was in doubt was whether it was appropriate to lionize an entire *profession*, especially when the data suggested it wasn't always worthy of the blind adulation.

Numbers, however, are what the public received following the events of April 12, 2015, when Freddie Gray was arrested in West Baltimore for carrying a switchblade, placed in a police wagon, and arrived at the station in a coma. Gray never regained consciousness and died in the hospital a week later. After his funeral a couple of weeks later, disturbances broke out and a CVS pharmacy in the area was burned and looted (an image CNN seemed to keep on a continuous loop). Thirty-four people were arrested. As in Ferguson, the black community saw another one of its own killed. Freddie Gray was dead, and of the six officers who were in the van with him, none reported foul play that could have led to his death—yet the city coroner said Gray's death was not an accident and ruled it a homicide.

And as with Ferguson, the armchair quarterbacks, protected in the pockets of their safe communities with police they trusted, couldn't understand how people could erupt yet again. Yet when the Justice Department investigated the Baltimore Police Department, it found a force that seemed to spend a fair amount of time harassing the black community to such a degree that it wasn't surprising that the black public believed the police killed Freddie Gray:

> Arrests without probable cause: From 2010–2015 supervisors at Baltimore's Central Booking and local prosecutors rejected over 11,000 charges made by BPD officers because they lacked probable cause or otherwise did not merit prosecution. Our review of incident reports describing warrantless arrests likewise found many examples of officers making unjustified arrests. In addition, officers extend stops without justification to search for evidence that would justify an arrest. These detentions—many of which last more than an hour—constitute unconstitutional arrests.

Another federal report had concluded law enforcement mistreated its citizens, especially those in the black community, and in a similar response to Ferguson, the armchair quarterbacks who lived in safe, just communities felt comfortable in criticizing the black community. The fans cheered for cops at the ballpark but suddenly had no time for data showing that police routinely violated the Constitution. Under the heading "Unconstitutional Stops, Searches and Arrests," the Justice Department report noted only 3.7 percent of pedestrian stops in Baltimore resulted in a fine, arrest, or citation, yet the officers would search, stop, and frisk citizens without cause to do so, a violation of the Fourth Amendment prohibiting unlawful search and seizure. Or put another way, 96.3 percent of the pedestrians the Baltimore Police Department stopped were frisked for nothing, just being harassed without cause. The Justice Department found a runaway police department that did not discipline its officers. In another section of the report, the Justice Department determined that several Baltimore officers in the BPD sex crimes division on multiple occasions were found to be having sex with prostitutes and went undisciplined.

The culture within the police department was bad enough, but what came next was worse. After the Justice Department report, the police commissioner, city council, and several members of the Maryland state legislature introduced a bill that would address reforms. It died mysteriously in committee.

"If the Baltimore City Council could do it alone, we would, but we cannot," wrote city councilman Brandon Scott. "However, as chair of the city council's Public Safety Committee, I pledge to work with all of my partners in government to make these much needed actions a reality. We may not have achieved our goals during this session, but eventually we will. For now, however, we are left to ponder who opposed these simple yet needed pieces of legislation and why."

New York Knicks star and Baltimore native Carmelo Anthony, raised in the same part of town as Freddie Gray, watched the events on television—his people in the streets, grieving, angry, frustrated. He received hundreds of text messages from friends and family. He made a decision. He was going to join them.

"I'm like, 'Naw, I'm going home.' You know what I'm saying? Like, 'If you wanna come with me, you come with me, but I'm goin' home,'" Anthony recalled. "I'm not calling reporters and getting on the news. I'm actually going there. I wanted to feel that. I wanted to feel that pain. I wanted to feel that tension."

And so Carmelo Anthony did something remarkable, something Patrick Ewing never did during Howard Beach or Bensonhurst, something Magic Johnson didn't do during Rodney King, something no player of his stature had done in decades. He reached back into the Heritage not by writing a check to the nearest historically black college but by showing his face, walking elbow-to-elbow, arm-in-arm, with the Baltimore residents who were the ones actually living the data. Walking with his people and not the celebrity class or the millionaire class only increased what was becoming a personal awakening. Anthony felt for Eric Garner and his family, for Michael Brown and his family. But Freddie Gray was different. Freddie Gray was Baltimore. His Baltimore.

"When you're in that environment, it happens. It's a part of your life," Anthony recalled. "And it's not until you step outside of that environment and start looking back into that environment when you're like, 'Oh, this is messed up.' I get so passionate talking about it with different people that I grew up with. And we sit down and start reminiscing. Before, when I used to tell that story it was, you know, funny. It was laughing, joking, and funny, and 'Yo, remember when we got pulled over? Remember when the police put us on the ground? Or they chased us?' It was funny. Now, that shit ain't funny no more."

There were disturbances in the street. Major League Baseball feared the worst. The night of Freddie Gray's funeral, the Red Sox and Orioles played a night game at Camden Yards, and fortuitous timing avoided major overlap between demonstrators and fans leaving the yard. The Orioles were next playing the White Sox and could only envision the reality of the nightmare scenario they had narrowly avoided: the white suburban ticket buyer spilling out of the stadium (maybe with a few too many beers in him), clashing with black protesters grieving another dead body with low expectations of justice and rising frustration. Baseball was aware of the Ferguson clashes between protesters and fans both at the St. Louis Cardinals and Rams games and made the executive call to not only cancel the game against the White Sox but to play it the next day in the daytime—with no fans.

And as Carmelo Anthony walked the streets of Baltimore, something special happened at 333 West Camden Street, site of the offices of the Baltimore Orioles Baseball Club. Unlike the Rams and the Cardinals, neither of which said a word of support for the people of Ferguson, many of whom rooted for the home football and baseball teams, the Orioles, or more specifically Baltimore team executive vice president John Angelos, released a statement saying that the Orioles belonged to every person in the city of Baltimore. It was subtle, yet important, that Angelos wasn't placing his baseball team on the side of the police. Nor was he saying that the feeling of African American baseball fans meant nothing to him because they couldn't afford season tickets or weren't the ears talk radio was trying to reach. The Orioles were the first and only professional sports team to date to acknowledge, in any way, the difficulty of the African American community. While the rest of the sports world encouraged the symbols of authoritarianism and feared the inevitable backlash from the police union, in a series of posts to social media, Angelos connected the attitudinal dots of what was happening in the culture that his peers were either too afraid—or too busy financing—to confront, writing:

> My greater source of personal concern, outrage and sympathy beyond this particular case is focused neither upon one night's property damage nor upon the acts, but is focused rather upon the past four-decade period during which an American political elite have shipped middle class and working class jobs away from Baltimore and cities and towns around the U.S. to third-world dictatorships like China and others, plunged tens of millions of good, hard-working Americans into economic devastation, and then followed that action around the nation by diminishing every American's civil rights protections in order to control an unfairly impoverished population living under an ever-declining standard of living and suffering at the butt end of an ever-more militarized and aggressive surveillance state.

July 2015. In Walker County, Texas, a woman named Sandra Bland died mysteriously in police custody after what appeared on video to be a routine traffic stop. The players watched. Sports had made its choice: it was going to sell the valor of police to the white public, even as federal investigations proved that police departments acted in many instances unlawfully and in many deadly cases unprofessionally. The players made a decision in return. They were going to show their faces, on the field, to tell their country that times needed to change.

9

A SEAT AT THE TABLE

AT ITS CORE, the Heritage was always about revolution. That was a scary word, and everyone did their best to dance around it, but it was nevertheless true. Whether it was Robeson advocating universal health care in the 1930s (he did) or Jackie Robinson refusing to accept segregation at Fort Hood or sending urgent telegrams to John F. Kennedy telling him it was time to protect black people against mob violence, the revolution was in destroying Jim Crow. Curt Flood sought to kill a century of how baseball did business. The Heritage was about turning over the soil and remaking the culture for people under its boot. What started with LeBron James and the Miami Heat wearing hoodies after Trayvon Martin's killing came with another message: it was time for athletes to return to their inheritance and use their power beyond cashing endorsement checks.

Players had unique talent; the public appetite for it was insatiable. Athletes were the most powerful black employees in the country—but, really, what had they done with that power? They hadn't even revolutionized their own sport in nearly fifty years. Football players took on the NFL twice with the strikes of 1982 and 1987, and got demolished both times, especially in 1987 when the superstars abandoned the cause faster than the rank and file. NBA players were now super-rich, but the money did not translate into front-office or coaching jobs or in any significant shift in team ownership. Until 2017, all four major professional sports leagues combined had one black owner.

LeBron James spoke of the NBA in terms of player ownership of the product, if not the financials. He assumed a partnership, referring to the league as "our game," but he owned no financial percentage of an NBA team. Michael Jordan was the only ex-player in the history of three major North American sports, of which African Americans composed a significant percentage of the players, to become a majority shareholder. Magic Johnson wrote a check for $50 million to join the Los Angeles Dodgers ownership group, but that was $50 million of a *$2 billion* purchase. The headlines called it "Derek Jeter's $1.2 Billion Bid," but when Jeffrey Loria sold the Miami Marlins to Jeter's group, it turned out that Jeter owned a 4 percent ownership stake, or $16 million of equity. The NHL had Mario Lemieux, who as owner of the Pittsburgh Penguins was the only other modern, post–free agency ex-player to own all or part of a major sports franchise. In history.

Besides, full or partial ownership wasn't *revolution*; that was *assimilation*. If the players could just think beyond their short-term salaries and be a little bolder in their vision, Carmelo Anthony thought, true partnership in a game where they were the prime performers was, at long last, a real possibility. Not doing so would continue to create easy wealth for the players, but they would never have any of the power that came with the money the owners had. "Their billions," Anthony said, "outweigh our millions."

Whether it was rooted in protest in the streets, the players after years of cashing the checks, sensed a growing anxiety about using their power. The public might have wanted them to be grateful for their millions and show gratitude toward authority, and media may have used the image of the sacrificing veteran or cop risking his life every day as a device designed to pressure players to *shut up and play*, but the players didn't see it that way. They weren't cops or soldiers, electricians or plumbers. They were world-class performers who had made the game. The NFL was a 70 percent black league whose annual revenue was roughly $13 billion. Eighty percent of the players in the NBA were black, and *Forbes* reported that the league had generated $5.9 billion in revenue in 2016, and that thirty teams had averaged a value of $1.36 billion; in 2017, revenues were expected to top $8 billion. Over a ten-year period, Major League Baseball, with its heavy Latino workforce, saw revenues nearly double, from $5.5 billion in 2006 to more than $10 billion in 2016. Revolution, though, wasn't always (or ever) only about receiving more money. It was about power, and the basic business structure of professional sports had remained unchanged: there were players and owners, unions and commissioners. The players didn't choose the commissioner, and they never sat in at the owners' meetings. They were still just employees. The players knew they were the product. They were also starting to believe what they'd been hearing for decades but refused to act upon: they had earned the right to be partners, and partners could make demands.

During the final few months of the lives of Eric Garner and Michael Brown, V. Stiviano, the thirty-one-year-old mistress of Donald Sterling the notorious, eighty-year-old Los Angeles Clippers owner, secretly recorded an argument between the two during which Sterling made horribly racists comments about black customers and one prominent black player in particular—the legendary Earvin "Magic" Johnson. On the recording, Sterling asks Stiviano, "Do you have to bring them to my games?" He is also heard demanding that Stiviano associate with African Americans "in private" and refers to the players as charity cases who should be grateful for his benevolence.

"I support them and give them food and clothes and cars and houses. Who gives it to them? Does someone else give it to them?" Sterling says. "Do I make the game, or do they make the game?"

Usually, the money people knew to keep their traps shut, but periodically the owners would get sloppy. This was one of those times. The ruling class dropped its guard and let the world see how it really felt about their millionaire hired hands. Sterling on tape revived memories of the time the Cincinnati Reds won the 1990 World Series and the owner, Marge Schott, referred to stars Eric Davis and Dave Parker as her "million-dollar niggers." If it hadn't been abundantly clear before, it was now: the players were not partners.

Everyone in basketball knew that Donald Sterling was one of the worst owners in the history of professional sports, a guy who for nearly three decades, no matter how many number-one overall draftees he received, ran his team into the ground and treated people like garbage. Though unsuccessfully, the legendary Laker Elgin Baylor had once served as his general manager and sued Sterling for racial discrimination after Sterling fired him in 2009. Angelenos knew Sterling as the man who settled a $2.7 million housing discrimination lawsuit for not renting to blacks or Latinos. Now the whole world knew Sterling as the racist owner of a team that played in a league where 80 percent of the players were black but who didn't want black people attending his games. Sterling then went on CNN and insulted Magic Johnson further, saying that Johnson wasn't a role model because "he's got AIDS."

Players texted one another about boycotting the playoffs. Doc Rivers, the coach of the Clippers, looked as if he needed a bottle of Tums doing his daily press sessions, trying to be diplomatic while still having to refer to Sterling as "his owner" or at least the owner of the team.

Adam Silver, the new NBA commissioner, hadn't even been on the job three months. While the Clippers players talked boycott, NBA old-timers were convinced that had David Stern still been commissioner, he would have wasted no time in crushing the would-be rebellion because no threat to ownership would be tolerated.

Everybody waited for the Clippers' response. They were playing the Golden State Warriors, and as tip-off neared, tension mounted—but the players did not mount a boycott. Neither did James's Miami Heat or any of the other teams in the postseason. During warm-ups, the Clippers arrived on court wearing their warm-up sweaters inside out, a statement that they played not to represent the Clippers but themselves. The players then dumped the sweaters in a pile at half court.

The Knicks did not make the playoffs that year, but Carmelo Anthony believed the Clippers players' warm-up gesture to be weak. Players expressed their disgust, but outside of maybe a higher laundry bill, the owners not only did not lose any money but *gained* the revenue of the playoff box office and probably a bit more in higher TV ratings from the suspense. If the players had been serious, Anthony believed, they should have boycotted the game.

"The way I woulda did it if it was close to me is I wouldn't have come out. Like, that was the opportunity right there to say, like, 'I'm not playing.'" Anthony said. "That was a real moment right there. It wouldn't have been about basketball at all. That was a race issue right there. And that was where you coulda put your foot down and said, 'No, we're not havin' it.' It wasn't no gestures. It was me saying, 'I'm outta here.'"

Instead, the players in the playoffs decided to work within the system. They decided to trust NBA commissioner Adam Silver. Silver knew he couldn't be weak on Sterling, lest he risk the players actually making good on the threat and walking out during the playoffs—a colossal disaster. Nor, however, could Silver give the impression he was willing to sell out another owner. The owners were his bosses.

Two days after the Clippers tossed their warm-ups in a pile, on April 29, 2014, Silver took the podium for an afternoon press conference and announced that Sterling was being banned from the NBA, fined $2.5 million, and forced to sell the Clippers, which he later would, to the Microsoft megamillionaire Steve Ballmer.

Sterling was out, and by refusing to shut up and play, the players had won. Silver had needed to listen to them. "I thought they handled it perfectly," Charles Barkley said of the players.

Carmelo Anthony and several other players were embittered, though. They viewed the Sterling incident as a missed opportunity. They would never know how much power they really had—and the owners would continually believe the players would not fight. They chose to stay in line, opting for partnership over battle. The players would never know if they really would have been willing to shut down the game and, in Anthony's most radical vision, sent the message that a player-owned league was one day a possibility. Anthony was offended by Sterling's racism and believed that though Sterling was the one who'd been caught, his attitude represented all the owners; otherwise, Sterling's well-known views wouldn't have been tolerated by the other owners for more than thirty years. For all the talk of revolution, the players had chosen compromise.

"I can only speak for basketball players, but we're powerful enough if we wanted to, to create our own league—if we wanted to," Anthony said. That was the kind of the talk that had percolated in the late 1980s, when the principles of the Heritage combined with the new reality of players amassing the kind of wealth that should have translated into economic autonomy but rarely did.

Craig Hodges had pleaded with Michael Jordan to consider the possibilities: player-owned, predominantly black initiatives could open a range of opportunities currently closed to players. Jordan, who by 2016 would join Oprah Winfrey as the only two African American billionaires, always remained practical. Creating startups to challenge the institutional power of the NBA, Nike, or Reebok sounded romantic, revolutionary even. But it couldn't win. The smart money didn't bet against the big guys. It joined them.

Now the ground was shifting. Carmelo Anthony and LeBron James were part of a new generation of athlete who had succeeded professionally and rejected the Jordan template of apolitical athlete-as-CEO, but what had they actually won? Would players ever be willing to take the risks of ownership, of economic responsibility and freedom, and discover if the revolution Craig Hodges once implored Michael Jordan to lead could ever be real? Thus far, the answer was no.

"Without the athletes, there's no league. But they don't think like that," Anthony said. "[Owners] look at it this way: 'We're your main source of income, so you're gonna need me before I need you.'"

THE REALEST DUDE

When the Heritage collapsed, it did so because the stars were unwilling to carry its responsibilities. With new superstars, its revival not only reconnected the present day to its origins but started the repudiation of the Jordan mandate. If the forty-year hold of the OJ-Michael-Tiger attitude on pro sports wasn't completely dead, it at least had competition now.

"It was all about a corporation, and about building that corporation," Carmelo Anthony said. "And it was about building the perfect athlete. And Michael Jordan came in. He transcended the game to another level on the court and off the court. You know? Be like Mike. So everybody wanted that typical athlete, that clean-cut athlete suit. You know what I'm saying? Never not politically correct. Never spoke outside of his message and what people want. That was the athlete that was being built from the '70s to now."

But in a time of Ferguson, Michael Jordan, with his apolitical message and inoffensive corporate packaging, was not the perfect model for this new group of players. The initial challenge to the Jordan model was not a socially principled player, the second coming of Bill Russell or Jackie Robinson, but an antihero who didn't care about trying to make white people believe he was one of them because he could wear a $2,000 suit and look like a black CEO. The antihero attitude who wasn't trying to gain the approval of anyone was embodied by the great Philadelphia 76ers point guard Allen Iverson. It was Iverson who first began pulling the athlete from the boardroom back to the streets, back to the people.

It was Iverson who captivated the public, black and white, Asian and Latino, with his relentless play, his toughness, and, most of all, his liberation, of *not* being beholden. Iverson was unique because of his slight build, fearlessness, and patented crossover dribble. He played as if he didn't care

about the established hierarchy in the game, whether Michael Jordan or
Shaquille O'Neal was on the court, or about the owners, the coaches, or the
media. Not caring what the establishment thought resonated with younger
fans, who themselves may have felt a growing disconnection with the traditional world. There was another reason Iverson connected with even the
hardhats, the white fans who, regardless of income, identified themselves
as the white working class, who so often denigrated black players and tried
their very best to resent him and called in to talk radio about black players
playing the game *the right way*: he so obviously busted his ass on the court
every game, every night, the same way they envisioned themselves doing at
their jobs.

Iverson uncoupled from the Jordan mold. In many ways, he made
the machine adapt to him. Iverson's force of personality was so powerful and authentic that Madison Avenue came to him, without asking him
to make the same greenwashing deal so many black athletes had been
forced to make since O. J. Simpson drew the first blueprint of crossover
appeal. Iverson disrupted both the racial and class norms of a superstar,
and there was no reason to dance around it. What did the big words really mean? Corporate and mainstream comfort? Appeasement *at the cost
of individuality?* Everyone knew what they meant but no one—especially
players—could say them out loud: it meant taking the money at the cost
of blackness. It meant making white people comfortable.

It also meant controversy when Iverson wore cornrows, because at the
time, in the 1990s, cornrows were associated with the ghetto, prison, and
urban black life. It meant controversy when Iverson didn't abandon every
childhood friend, which was what black players who'd "made it" were
expected to do publicly (even though the gap in money between themselves and their old lives was a conflict that devoured athletes of all races).
It meant controversy when Iverson wore jeans and gold chains to awards
ceremonies. Iverson sent the message that he would not be greenwashed.
If the sports industry was going to scour the ghetto for black talent, Iverson seemed to say, it would have to take the blackness and the personality
and black culture that came with it. That meant a high-speed collision
with the white owner–white coach–white media–black player structure
that was pro sports. To the mainstream sports culture, that blackness only
translated into the commerce of the "dead or in jail" black narrative that
had become the *only* black narrative when it came to athletes, never mind

that Iverson also connected with the people in ways that were uplifting and inspiring. He did not turn poor communities into cliché. He gave them the dignity of being treated like everyone else.

"When I started doing it, I was criticized so much. I was beat up for it, and I was so young. Back then, my skin wasn't as thick as it is now. So it used to bother me a lot," Iverson said. "Even articles and things people used to say. . . . Then, I had to grow and learn to understand that that's the way it's going to be. A negative story about Allen Iverson is going to sell more than a positive one. Me giving out turkeys, or giving out gifts for Christmas, and stuff like that, don't nobody want to hear about stuff like that, when it come to me. They want to hear about the renegade story."

This was the game, even though blackness had been appropriated by white culture since the birth of the cool. Black style (at least the stereo-typical elements whites felt they understood) was more marketable than Iverson's crossover, and the price of stardom, endorsements, and market-ability was to code-switch from being fetishized for the sweat, the speed, the snarl of competition into the white mainstream living room. Shaquille O'Neal was a master at it, which is why he could sell anything from energy drinks to foot powder. Charles Barkley, too, knew how to disarm a public that loved his end-to-end ferocity on court but wanted him to hug their grandmothers when they saw him in a restaurant. In particular, Barkley, outspoken but of moderate politics, had parlayed his code-switching skills into an entertaining, lucrative broadcast career (and a $2 million a year en-dorsement deal with Weight Watchers). He even titled one of his autobi-ographies *Who's Afraid of a Large Black Man?* These players could rip down backboards but still flash the pitchman's smile that told Middle America that *this black giant won't hurt you.*

Iverson was totally different, and though he was virtually never polit-ical (or violent) during his NBA career, in his own independent way, he represented one of the first reconnective bridges to the Heritage because win or lose, rich or poor, Allen Iverson was not going to make the deal that had been central to the black athlete's survival since O. J. Simpson: he was not going to sacrifice himself, the identity in his blood, to make the white mainstream like him. And instead of turning on him, which had been the great fear of black athletes (and their agents, handlers, and mar-keters) for two generations, the public loved Iverson more.

CHECK, PLEASE

As the Heritage began its slow revival, the larger question was *"What did it mean?"* Did it just mean athletes tweeting out words of support and encouragement after a confrontation between the cops and an ill-fated black kid? Did it mean speaking out during political campaigns? Did it mean becoming more active in labor-management issues? Did it mean owning the shoe company instead of being sponsored by it? Did it mean destroying the old model of sports and creating a new one? What it meant above all was control, and when it came time for the black athlete to be faced with politics once more, Iverson's independence had created a pathway to reconnect the athlete simultaneously to his individualism and his people. It was Iverson who told a new generation of young black athletes that if wearing a $2,500 suit wasn't who you were, you didn't have to be that person, even if Michael Jordan was. It meant that if a Freddie Gray got killed and you wanted to get involved, you could—even if Michael Jordan didn't. And it meant that if you were comfortable with the cost—because there would always be a cost—you didn't have to play along.

Iverson also proved that black authenticity could sell—as is. Nike had already profited from creating an antihero campaign to counter its own Jordan hero-making a few years earlier with its Charles Barkley "I'm not a role model" ads. As Nike recognized the potential power of Jordan in the 1980s, Reebok saw value in the counterprogramming of Iverson to a more irreverent, nonconformist generation of basketball fans. Whether any of this irreverence was real or just the same lucrative trope from an "edgier" angle was a different story, for as much as one corporation may have feared the Iverson effect on their product, Reebok saw Iverson as an asset.

"It's the best. I mean, Reebok let me do me. Everybody, when I came into the league, was afraid of me being me, afraid of me just being like the dudes I grew up with. I didn't come up with the styles. A lot of styles I bit off dudes that I hang with. I didn't want to be somebody else because I was in the league," Iverson said. "I wanted to be myself. I thought it was cool, and I wanted to be the person that my mom looked at and said, 'That's my baby.' For my homeboys and people that I grew up with and went to school with, you know, I didn't want to change who I was because of where I was at. Reebok let me be myself; they invested in me and marketed me like I wanted to be marketed. That's why I'm loyal to them, and I'll always be there with Reebok, and it's real."

It was a liberation, a power that opened up possibilities, a newfound self-determination of control of image—how black men were portrayed in media, in interviews—if they were willing to demand control. Technology would aid the possibilities, as the rise of social media assisted in wresting control of a player's image from traditional media. Players could be their own messengers. What it also signaled was a challenge to the greenwashing of the black athlete, the notion that money was ample compensation for the black identity. A conscious athlete who drew strength from his identity and was not willing to barter it for money, as so many players either did willingly to increase their chances of endorsements or unwillingly on the advice of an industry that only knew one speed: to make talented black men comfortable to white ticket buyers. Comfort didn't only mean "disarming." It also meant reinforcing the comfortable stereotypes that the white mainstream expected of black players, stereotypes that diminished black men even as they profited from them. It meant, in today's world, that athletes were individual, multimillion-dollar corporations and could now hire and promote black professionals that, in the past, did not have opportunities to enter the league, as Chris Webber discovered when he wanted to hire a black agent. It also revealed just how little control black athletes had over their images.

Take, for example, the April 2008 cover of *Vogue* that featured Brazilian supermodel (and wife of Tom Brady) Gisele Bündchen and with his left arm around her, right hand dribbling a basketball and face roaring into the camera, LeBron James. James was four years away from making his political statement after Trayvon Martin's killing, years away from his becoming a major political sports figure and powerful businessman. The cover, shot by the famed celebrity photographer Annie Leibovitz, inflamed black readers, conjuring images of King Kong, of the same insulting racial encounter between the frail white woman and the animalistic black male. It was a formula that became a business model in sports: the sports show hosted by the white (often blond woman) flanked by two black ex-athletes. In one way, the photo was held as proof of a changing industry and greater opportunity. In another, with both women and black men, it represented still more of the same, not only the selling of body over mind but of the bedrock black currency: anger. It was proof again of the value of the black body and the devaluing of the black mind that had created the importance of the black athlete in the first place. If an athlete at the level of James would allow himself to be depicted in such a reductive manner, for money, what was the point of being awakened politically?

As culture changed, and the change in the demographics of the American population became undeniable, the popular culture began to sell an odd product: the positive stereotype, which at first glance appeared to be an oxymoron. As demand for diversity increased, different faces appeared, as humiliating caricature where the minority gets lampooned. The gay man is being neat and creative, the interior designer, the natty dresser or gossipy hairdresser. The Indian tech whiz, the Asian math whiz. The white computer nerd. All are lampooned. None get the girl. All provide the comic relief that reinforces the white storytelling structure while scoring points for hiring minority actors. Yet while offensive, each also emerges with a reputable, white-collar, non-threatening and marketable *skill*. We may laugh at the gay guy, but he has a career. The Indian tech whiz might not get the girl and the rainbow, but he's a computer professional and works at Apple, one of the greatest companies in the world. The math whiz may never get a date, but he's a top scholar at MIT.

Not so for the black guy. The black guy kicked your ass. The black guy scored the touchdowns. Black athleticism sold. Black anger sold. Black hypersexuality sold. Black stereotype sold, in music and sports and Hollywood. The black value then, now, came from the black body.

There was always room for the physical, aggressive black voice or body. In fact it often appeared as if aggression was the only lane—in advertising, in the music, the movies, in the American imagination—for black men. James reinforced as much through his *Vogue* cover, and that was why the reaction was no exaggeration. Unlike the "positive stereotypes" of other lampooned minorities, there was nothing positive, no white-collar skill, about the black guy snarling like he was either going to dunk on you or steal your wallet—and in real life, that expectation of aggression was being used as an adequate defense for shooting black men both by police and citizens.

Periodically Al Sharpton and music titan Russell Simmons would spar over the messages being sent through music by black artists and whether the words "bitch" and "nigger" could be declawed through pop-culture ubiquity. Sharpton would tell Simmons it was not possible, that some words would always be a weapon, no matter who held that weapon, and in the black community the weapon being fired outward to the pop culture for profit was backfiring on young black people, who now used hateful, reducing speech as a matter of course, often on each other. Where, Sharpton asked, was the value in white hip-hop fans repeating lyrics with the word "nigger" or young black boys and girls referring to themselves and their friends as "niggers" and "bitches" as a cavalier substitute for their first names? Simmons would counter that words could be used enough to be co-opted by a benign culture and thus changed, softened, massaged, *normalized.* Then, during the 2017 NBA Finals between the Warriors and Cavaliers, vandals defaced the front of LeBron James's Brentwood estate with the word "nigger." As the country lamented this racist act against the superstar, Sharpton called to tweak Simmons with a mic drop of his own. "Hey, Russell," he began, "I thought that word didn't have meaning anymore?"

ASE!

If the professionals were idealistic about one day having greater control of their shoe deals, contracts, and images and being partners in the sports machine, the coaches, administrators, and athletic directors at the collegiate level were equally idealistic about the supposed virtues and benevolence of amateurism and keeping all the power that came with it for themselves.

The college game had always been fertile ground for revolution. High-level men's college basketball and football were dominated by black men who were paid nothing while their universities reaped millions. Both college football and basketball brought in revenue for schools and the coaches a lot of money, but the players were growing increasingly frustrated. In January 2014, the Northwestern University football team took steps to unionize college players. After decades of dismissal as being unfeasible, paying college players was becoming a popular opinion.

The NCAA was a dirty business. Don Yee, agent to superstar quarterback Tom Brady, kept a database—spreadsheets, white papers, the works—on just how dirty. He compiled the ratios of what college coaches earned and how much revenue the players were generating. He kept statistics on how much future income college athletes were losing to injury and potential alternatives to the college game in which the players got to share in the wealth. There was more dirt: Yee kept another database tracking the virtually nonexistent head-coaching opportunities for African Americans at the collegiate level. The black players didn't become coaches. They played and were discarded. The college campus was supposed to be the place where the American black body was to be transformed from unpaid, uneducated slave to poorly paid, exploited laborer, to the black professional. It was a can't-lose proposition: the athlete would either become famous in the pro ranks or, if he didn't make it, educated on the pathway to the American Dream, using his access to the full university education that had been denied so many of his people who didn't have superior athletic ability. It was such a powerful idea, everyone believed it. The promise of pivoting from muscle to mind, opening the doors that had been closed in the sciences, the arts, and business was really the root of why sports was so important to black America in the first place. Indirectly, it was why, if the blueprint was to be successful, sports would rightly one day lose its importance as more African Americans were exposed to the opportunity of a college education and the options that came with it. Had this blueprint actually worked, there would be no need for a Heritage. It would have meant, for the first time in American history, that the black brain had become more valuable than the body. In 1968, *Sports Illustrated* highlighted the potential dangers of the black body on the university campus without a pathway to careers that didn't include shooting baskets.

Are there impediments? Of course. One is that these reforms will cost money. They sure will—but, as any manufacturer can tell any college president or athletic director, since 1863 it has not been considered acceptable in the U.S. to make profit margins dependent on the labor of slaves. Sport has increased the opportunities for the Negro to go to college. It must now make certain that what is inside that open door is more than a basketball court, a football play book—and a fast exit to oblivion.

As for professional sport, it must recognize that racism, on the field and off—subconscious, subtle or overt—still exists and that it must be stamped out. This is not only the right thing to do but, as Green Bay's Vince Lombardi has demonstrated so spectacularly, it is the efficient thing to do. It is good business. Beyond that, black men who are finished as athletes must be given opportunities as coaches or in the administrative structure that surrounds both professional and college sport.

For the gifted ones who lived in that millionth percentile, the Ones Who Made It, the blueprint changed the lives of thousands of black athletes. For the rest, the whole promise of the sports-to-education nexus collapsed, which was why when the fractures widened, the rhetoric grew more overheated and words like "servitude" and "chattel" and "slavery" were tossed about like one of the footballs used to exploit the players. In theory, the players received a "free" education in exchange for their athletic gifts, but there was so much fine print that had been smudged and glossed over for so long that the public, not wanting to feel badly for rooting for the old alma mater, bought it—even as the academic scandals and vacating of records would become as common as the multimillion-dollar contracts of the coaches.

And the education wasn't free. The college system was actually similar to the reserve clause that Curt Flood had fought in Major League Baseball back in the 1960s. College athletes did not receive four-year scholarships but four one-year renewable scholarships, and they were prohibited under the terms of those scholarships from receiving outside revenue in the form of cash or goods (buying a kid dinner was an NCAA violation, and yet the best players on a given campus tended to drive luxury cars). Thus, an injured or unproductive player risked losing his scholarship, which exposed black athletes who wouldn't be able to afford attending school or keep up with the coursework a regular student without a killer jump shot was required to. The players were there to generate revenue for the school by playing sports. They weren't students nearly as much as they were employees.

Everybody knew it, and everybody laughed about it (as long as their teams were winning). They laughed about the gut classes with silly, generic majors. They made examples of the bad apples like legendary college basketball coach Jerry Tarkanian and made excuses for the "good ones." (The University of North Carolina, for example, was caught in a cheating scandal that would have put a monitoring bracelet on Tarkanian's ankle.) None of it really made sense, how these black athletes did not appear to be educated yet were admitted to these institutions. Very few people listened to those trying to explain why.

In reality, the entire setup of amateurism in the NCAA was an insult to thoughtful observers, even though several searing indictments (Taylor Branch's *The Cartel* and Joe Nocera's *Indentured* are just two) laid bare the exploitative nature of it all. Nothing exposed the NCAA more than the raw numbers themselves. The top basketball and football conferences were signing television deals worth hundreds of millions. ESPN paid $600 million annually to broadcast the college football play-off. The coaches were making professional-level salaries. Former Florida State coach Jimbo Fisher's five-year contract topped $20 million total. The money generated from sports produced new facilities, new athletic dorms, new equipment for schools all over the country. In 2017, the Big Ten Conference signed a six-year, $2.64 billion television deal with Fox, ESPN, and CBS to broadcast football and basketball. According to *Forbes*, the fourteen member schools will split $440 million annually, or roughly $31.4 million per school every year. The machine was humming, fueled by the largely black and brown athletes who couldn't accept a sandwich as compensation and were emerging from some prestigious universities without an education.

They were everywhere, the black players who tore up their knee or just weren't that good who attended the very best schools in the country—and wound up stacking shelves at the Home Depot. The word "slavery" made everybody wince, and no, it wasn't slavery, but college sports was a billion-dollar machine underwritten by uncompensated, often uneducated black men who instead of being sent into the world armed with the benefits of the university experience, were often equipped with only the magic bullet of their athletic talent. Instead of feeling grateful, the players knew that, for all the rhetoric, they were the same mules of their ancestors with nicer sneakers, better dorms, more perks.

"The NCAA today is in many ways a classic cartel. Efforts to reform it . . . have, while making changes around the edges, been largely fruit-less," wrote Taylor Branch in *The Cartel*, his takedown of big-time college sports. "The time has come for a major overhaul. And whether the powers that be like it or not, big changes are coming. Threats loom on multiple fronts: in Congress, the courts, breakaway athletic conferences, student rebellion, and public disgust."

For all the talk of access to college, for the less than 1 percent of play-ers who will be set for life in the pros, the college game was, outside of making a few athletes super-rich and many coaches even richer, a failure. The failure of education was why players, the media, and the general pub-lic still viewed the athlete through the stereotypical narrative of "dead or in jail," even though these athletes attended some of the best universities in the country. It was why the athletes would market themselves within that magic bullet narrative of sports or death, and the failure of the public educational system explained why the athletes from impoverished communities were so heroic and special to the kids back home. So much of the sports narrative punctured the myth of progress. If the players were educated and progress has created the better life, why was "dead or in jail" the only options if sports didn't work out? The truth was the college game, comprising predominantly black players, was going to be used as the financial engine of a university system. That meant the players possessed power, and if they ever chose to exercise it, the people in the big offices would have to listen.

———

AFTER A SERIES OF racial incidents over a two-month span in the fall of 2015 went unattended by the University of Missouri, its football team dropped the hammer on the campus, the state, the NCAA, and the country. The optics had been tense. The members of the student group Concerned Student 1950, the name a nod to the university's first African American student from seventy-five years earlier, camped out on the university green resolute in their demand that the university president, Tim Wolfe be fired. The university, having never listened to the students in the past as the recent campus incidents compounded previous ones, said it was now paying attention to their concerns. A graduate student, Jonathan Butler, threatened a hunger strike until the university removed Wolfe. Of course, they weren't going to fire the head of the university just because black kids felt disenfranchised on campus. Of course, a graduate student wasn't *really* willing to die in a hunger strike over some name-calling on campus (or was he?). Everyone knew how the standoff would end: the university would *reach out* to the students, promise some *changes*, create a *committee* or two to *really look hard at the issues* facing African Americans on campus, and then everyone would *move on.*

And then, on a crisp November day, the seventh day of Butler's hunger strike, the Heritage arrived on campus. Black members of the football team contacted Concerned Student 1950 and told the protesters they would not play or practice until the student demands were met.

The next day, a group of players arrived at the tents. "As the football team, we're here to support the movement and use our platform," said cornerback Aarion Penton (who went undrafted but later signed with the Los Angeles Rams). Defensive end Charles Harris (who would be a first-round draft pick of the Miami Dolphins), spoke next: "Let this be a testament to all other athletes around the country that you do have power. It started with a few individuals on our team, and look what it's become. This has become nationally known, but it started with just a few." The head coach, Gary Pinkel, himself fighting for his job because of his record and the protest (he would lose), saw his players make a stand. In one instance, he told the players he supported them. In another, he walked back and said he supported the players' loyalty to their fellow students but not the cause of Concerned Student 1950. "He's backpedaling faster than I did when I played," said Demetrious Johnson, a Missouri alumnus from the early 1980s. "Now he doesn't support the damn issue, just the kids. But you know what's happening—he's getting his ass whupped by the white alums."

The Missouri protests were extraordinary, another link to the Syracuse 8 and Black 14. A version of their grievances existed in every corner of the black American experience, from the boardroom to the classroom and locker room, but especially on a Missouri campus that had struggled with race for decades. But the post-Ferguson zeitgeist had activated the football team, linking its power to the student struggle. Maybe it was the players watching how the NBA players had ousted Donald Sterling months before Ferguson. Maybe it was Kenny Britt and the Rams taking a stand. Maybe it was the litany of names too long to count of black Americans being shot by police in what was supposedly a postracial nirvana, black president and all. Or maybe it was the joy and heartbreak of youth, students thinking their story was going to be different than that of their aunts, uncles, and parents (after all, it was 2015!) only to find out that isolation of a minority was perennial, black man in the White House or not. Maybe it was just their turn. Maybe it was all of the above.

But there was no "maybe" about the influence of the football team. The Southeastern Conference was the power conference of college football, and though Missouri was a new member, often more chum than dominator, each school divided the dollars equally. The Missouri football program brought roughly $35 million to the school. The team not playing cost the university an estimated $1 million per game. Now the university had to pay attention.

The students hardened their position, and national attention focused on the administrators of the state university system (and the students expressed need for "safe spaces" launched them into the national culture wars). It was a clear battle for power and leverage. The mathematics and economics created a simple dynamic across big-time sports schools around the country: you didn't mess with sports, because, even though the data would disprove the orthodoxy, football supposedly paid for virtually everything, from the new science lab to the renovations to the Quad.

It took less than forty-eight hours after the player-boycott announcement for Wolfe and chancellor R. Bowen Loftin to tender their resignations. It was over, and as in the NBA with Donald Sterling, the players had won. On campus, in the safe space of their tent city, which would be lampooned as precious by conservatives as part of an ongoing culture war that would engulf sports, the black students rejoiced. Throughout the protest, the students had used the word *ase* (pronounced ah-shay), which referred to a Nigerian concept of the power of change through action. They had won, but it was the enormous financial leverage of the football team that had forced the university to take the protest seriously. At the campsite, students made a ring and danced, and with a nod to the football team, who used its financial muscle, did a swag surf.

This was what power looked like: a football team—the supposedly protected, coddled jocks detached from daily campus life because they were the university superheroes—joining a campus protest of African American students not with a symbolic gesture but with a devastatingly financial one. By threatening not to play, the Missouri football team had invited itself to the table of power and demanded a seat. The Missouri state legislature responded quickly with a bill that would strip any athletes of their scholarship if they attempted a similar protest tactic. The bill was just as quickly withdrawn.

In the months before Ferguson, the players toppled a notoriously racist NBA owner who had been allowed by his supposedly upstanding cartel members to exist in their club for thirty years. A year after, the financial leverage of black college football players forced the ouster of a university system president and its chancellor. Players had threatened boycotts before, sometimes successfully, but in a multibillion-dollar industry, players now possessed leverage the original Heritage never could have imagined. Still, the end result was the same. Whether in the 1960s or in the 2010s, power respected only one thing: equal or greater power. In the minds of people like Don Yee, the agent to Tom Brady, the possibilities of the college football or basketball player only ended at their vision. They had shown what they were capable of when they were focused and unified. The financial disparities between the players and college coaches only exacerbated the issue, a wealth gap and cognitive dissonance that would inevitably force change.

"What the players don't realize is that they are the game," Yee said of the college students. "And when you are the game, you are everything. No one else has the talent to do what they can do. That gives you immense leverage to create something better for yourselves if you have the vision and courage to do it. The players, I'm telling you, have no idea how much power they really have. If they wanted to, they could take the whole thing down."

10

"WHO IS THE PATRIOT?"

A patriot has universal values, standards by which he
judges his nation, always wishing it well, and wishing
it would do better.

—TIMOTHY SNYDER, *On Tyranny*

MAYBE IT WAS ALL THE COMMERCIALS, well-intentioned and heartbreaking, of wounded soldiers and foundations. Or maybe it was the insistence at every turn that the paying customer acknowledge, multiple times
in multiple ways, the generic umbrella of "the troops" without going beyond the photo op. Even little kids at baseball games couldn't run the
bases after games without paying homage to some military-soldier tie-in.
Maybe it was the smothering corporate influence on gestures that felt
orchestrated. Maybe it was every jersey, for every occasion, being sold in a
desert camo version, along with camo caps and coffee mugs. Or maybe it
was just that good old-fashioned American bullshit detector that came out
when we were having too much of one thing crammed down our throats
with no counterbalancing criticism that made it all feel just a little bit off.
It was all of the above, naturally, the overdone deference, the ubiquity of
soldiers while erasing the word "war," being treated like a traitor just for
voicing an opinion, the nonstop commercial milking of 9/11 sentiment
nearly *twenty years* after the Twin Towers fell.

Then came the day when all the dissenters, the ones who fought and
the ones who didn't, the ones who were pissed off when after 9/11 the
president told America not to sacrifice but to shop, and the ones who
didn't even *want* to be called dissenters but were nevertheless offended

that it looked like sports teams were using the military for optics but not jobs, finally saw the numbers on the page. It was a bitter vindication and a swift punch in the gut. You could run or sit and take it, but the truth wasn't going anywhere: so much of the patriotism at the ballpark was a deception, part of a big hoax.

On November 4, 2015, US senators John McCain and Jeff Flake, both of Arizona, released a report titled *Tackling Paid Patriotism*, which in 150 pages detailed what was really behind the rituals Americans had become accustomed to in sports after September 11, from American flags across the fifty-yard line to all those soldiers at the games to the heart-wrenching surprise homecoming ceremonies at halftime. The report came to a devastating conclusion: These weren't home-grown, self-less shows of support for the troops by the local team on board with local soldiers. This was about money. Sports teams had been charging the military to stage their events at ballparks, and the Pentagon had been paying the teams millions in taxpayer money—at least $6.8 million, to that point—to do it.

And just as the Justice Department's 585-page *Federal Report on Police Killings* revealed routine violations of the Constitution and of the rights of primarily black citizens across the country, *Tackling Paid Patriotism* did not originate from some commie think tank or the Bernie Sanders wing of America. It came from two conservative Republican senators from a state that had voted Democrat in a general election exactly once since 1952. People could say what they wanted about John McCain, but you had to be a ghoul to question his service credentials.

The surprise homecoming ceremonies at halftime? Staged. The throwing out of the first pitch by a returning soldier?

A deception.

"It is time to allow major sports teams' legitimate tributes to our soldiers to shine with national pride," the report read, "rather than being cast under the pallor of marketing gimmicks paid for by American taxpayers."

When the report was released, McCain and Flake connected the dots the public wouldn't. The dissenters who saw state-sponsored nationalism at the games were no longer easily dismissed as conspiracy theorists but rather as rightfully insulted citizens. What had happened? The Army National Guard, air force, and navy, especially, had clearly been watching what sports had become in the years following 9/11 and, combined with falling enlistment rates, saw an opportunity. Before 2009, NFL players often remained in the locker room during the national anthem. Afterward, the secret embedding began, deceiving fans into thinking NFL teams were supporting the military because individual owners believed it was the right thing to do. It was, in fact, a deception that permeated virtually every sporting event in the country. There was no taxpayer money for schools or roads, but there was $280,000 for the Massachusetts Army National Guard to sponsor Boston Bruins Military Appreciation Night. Now it made sense why a team like the Yankees would try to have a guy removed from the ballpark for not playing along with the patriotism game. The Wisconsin Army National Guard in 2014 paid the Milwaukee Brewers $80,000 for military perks, and during every Sunday home game, and this wasn't a misprint, *$49,000* was the price tag to sing "God Bless America."

The Brewers Military Appreciation Day was no organic outpouring of the home team doing the right thing to support the troops. The team charged the National Guard $10,000 for a "promotion to recognize soldiers and their families and provide 12 vendor passes during each of four Brewers home games," strategic plants for the crowd shots of the armed forces at the ballpark. The Brewers charged $7,500 for the honor of a service member throwing out the first pitch.

So, when racecar driver Richard Petty came out to see the troops, signature cowboy hat and all, to shake hands and thank the men and women for keeping the country safe, it was a fraud. In 2015, the Air Force paid NASCAR $1.56 million for the racing star's grip-and-grins that made everybody bleed red, white, and blue.

They were all in on it: NASCAR, MLB, the NBA, the NFL, NHL, MLS, and the NCAA. The military was using sports to sell the business of war. And the teams? Well, they were in the business of making money—and you could make even more money if it looked like you were acting out of a sense of duty. And there were, as is always the case, unintended consequences to this little game: what was happening at the ballpark was splitting the country apart, by forcing an ersatz patriotism on the public. Unwitting fans arrived to stadiums across the country believing their favorite sports teams were genuine in their concern for servicemen and -women. While sports and the military may have been using one another—the armed forces to buy support for the wars and recruit soldiers, the teams to buy goodwill from the public, open up marketing opportunities, and force the players into an obedient position—the fans were being used as well.

If the military wasn't being used because it willfully targeted sports to recruit and burnish its image, then the individual soldiers were being manipulated by its military and the corporate power of sports as shields against dissent. Soldiers were Americans who joined the armed forces for a host of reasons, usually out of the desire to improve themselves economically and educationally, were distorted into a class of monolithic super-patriots whose only mission was to obey their government. A polarized climate turned soldiers into political pawns, the guise of patriotism used to mask the lack of economic choices that prompted their enlistment.

So much of this deception came back to Pat Tillman, whose enlistment served in part as a catalyst for the Department of Defense to hone in on sports at a potentially fruitful recruiting ground. His death and its subsequent cover-up by the army magnified this subsequent twisting of reality for the sake of propaganda. Was everything about this period a cynical ruse for profit?

"What's so disturbing is that the Bush administration used Pat Tillman in death in a way that he would not allow them to use him in life. He refused all efforts for the Pentagon to turn him into G.I. Joe or for a recruitment poster at a time when recruitment was dropping dramatically," the *Nation*'s Dave Zirin said. "Then in death, this government lied to his family about how he died. They held a nationally televised funeral, and they lied about the matter of his death over his grave. It wasn't a funeral. It was a desecration. The family tried for years to find out the truth about his death. And even though NFL owners are some of the most politically connected people in this country, and even though they have a Pat Tillman jersey encased in glass at the NFL offices, they have not lifted one single solitary finger to help his family get the truth."

When McCain and Flake's report was released, the sports leagues were alternately embarrassed and enraged. The NFL promised to return some of the money. MLB didn't like looking as though it was ripping off the public. The baseball argument was that yes, teams were charging the military to hold a promotion, but the dollar amounts were at such a discounted rate that it amounted to a giveaway, and McCain and Flake's report was unfairly distorting them. It wasn't as if teams were getting rich off the military. (So what if the air force paid the Dallas Stars hockey team $10,000 for season tickets and "promotional rights"?) Of course, the real benefit to teams wasn't from whatever check the Pentagon sent over but from the embedding of military into the minds and wallets of the customer.

"Look, they shouldn't be paying the NFL. That is corruption, any way you call it," Lieutenant General Russel Honoré said. "Somewhere along the line, one of these contract agencies, ad agency, or some retired dude said, 'We could get the Army to pay us if we let them carry the flag out.' Or 'We could get the Marines to pay us if we allow them to take the flag out.' Everything gets screwed up if we're not doing our jobs and holding ourselves accountable, but I don't think the military ought to be paying to participate."

Now fans could feel like they were part of the effort, buying that $250 camo jersey or coming to Military Appreciation Night instead of staying home or buying the $25 desert camo hat with the pink logo for the ladies instead of a foam finger. The teams would also receive all kinds of shine for being patriotic when all they were doing was ripping off taxpayers and fooling their own fans at the ballpark. Most thought Bob ("We're all Patriots") Kraft was reaching into his own pocket when the team honored a member of the Massachusetts Army National Guard as part of its "True Patriot" program. Turns out, the Patriots charged the guard $700,000 from 2012 to 2014 for the promotion. There was the air force, which in 2012 paid $20,000 to perform a "full-field flag detail" at Indianapolis Colts home games.

On the football field, the baseball diamond, the hockey rink, the basketball court, and even the tennis court, the culture sold this message: the only people who deserved thanks or discounted tickets or who could be considered unquestionably American were the ones who carried the guns.

Even the optics were paid for, as all those crowd shots of our brave men and women in uniform taking in the game were included in the twenty grand: three hundred tickets for two home games a year. So, the soldiers may have been diehard football fans, but they were also plants. McCain and Flake's report offered a scathing admonition:

> Consider this: honoring five Air Force officers put $1,500 into the pockets of the LA Galaxy. In another example, taxpayers footed the $10,000 bill for an on-field swearing-in ceremony with the World Series finalist

New York Mets. And the list goes on. By paying for such heartwarming displays like recognition of wounded warriors, surprise homecomings, and on-field enlistment ceremonies, these displays lost their luster. Unsuspecting audience members became the subjects of paid-marketing campaigns rather than simply bearing witness to teams' authentic, voluntary shows of support for the brave men and women who wear our nation's uniform. This not only betrays the sentiment and trust of fans, but casts an unfortunate shadow over the genuine patriotic partnerships that do so much for our troops, such as the National Football League's Salute to the Service campaign.

As tough as the report was, McCain pulled his punches because the NFL's Salute to Service, which he lauded, was just as bad. It was one of the biggest hoodwinks in sports, riddled with examples of the military paying for the ceremony—such as the Baltimore Ravens paying $89,500 in 2013 for the "production of 30,000 co-branded rally towels and 20,000 co-branded hats." The NFL was the sport that most closely aligned itself with the military with its grotesque war metaphors. And those little video clips between innings from those homesick soldiers cheering the home team from somewhere around the globe, like the ones marine Cecilia Evans recorded to be played during Steelers games at Heinz Field when she was deployed to in Iraq? Staged.

Here's how it worked in the case of MLB and the NFL: Inside the Defense Department was a division called "DVIDS," which was responsible for the satellite hookups from the remote military bases fans saw during games. DVIDS oversaw a program called "Shout Outs," in which the military would invite enthusiastic service members to record videos for the military-appreciation days that sports teams would promote during the season. Take, for example, a 2017 email DVIDS sent to service members in an effort to accommodate their staged promotions:

We have received an urgent request for shout outs for the July 23rd Minnesota Twins Military Appreciation Game. If you have any service members who are Twins fans and would be interested in recording and submitting a shout out, please reference "Request #1" in this email. If you have any questions, please do not hesitate to reach out. Thank you for your time and support.

REQUEST #1

Need: Minnesota Twins Baseball Shout Outs

Event: Minnesota Twins Armed Forces Appreciation Day & other games

Requests:

1) Generic Minnesota Twins shout outs may be used for future games if they aren't used for the Military Appreciation Game.

*** Make sure to have fun and show your enthusiasm. Military service members can wear sports gear/fan paraphernalia if they desire.

*** Group shout outs are also acceptable and remember your background is more interesting if it conveys a sense of anything "military."

REQUEST #2

Need: Oakland Raiders Shout Outs and Live Shots

Event: Oakland Raiders Salute to Service Members and Home Games

Requests:

3) The Oakland Raiders would like multiple shout outs from military service members showing their fandom for the Oakland Raiders. Feel free to wear your sports gear and get creative. The important thing is to show enthusiasm and team spirit. Shout outs will be used for their Salute to Service member game on Nov. 26th vs. the Broncos, and also for the remainder of their home games.

*** Don't reference an opponent in your shout out. This allows your shout out to be used for different games.

This wasn't patriotism. This was capitalism. There was nothing organic about having, nor was there any particular demand to have, the military be part of a July 23 Minnesota Twins game.

As for the Raiders, the team was simply fulfilling a contract with the military to make the game look patriotic, to sell patriotism to the public. And of the fan who just wanted to take his twelve-year-old to the game and not think about weapons of mass destruction or the Islamic State? Too bad. Now the kids were being beamed military images so when they got out of high school, maybe they'd sign up too.

That the army was surreptitiously recruiting was hidden from the public, but Lieutenant General Honoré had no problem with this. "Oh no, we gotta recruit them little SOBs. Mom and Dad, we're gonna recruit

'em. You better hold on to them if you don't want them in the Army,"
he said. "We're gonna recruit the hell out of them. That's how we man
the force. We only get two out of every ten that qualify. And [sports] is
a good place to recruit them. . . . About 65 percent of our soldiers come
from rural communities, and any exposure we can get to that population
is very important, and important that people see the esteem that people
hold those in uniform who serve. It may start a conversation with a kid
that may show some interest when the recruiters come around the high
school to get them to come to one of the service academies or enlist them
to come into the military. This is a source of how we play the game."

The military had made it a deliberate strategy to target kids watching
their favorite team as potential soldiers. The leagues should have been
transparent about this.

"The kids that go to [sporting events] have a pretty good tendency to
play sports, and to be a warrior you need to be what we call the 'warrior
athlete,' Honoré said. "You gotta be able to run. You gotta be able to jump.
You can't be no fat ass. We need the warrior athlete. And the people who
say they want to go to a game and don't want to see the color guard on
the field, I feel sorry for them, but we've got to recruit every opportunity
we get to get the right young people who want to serve and participate."

When McCain and Flake's report was released, the Department of
Defense didn't even try to hide from it. They were just looking to recruit
soldiers, and the ballpark, NASCAR, post-9/11 with all its ceremony,
seemed to be a great place to find tomorrow's infantrymen and officers.
The leagues, meanwhile, didn't acknowledge it was subjecting its fans to
surreptitious recruitment, and the scam continued unchecked.

It was also bad enough that within this climate, leagues were profiting from the images and memorabilia from third-party relationships
with shady affiliates like GovX designed to build a mailing list to sell
military-grade equipment to veterans in exchange for discounted tickets
to veterans and first responders. Each new revelation eroded the enjoyment of watching a game that was supposed to be a diversion from the real
world. Everybody, it seemed, was cashing in.

When all the dots were connected, the finished picture was an ugly
one. The ballpark was the place where the Pentagon sold its endless war
to the public, and while sending out emails to servicemen to stage "watch
parties," neither the military nor sports teams had the stones to admit

it publicly. When McCain and Flake exposed the relationship, the UK *Guardian* newspaper reported that the Defense Department was concerned that declining unemployment and better access to college were depressing enlistments, and that it believed recruiting through sports might be fertile territory.

A Defense Department memo from the same time referred to pro sports games as a "neutral environment" where recruiters could talk with potential soldiers, including the 32 percent of eighteen- to thirty-four-year-olds who watch the NFL.

NOBODY CARES, OR DO NOT OBEY IN ADVANCE

The *Paid Patriotism* report was damning, insulting, indicting. It was about phony patriotism, phony concern for veterans, a con. So, naturally, having been taken for a ride by the military-industrial complex and by sports owners who couldn't keep their watery beer under ten bucks but were willing to sell you the special Memorial Day alternate jersey to keep the war machine going, the angry American public revolted, hoisted Flake and McCain on its collective shoulders, and thanked them for being the public watchdogs keeping the power in check, right? Wrong.

Nobody cared.

America was so immersed in the reality show that it didn't mind that the reality wasn't real. Nor did McCain and Flake's revelations force the public to even rethink its part of the whole hero business. That was the power of 9/11. It still lingered, and the promotions continued. Nobody wanted the truth about the cost of war on the warriors or a third-party company like GovX selling bowie knives to returning soldiers who might be suffering from PTSD in exchange for a couple of Celtics tickets.

What the fans were really expressing by embracing a fraud, Lieutenant General Honoré thought, was the guilt they carried around for not having served. At the game, with sixty thousand other people who felt similarly, fans could feel better about their place in a world with no draft and wealth inequality so great (and increasing daily) that only the Americans with virtually no other options or alternative way to afford college did the fighting. Collective guilt from not doing one's share became a large part of the culture, and because of that, the fans were complicit in this deception of patriotism for money. Honoré felt the guilt was misguided.

"That was the objective of a volunteer army. It was a political objective, and that's what we've got. It's not something to feel ashamed about," he said. "There's more than one way to serve. Telling stories is one way, respecting your country, holding your government accountable to what's in the Constitution. And we all have a responsibility to do that, to vote, to pay our taxes, and to volunteer and help those who need help in our communities, and there are a lot of veterans who need help."

The jig was up, and veterans would write about feeling used. "Those planes fly overhead and cannons salute to glorify the casualties of our children, friends, sisters, fathers, mothers," wrote one former marine. "And all of it paid for by the United States Government."

No matter. The public didn't even listen to the guys doing the fighting. The selling of patriotism, of healing the wound of 9/11, of participating in something that *felt* unifying, even if it was inauthentic and bred an encroaching authoritarianism, were more important than the effects of war.

"I guess I'd feel deceived if I thought about it in those terms, but I don't think about it that way," said WFAN New York Yankees reporter Sweeny Murti. "It's pretty obvious almost everyone is on the same side of the patriotic argument, so you're not creating any controversy, and you're not looking to create controversy. Maybe you're trying to create the Christmassy atmosphere and make a show of it. Sure, it's furthering a political agenda that doesn't have a controversy attached to it, and if it did, you wouldn't be doing it. If you knew you were alienating half your audience by doing that, you wouldn't even think of doing it.

"When I watch the homecomings, I bawl like a baby," Murti continued. "No matter what part of it happens to be staged, the actual child and the dad getting reunited isn't staged. That part is authentic. I buy into it, and if it is staged, I'm guilty. They've got me in a movie, and I'm guilty. They got what they paid for."

Murti's position was a common one, emblematic of where America found itself in the dozen and a half years after 9/11. *It's furthering a political agenda that doesn't have a controversy attached to it* and *creating a Christmassy atmosphere* sure were a hell of a way to describe seventeen years of war, but that's how disconnected war all felt—and that was precisely the emotion this concoction was intended to produce. Though you'd have to be a monster to not feel sympathy and support for soldiers, an important part of patriotism—for the sake of the soldiers—was the public holding the government accountable that it was fighting for the right reasons.

The more soldiers became a part of everyday life—at the airport, the train station, Times Square, the Pantheon, or any world landmark that was a target for attack—the less you heard the word *war*. It was a word scrubbed from whatever limited national conversation was taking place. Post-9/11 America killed the neutral sporting event, but it also killed the traditional antiwar movement. America didn't even feel as if it was at war, and when soldiers were trotted out to the pitcher's mound—the wounded, the maimed, the broken by PTSD—the public never reconnected them to the trauma and to the *politics* that had maimed and broken them in the first place. That part disappeared. "If we want to be a nation that supports our all-volunteer military, then we have to start bridging the gap between the less than 1 percent that serves and the rest of the population," Sean Doolittle said. "These displays can serve to widen that divide by inadvertently illustrating [that] only a very small percentage of Americans will volunteer to serve in our military."

Bill Astore had it right: after 9/11, the president told the public to go shopping, have fun, support the troops at the ballgame, let the experts handle it, and all the public had to do was stand when told, cheer when told, and not think.

"Am I a 'dissenter'? It's a weird label to wear," Astore said. "I like to think I'm being patriotic when I call attention to the corporate military's blatant propaganda and manipulation of the masses. I see them—with all their 'warrior' and 'warfighter' talk—as dissenters from the proud tradition of a citizen-soldier military.

"What I mean is this: if we label ourselves as 'dissenters,' we are automatically dismissed by many as un-American. Terminology is critical, and I don't have an easy answer. Again, who is the patriot? Isn't dissent patriotic?"

WOKE-A-COLA

At times, it appeared the deception that the military and pro leagues put over on the public gave automatic vindication to a revived Heritage. Both institutions were exposed, revealing an adventure in cynicism for money and support of an ongoing war, while the Heritage built on the traditions of boundless, sturdy courage in the model of Paul Robeson, Jackie Robinson, Curt Flood, and Muhammad Ali.

Or did it? Colin Kaepernick's worldview as a man changed after Ferguson, and there were several clear moments of authenticity. But *activism* in post-Ferguson America became as trendy as *patriotism*—and potentially as lucrative, both in cash and street cred—and it was important to remember that the Heritage was built on sacrifice, not speeches. Marketers wanted in on the wave, and by capitalizing on the optics of young people taking to the streets, activism was no different. Madison Avenue saw a way, no matter how clumsy and tone-deaf, to connect to that coveted demographic of young people who moved the advertising needle. Take, for example, Ieshia Evans, the young black woman who, during a June 2016 protest rally in Baton Rouge, Louisiana, stood peacefully in the middle of the street in front of rows of state police clad in full riot gear. Reuters photographer Jonathan Bachman captured the moment of two officers in body armor descending on a lone black woman wearing a summer dress.

Less than a year later, Pepsi attempted, disastrously, to capitalize on the cool of protest by recreating Bachman's iconic image, substituting Evans with the white model Kendall Jenner, protesters behind her, law enforcement in front, brokering the peace by handing the cops a Pepsi. In the ad, the cops are dressed not in menacing, ready-to-kick-some-ass body armor, as they had been in confrontations with citizens in Ferguson, Baltimore, and a host of other places, but in standard-dress police uniforms, humanizing baseball caps, and smiles. A corporation distorted the images of a menacing militarized police presence in the streets, just to sell a can of soda.

The ad drew so much scorn that the company fell into full retreat, apologizing and quickly pulling the ad. It was one of the great boneheaded plays of the year, straight out of the *what were you thinking?* playbook. Of course, everyone knew exactly what Pepsi was thinking. The company was thinking of profiting off the cool, off the optics of protest. And to the suits who weren't the target of the police, *cool* meant standing up to the cops. It was all a game now, a show of images and sensations the suits could exploit. Money could be made from it, and no one wanted to miss a branding opportunity.

And that was the danger. Now all the Big Boys were getting involved, showing support, in hot recognition of the money that could be made off the zeitgeist. Maybe their interest was out of conviction, out of making the world a better place . . . maybe . . . but *definitely* Coke and Pepsi were in it for the money.

In February 2017, Nike released an ad supporting the revival of superstars taking an active role in the Heritage in a spot called "Equality," which featured all the "right" hallmarks. It had the activist stars representing the diverse constituencies (the openly gay Megan Rapinoe) and the superstars (LeBron James, Kevin Durant, Serena Williams). It had the authoritative narrative for the Better Tomorrow (voiced over by the actor Michael B. Jordan) and, to give it that mourning, soulful depth, the gospel piano and voice of Alicia Keys covering Sam Cooke's elegiac "A Change Is Gonna Come." The ad was shot in slow motion, in black and white, each set piece attempting to give the inner city a dignity in a commercial that it did not often receive in real life (like the shot of kids playing basketball and a police cruiser, lights on, rides slowly and menacing into the foreground, or the black and brown women and men sitting on the courthouse steps under the chiseled words "And Equal Justice Under Law"). The ad rises to a crescendo with James, his face in close-up, with the last words of the change that is possible. As the best player in America, he gets the final image and the last word of the ad, representing a philosophical break with OJ, Michael, and Tiger, the best players of other eras who had no interest in the front lines. James is the leader, the face of the twenty-first-century chapter of the Heritage.

Of course, Nike received praise for "Equality" because it was glossy, inspiring, well-produced, and packed with the kind of star power that stirred people and made them believe the Heritage was back, invoking daily comparisons of the athlete *du jour* to Muhammad Ali. It hit all the right notes to suggest irreverence, independence, and an idealism that progressives wanted to believe, but the more hardened dissidents knew not to bet on corporate courage. In a time when sports wouldn't say a bad word about cops regardless of how many "officer involved shootings" took place, Nike didn't shy from depicting a menacing presence of the police. That gave them street cred. And street cred made them more marketable.

Yet, as with paid patriotism, whether any of it could really be trusted was another story. Nike, like Pepsi but to a lesser extent, was taking advantage of an opportunity. The NBA All-Star Game had just been moved from Charlotte to New Orleans in protest of HB-2, the state's notorious "bathroom bill," which sought to deny transgender people from using the public bathroom of their choice. If protest was now marketable, then it ceased to be protest. If activism was cool, full of celebrity and corporate backing, it lost much of its purpose, its dissidence, and you could count the minutes before the hipster protesters moved on to the next hot thing. If the corporations were getting involved co-opting, mainstreaming dissent, it wasn't really dissent. It was just another way to win optics and dilute a cause that wasn't a game.

Besides, Nike wanted it both ways. Just two years earlier—less than a month after Freddie Gray's death and at a time when police had killed 420 people, and it wasn't even yet June 1—Nike announced its Law Enforcement Appreciation Day promotion, offering a 30 percent discount off all apparel to police and other law enforcement officers. Maybe "Equality" was just Nike performance art.

So how authentic was the awakening? Was it just companies competing to market being *woke*, a flimsy attempt to use Ferguson anger over life-and-death issues as a way to steal a little market share with ballplayers joining in to burnish the image without risk, while the underlying structures that have been predicted since the Kerner Commission remain in place? It was true that the players, too, were not yesterday's Heritage. They were of a different social class but by race and lineage to the struggle were expected to be present. Even Colin Kaepernick, for all he endured and risked, did so with millions already earned. He was not John Carlos, who had to take odd jobs below minimum wage just to pay his rent. The children of the modern player did not attend public school, and the athletes were super-rich. When he played for the Yankees in the mid-2000s, Gary Sheffield would talk about the difficulties of keeping his kids off the streets in Tampa when they were home from attending the nation's most elite prep schools, where they were classmates with Saudi princes and princesses. Sheffield earned nearly $150 million in salary alone over his career. Could these public shows of support be called activism when no one really seemed to be risking anything?

To join the Heritage, you had to pay the cost. Jackie, Muhammad, Smith, Carlos, and Flood all risked, and all lost something. With the exception of Colin Kaepernick, many current players made political negotiations with the leagues, wore T-shirts, and asked permission to protest without direct skin in the game. Yet, being black linked them, in some ways, to the same fights of old, because despite their celebrity, the players were fighting for the same group of people, still on the bottom, still at the mercy of the service revolver.

"I think we're born into the Heritage, but I think what we're talking about is reclamation. Do we reclaim it by wearing a T-shirt? No, you're nodding to it," said De Lacy Davis, who founded Black Cops Against Police Brutality and believes the constant sparring with and scrutiny of fellow officers ultimately cost him his career in law enforcement.

"The real reclamation is when you decide to get on the bus. Where do you get on the bus? Where will you participate? The question will be, 'What did you do for the people? What did you do with your wealth? Can I impact the life of a young person when it counts, not when it's safe?'"

THE POLITICS OF POISON

Donald Trump did not create the fractures that have ripped sports away from its unifying moorings, but he exacerbated each strain by his nationalism, divisiveness, and appeal to authoritarianism. While the black players knelt, Trump's first year included his attorney general, Jeff Sessions, vowing to undo, roll back, or ignore the recommendations and data the Obama White House had compiled regarding constitutional violations by police departments across the country.

Trump began his presidency by attacking dissent, arresting 200 protesters of his inauguration and charging 194 with felonies that could lead to serious jail time. He spent the year pitting protesting black players against their country and shaped sixteen years of post-9/11 pageantry into an ally of whiteness against black citizens who challenged him, calling them disrespectful to the military, even though the country employed a multicultural, voluntary fighting force that was heavily minority. That fact was secondary to the television optic of black players kneeling while white fans stood with their hands on their hearts. White fans owned the flag and, by extension, were real Americans. During a high school basketball game in Connecticut, white fans taunted a team of predominantly black and Latino players with the chant "Trump! Trump! Trump!" when the team shot free throws.

In the theater of easy visuals, the black players knelt in protest were un-American, and Trump provoked this by using soldiers as the object of the players' perceived disrespect. Like *patriotism*, the military also took on the characteristics of the white, mainstream ideal—even though the concerns of the players were universal across all races. Trump portrayed the military to his supporters as if it needed his defense against black dissidence, even though players had never protested the armed forces.

The entire 9/11 ceremony, in truth, contained those very characteristics from the day the Towers fell—the hero narrative in New York always contained elements of the old ethnic battle lines because of the historical grip the city's Irish and Italians have held on police and fire—and Trump weaponized those old characteristics further. Within the framework of sports, thanks in part to Trump but mostly to the unwillingness of white athletes to engage in social movements that aren't sanctioned by the team or league—and to a corporate media that aided heavily in the misdirection—*patriotism* has been turned into a white ideal. Protesters, African American athletes especially, constantly find themselves on the defensive. The consequence of the post-9/11 coupling of police and military now meant challenging the police for killing LaQuan McDonald or Akai Gurley, which now meant challenging the flag's authority—so now players challenging cops were unpatriotic. The effects—of paid patriotism, embedding police in the games, and attacking black players from the White House—were cumulative, and the president of the United States intended to pressure protest right out of the game.

The appropriate pressure valve was represented by the owners, several of whom, including Dallas Cowboys owner Jerry Jones and New England's Robert Kraft, gave more than $1 million each to Trump's presidential campaign. During one particularly contentious meeting between players and owners held in Washington, DC, players' union head DeMaurice Smith, aided by a few players, called out a few of the owners for supporting Trump financially while at the same time pledging money to combat issues in black communities.

"You've been fine with the players being out front on this issue," Smith said. "And you were happy with our players taking a beating from the right and being characterized as anti-cop, anti-America, anti-military, and that's bullshit, and the reason why you did it is because I think you let your politics get in the way of our business."

THE MARCH ON 245

Paid Patriotism represented a military-corporate collusion that has applied enormous pressure on citizens who disagree with their government. The sheer volume of nationalistic themes would give any thinking person pause before challenging authority. There was a time when Americans broke out the American flag between Memorial Day and the Fourth of July. Today the American flag is a year-round accessory.

Over the history of sports, the disagreeing constituency has overwhelmingly been black players. Before shifting to advocacy for African Americans, the Heritage was built originally on black players speaking out on issues to reflect their patriotism and fidelity to the country. Today, as the nation continues down its path of demonizing dissent as un-American, the stamina of the athlete to be vocal about causes will be even more greatly tested.

Before Ferguson, Adam Jones of the Baltimore Orioles once took a selfie with the cops for the cover of *ESPN the Magazine*. Two years later, when asked about the NFL protests, Jones said that baseball would never engage in such a fashion because it was essentially "a white man's sport." The game that created the Heritage had a population of African American players perennially under 10 percent, and the black impact in baseball was diminishing rapidly. Managerial and front-office hiring had always been slow, but black stars had been the face of the game since Jackie.

Once, in 2009, Jimmie Lee Solomon, then baseball's highest-ranking African American in the Commissioner's Office, called a clandestine summit of players to discuss what felt like the erasing of black participation from the game—from hiring to marketing to advertising to outreach. The meeting was initiated by Solomon but also by players, from veteran second baseman Orlando Hudson to centerfielder Torii Hunter to the first baseman Cliff Floyd. The issues of declining black participation had become an annual cliché. Solomon's plan was to keep the group small. He also wanted the group to be contemporary, with younger veteran players, like Hunter, who would feel more empowered to take a leadership role without the elders from previous generations. The meeting would occur on a neutral site so it could be informal and unofficial. He also had the players pay their own way to the meeting as a sign of their personal commitment. Though Solomon never played in the big leagues, his reaching out to the players was reminiscent of the old traditions in baseball, where blacks in the game kept a tight, informed group.

Solomon's plan backfired badly. Little details of the potential meeting leaked out, and both the Players Association executive director, Donald Fehr, and MLB commissioner Bud Selig, were furious at Solomon for, as they saw it, going rogue. Solomon contacting players on his own represented a serious breach in a relationship as adversarial as the one between the league and the union. Tony Clark, who had just retired as an active major league player and would one day become the union's executive director, wasn't on Solomon's original list at the time—which represented another breach in protocol, as the union was grooming Clark for a major role.

Suddenly, Solomon's secret, off-the-record meeting with a few key black players turned into an official summit at the MLB headquarters on 245 Park Avenue. All the heavy hitters were there: Fehr, Selig, and legendary players such as Hall of Famers Eddie Murray and Frank Robinson.

"We called it the March on 245," MLB Players Association executive director Tony Clark remembered. "The players were all staying at the same hotel, and the sight of these black men in well-tailored suits walking down Park Avenue. It was a fascinating visual."

For the players, the meeting was a disaster, for instead of an authentic discussion of issues, the hierarchy spoke. One person at the meeting recalled Selig talking about his long relationship with black people, how many friends he had, and how many black people were also concerned about African Americans in the game—to applause from the room. No one spoke spontaneously.

"I definitely got slapped on the wrist for this," Solomon recalled. By trying to reach across the aisle, tapping indirectly into the traditions of the Heritage, Solomon had violated the protocols of communication between the Commissioner's Office and the Players Association, and a tight, open session at an off-site location where players could be candid turned into an officially sanctioned dog-and-pony show at MLB headquarters, where no one spoke out of turn, the bosses said all the right things, committees were formed, and nothing got done. Jimmie Lee Solomon learned the oldest rule book the hard way: no good deed goes unpunished.

In the years since, the spirit of the Heritage in baseball is weakening as rapidly as the player percentage decline. There is a cultural effect at work. Perhaps it is because of the money, but as the elders age out of the game without being replaced by a new generation, the players are not communicating and connecting as black men with a special heritage in the sport.

The pressure is constant, to not discuss racial issues, to be greenwashed by their millions, and, in today's climate, to not get involved the political discussions occurring in basketball and football.

On September 29, 2017, a week after Donald Trump referred to kneeling NFL players as "sons of bitches," the Oakland A's biracial rookie catcher Bruce Maxwell took a knee during the national anthem. He was the only baseball player to do so, and to his disappointment, none of the elder black players—not Adam Jones or C. C. Sabathia or Justin Upton—joined him. Before the Washington Nationals began their playoff series against the Chicago Cubs, Dusty Baker called Maxwell, and the two talked for two hours. One former player, Coco Crisp, also called. Adam Jones did send a quick text, but the rest of the game, the established black players said nothing. Meanwhile, as baseball players distanced themselves from him, one of the first people to call Maxwell directly was Colin Kaepernick.

"They don't feel connected to it," Dusty Baker said. "You can see it, and there aren't enough of us in the game anymore, so you know you're going to deal with the backlash and not have any support. It's a different generation, but if you let your traditions go, you'll never get them back."

THE PEACEMAKERS

You want my politics out of sports? Take your politics out of sports.

—COLIN KAEPERNICK

THE REVIVAL OF THE HERITAGE has been made possible through the old cliché that, for the first time in decades, now works in favor of social justice: the player with the biggest number of zeroes on his paycheck shapes the culture. Today, that player is LeBron James.

James does not hide from his liberal politics. He loudly rejects Donald Trump and his policies. James pledged over $40 million to send children from his hometown of Akron to college, and unlike in the Michael Jordan era, he did not out of fear of offending the white mainstream write a check without showing his face. James has done what Jordan did not: he gave cover to the athletes without his talent or bank account to be more vocal politically. He sent the message that being politically active should not be radical but commonplace.

"I'm watching TV at five o'clock in the morning in the gym, and they're saying that LeBron got more points than Michael Jordan, but there'll never be another Michael Jordan," Al Sharpton recalled during the 2017 NBA playoffs. "But LeBron far excels over him in terms of standing up for causes by putting on that hoodie for Trayvon and that I Can't Breathe T-shirt for Eric Garner. I can't think of anything remotely close that Michael did."

Two months before Colin Kaepernick's awakening, James, Chris Paul, Carmelo Anthony, and Dwyane Wade took the stage in Los Angeles at the 2016 ESPYs, ESPN's annual glamourfest award show. Days before, James's representatives contacted ESPN president John Skipper on behalf of the foursome with a request: they wanted to use the ESPYs to make a statement to America after a week of violence between black communities and police so gruesome that it prompted even Michael Jordan, now part of the ruling class as owner of the Charlotte Hornets, to speak.

In St. Anthony, a suburb of St. Paul, Minnesota, thirty-two-year-old public school cafeteria worker Philando Castile was shot seven times and killed by police after being stopped for a broken tail light. In Baton Rouge, another black man, thirty-seven-year-old Alton Sterling was killed by police after they confronted him for selling compact discs on a sidewalk. Days after that, Xavier Micah Johnson, an Army veteran who had served in Afghanistan in 2013 and 2014, ambushed and killed five police officers in Dallas in alleged retaliation. In retaliation for the killing of Sterling, twenty-nine-year-old marine veteran Gavin Long ambushed police officers in Baton Rouge, killing three and wounding three more.

"The four of us are talking to our fellow athletes with the country watching, because we cannot ignore the realities of the current state of America," Anthony began. "The system is broken. The problems are not new, the violence is not new, and the racial divide is definitely not new, but the urgency for change is at an all-time high."

Paul, too, reclaimed his inheritance. "Decades ago, legends like Jesse Owens, Jackie Robinson, Muhammad Ali, John Carlos and Tommie Smith, Kareem Abdul-Jabbar, Jim Brown, Billie Jean King, Arthur Ashe, and countless others, they set a model for what athletes should stand for. So we choose to follow in their footsteps," he said.

James went last: "It's not about being a role model. It's not about our responsibility to the tradition of activism. I know tonight, we're honoring Muhammad Ali, the GOAT [Greatest of All Time], but to do his legacy any justice, let's use this moment as a call to action for all professional athletes."

The old ways were uncomplicated. Paul Robeson and Muhammad Ali were unambiguous: they fought for black people. Modern athletes, however, have not aligned themselves with the Heritage, but these players are now practically walking portfolios. As of 2017, Dwyane Wade had earned $179.5 million in salary alone; Carmelo Anthony, $206 million. Serena Williams's net worth, according to *Forbes*, was $150 million in 2016, and she owned a minority stake in the Miami Dolphins. Venus Williams owns her own clothing line. James, meanwhile, executive produces game shows, movies, TV programs. The *Motley Fool* investment guide estimated his net worth in 2017 to be roughly $400 million. Alex Rodriguez was never an activist, but he was so rich that he referred to Warren Buffett as "a friend," for goodness' sake.

Today's players are ubiquitous, shaped by the marketing muscle of some of the world's biggest corporations. They are the public possessions of an ostensibly postracial, commodified world. They are also financially conflicted, because maintaining the traditions of the Heritage means challenging the corporate mainstream—but today they *are* the corporate mainstream. They are the power they're expected to protest.

Their ubiquity within the culture has given black athletes a different mission: they are not expected to stand for black people but to make the world a better place. During negotiations with the players, ESPN edited their comments that sounded "anti-police," while the players worked with their individual teams and business relationships to ensure they were not harming their financial partners. The editing of the statements continued right up until the minutes before the curtain rose, John Skipper recalled. The message was powerful, but it was the result of compromise, concession. If the original purpose of the Heritage was for athletes, in Tommie Smith's words, to "support oppressed people around the world," the modern political black athlete more resembles a privileged, corporate bridge between the races whose job isn't to advocate for Pan-Africanism, for the black people of the world, as Ali and Robeson did, but to advocate for everybody. It is to be a peacemaker.

That means being caught in the middle during a time where there is no middle. Despite the high-profile killings by Gavin Long and Micah Xavier Johnson, widespread systemic black retaliation against police does not exist, yet Wade addressed the issue as if foreshadowing a race war. "The racial profiling has to stop. The shoot-to-kill mentality has to stop. Not seeing the value of black and brown bodies has to stop," he said. Then, he added a negotiated, balancing qualifier, necessary to accommodate a pro-police corporate obligation. "But also the retaliation has to stop. The endless gun violence in places like Chicago, Dallas—not to mention Orlando—it has to stop. Enough. Enough is enough." Wade's words underscored the corporate minefield today's players tread.

Days later, Jordan appeared, comfortable speaking out because the re-taliatory killings allowed him to appease that middle, simultaneously ad-monishing and supporting the black community—which played well with cops and an American mainstream that could not see beyond black people kneeling. In a piece for the ESPN website "The Undefeated" titled "I Can No Longer Stay Silent," Jordan reinforced his cautious, inoffensive public style, playing to both sides—and writing a really big check:

> I can no longer stay silent. We need to find solutions that ensure people of color receive fair and equal treatment AND that police officers—who put their lives on the line every day to protect us all—are respected and supported. . . . To support that effort, I am making contributions of $1 million each to two organizations, the International Association of Chiefs of Police's newly established Institute for Community-Police Relations and the NAACP Legal Defense Fund.

Chris Paul negotiated, prefacing his comments in the same qualifying fashion, either that not all cops are bad or by announcing his personal bona fides. Paul's uncle was a police officer, as if that special qualification were required for him to voice an opinion. In post-9/11 America, perhaps it was.

The white mainstream put critics of police and military on the de-fensive. A common, disjointed response to police killings was to decry so-called "black on black" crime, where the high numbers of killings in the inner cities such as Chicago were an epidemic—thus Wade's inclusion of the "senseless gun violence in Chicago" was personal as it is his home-town, but was also seen as a negotiated appeasement to the "What about black on black crime?" sect. It was always a false equivalence in a time of the declining value of facts. Crime ostensibly is committed by criminals, yet by this reasoning, police were compared with lawbreakers. It was actu-ally a rhetorical derivative of *Shut up and play*: black people killed one an-other, so why should anyone complain when the good guys kill them too?

James said the night should have been a call to action for all athletes, but just as in the 1960s, few if any white players accepted the challenge. The police unions reacted to player protests first by co-opting the name of the movement Black Lives Matter into their own counter-protest, Blue Lives Matter, and then by often ridiculing black victims and threatening to withhold services to events where they received criticism from black celebrities. When James said, "It's not about our responsibility to the tra-ditions of activism," he could not have been more mistaken. It was *precisely* that, because he stood in front of America for the same reason his fore-bearers had whenever they sought white support: pleading to be seen as full Americans with a public that only saw flag over grievance, authority over justice. It was about reclaiming a voice from an American public that didn't think they had ever earned the right to speak at all.

It was all complicated. James was a revelation, but when Tamir Rice was killed, he did not return to Cleveland and walk arm in arm with the people as Anthony did in Baltimore. Instead, he was curiously distant. Like the rest of the modern incarnation of the Heritage, James was ex-pected to be a peacemaker, urging calm, facilitating "dialogue." It was being a bridge, ironically, to nowhere.

PAYING THE PRICE, 2017

It is for this reason that Colin Kaepernick engenders so much anger: he is not a peacemaker. He did not seek the approval of the white public for his beliefs. He did not try to make them comfortable. There were no ride-alongs with cops or PR experts massaging the words until they found *just the right tone* that didn't offend the mainstream or the cops. For his fidelity, the NFL punished Colin Kaepernick just as the US government had punished Robeson and Ali, by eliminating his ability to work, in this case closing off the American pro football world to him. The blueprint of dealing with the Heritage had not changed. Activist players before him had all paid the price, and now it was his turn.

Invariably, it was the black players who provided the league cover. Mi-chael Vick said Kaepernick's job search could be aided by cutting his hair. Ray Lewis said Kaepernick needed to "shut his mouth." If Donald Trump provided the truth serum that embodied the backlash against eight years of a black president, Colin Kaepernick provided the truth serum for an unevolved sports industry. He exposed the limits of the Heritage and, per-haps most importantly, 125 years after Reconstruction, revealed America's unchanged valuing of the black body over the black brain.

The black body is so important that the NFL allowed Vick a pathway back after he did a year and a half in Leavenworth. When Vick, murderer of animals, was released from prison, the NFL awaited. He played for

Philadelphia, which steadfastly withstood the protests against Vick, then with the New York Jets and Pittsburgh Steelers before retiring. He was then hired by the Kansas City Chiefs organization. Michael Irvin, who as a player was busted for cocaine and settled out of court for sexual assault, is one of the most prominent faces on the league's television house organ, the NFL Network. Irvin was nearly sent to prison for twenty years after an altercation with a teammate could have resulted in a possible parole violation before the Dallas Cowboys owner, Jerry Jones, intervened to broker a truce.

Jones is the same man who threatens his players against kneeling and worked behind the scenes to adopt rules forcing players to stand for the national anthem. The year before, Jones signed defensive end Greg Hardy, who was found guilty of beating and threatening to kill his girlfriend.

The black body is so important to NFL owners that it allows the league to celebrate Lewis, implicated in 2000 as a witness to an unsolved double murder. Lewis pleaded out of a two-count murder charge in exchange for his testimony and a guilty plea to obstruction of justice. To this day, the murders remain unsolved, and Lewis was not only welcomed back to the NFL but never had to leave. The NFL fined him $250,000 but placed him in such high esteem that his team, the Baltimore Ravens, gave him a front-office position after he retired and even erected a statue in his honor. ESPN, a league television partner, made him a lead on the prestigious *Monday Night Football* broadcast team.

How could Vick and Lewis even be employed after what they'd done, let alone feel emboldened to offer Kaepernick advice on how to behave? Or how could an anonymous NFL executive say in 2016 Kaepernick was as hated a player as Rae Carruth, the former Carolina wide receiver sentenced to life in prison for ordering the murder of his pregnant girl-friend—and have virtually no players come to his defense? How could the football public accept such a vulgar incongruity? In a sense, it was easy: Vick and Lewis fit the stereotype of what a black man is supposed to be: violent, aggressive, criminal. It was easy for Steve Bisciotti, the owner of the Ravens, to navigate Lewis. Black male anger sold. It was what the public expected from them, and it allowed white male owners to seem benevolent without having their power threatened. The players were troubled, and paternalistic owners would provide post-playing careers for three convicted felons.

There was another reason that Vick and Lewis were welcomed by the NFL: Vick and Lewis knew what football meant to them. Football was their lives. They were not going to challenge the sport that had graciously given them a second chance after prison for Vick and an ugly trial for Lewis. They would never challenge the NFL in any capacity again. They could be counted on to be controlled.

Kaepernick was different. He traveled three weeks in Africa, to Morocco, Ghana, and Egypt. He helped raise $3 million that went to Somalia famine relief. Being on African soil, he said, was like "walking around not knowing there was a refrigerator on your back and waking up and realizing it's been lifted." He was surrounded by Africans who had nothing, no million-dollar contracts, no Beats headphones, and no private jets. "And you know what?" Kaepernick said. "They were connected in ways we aren't. They ate better and healthier than people in our inner cities. How can that be? We have all these things. How can they add up to nothing for so many people?" He was guided by the black brain, the black child with white parents who knew intimate truths about the American situation so much better than the people who booed him and once paid him. He was the black mind working. He was the threat.

The fans were not insulated from the indictment. They, too, indicated their appreciation of the black body over the black mind by forgiving Hardy, Vick, and players like Joe Mixon, the University of Oklahoma running back who punched a woman in a bar and broke an orbital bone in her face, but being ruthless toward Kaepernick for the crime of thinking. Not Vick, Lewis, Hardy, nor any in a roll call of others, none of their transgressions, moral or legal—nor the destructive nature of the game that was destroying the brains and bodies of their heroes—were sufficient reasons for fans to boycott the league. The Kaepernick threat was not disgracing the integrity of the league but challenging it to allow the black mind to think for himself.

"We've lionized Muhammad Ali from the days when he scared us," said the documentary filmmaker Ken Burns. "I wish we could see a little Muhammad Ali in Colin Kaepernick—and give him a fucking job."

In exile, *GQ* magazine named Kaepernick its citizen of the year. The ACLU honored him with its Eason Monroe Courageous Advocate Award. On December 5, 2017, the *Nation* awarded him its Puffin Prize for Creative Citizenship. That same evening, he accepted the Sports Illustrated

Muhammad Ali Legacy Award, presented to him by the music superstar Beyoncé.

"I accept this award not for myself but on behalf of the people. Because if it were not for my love of the people, I would not have protested," Kaepernick said that night. "And if it was not for the support from the people, I would not be on this stage today. With or without the NFL's platform, I will continue to work for the people, because my platform is the people."

Two days later, a jury in Mesa, Arizona, acquitted officer Philip Brailsford of the January 18, 2016, killing of Daniel Shaver, a twenty-six-year-old father of two who worked as a pest-control specialist. Shaver was showing off the air gun he used for killing birds to some acquaintances in his hotel room. The police were called after guests saw the gun pointed out the window. Bodycam footage showed Shaver in the hallway of the La Quinta Inn on his knees pleading for his life while the officers tell him on several occasions they will kill him if he makes any sudden moves. For nearly five minutes, the officers alternately scream confusing commands at Shaver, reminding him he will "not survive" the encounter if he doesn't cooperate. At the four-minute mark of the video, with Shaver on his knees sobbing for his life, Brailsford fires five shots from his AR-15 assault rifle at point blank range, killing him instantly.

Sixteen months earlier, Colin Kaepernick began his protest angry that "there are bodies in the street and people getting paid leave," and now an unarmed white man had been shot dead by another police officer acquitted of all charges by a jury that believed Brailsford's claim that he feared for his life. Charles Langley, the commanding officer at the scene, who had already had a checkered record as an officer, left the force three months after the shooting and was never charged. Brailsford escaped a twenty-five-year prison term, Shaver was dead, and Langley retired with a full pension—to the Philippines.

A RETURN TO UNOCCUPIED TERRITORY?

For as much as *Shut up and play* is a prevalent rallying cry, and a private wish of the corporations nervous about race, protest, and their bottom lines, it is not one practiced by the very entities—networks, leagues, advertisers, and fans—who claim to want the simplicity of touchdowns and base hits. On November 6, 2017, the ESPN show *First Take*, one of its signature programs, broadcast from the deck of a navy ship in honor of Veterans Day. Six weeks earlier, as Donald Trump portrayed his own citizens as unpatriotic, PBS aired Burns's eighteen-hour documentary *The Vietnam War*. The film's footage of the antiwar movement contrasted markedly with today's deference to the military.

"It's a question of having skin in the game," Burns said. "When you have a draft, no matter how unfair it was with its loopholes in the 1960s that benefited the well-to-do to avoid it, the poor with fewer options were going to serve a disproportionate amount. But a lottery system is a huge boon to the antiwar movement because everybody and their mothers, especially their mothers, has skin in the game.

"Today, we have a separate military class that suffers the wounds of war for the rest of us with no pushback. It permits the worst kind of 'patriotism,' where you get to grandstand and politicize and say 'Thank you for your service,' which is no longer a real thing, but just a way to end a sentence."

Perhaps the supreme irony of this part of the post-9/11 story is how the Twin Towers were destroyed and the ostensibly neutral field of sports was where the police and the military unified a country only to have those same ballparks, police, and military so heavily politicized and commercialized after almost twenty years of propaganda that it is their presence in the culture that now tears elements of it apart.

That is what happens, though, when a moment that once was organic is twisted into a cynical concoction, propagandized by corporations, the sports industry, and the Pentagon, a hero narrative built on inauthenticity. Since Emancipation, police have been a polarizing presence in black America, and depending on one's class, race, and circumstances in America in general, police are a friend to some, an occupier to others—and one of the most egregious uses of force has been when sports has demanded allegiance to police not just from paying customers but from the black players whose experiences with police have often been far from heroic. Police and fire departments, and unions, built the unskilled immigrant middle class—the Irish and the Italians, especially—and spent much of the twentieth century battling the black community at large and keeping African Americans out. As an institution, the police have never truly belonged to African Americans. The same is true, in a sense, of the military, whose fighting force has always been skewed toward the poor and the working class. It saw its ranks of minorities rise both out of opportunity and the desire to prove itself and be accepted as full-bodied Americans, only to have black veterans after World War I be unrecognized as soldiers, and after World War II be shut out of the middle-class opportunities of the GI Bill. The challenge becomes cultural—to encourage diversity of color and diversity of thought—otherwise the expectation will be as it is today: to have people of color join organizations that want them but also want to amputate their cultural inclusion and assimilate, a tension that exists in barracks and newsrooms and locker rooms across America.

"In the process of this public relations, we've actually forgotten the values the country was founded on. And we distort a person like Colin Kaepernick, who is genuinely and gravely concerned about what is happening to justice for African Americans in the United States," Ken Burns said. "That we've been able to contort this is the worst kind of behavior. When this happens, you've abdicated democratic response, and when you have a charlatan-in-chief, who lies in office every day, we end up with tribal responses instead of civil ones."

The gesture of protesting injustice through the American flag only exacerbates a tension that has always existed not just anecdotally but in real time. It is the black police organizations, Eric Adams's and De Lacy Davis's, that were most outspoken on police brutality, and it's the largely black and brown officers who publicly supported Colin Kaepernick—and their public support has been erased from virtually every conversation regarding his protest, their position diminished because it didn't conform. The black officers who decry police brutality are suddenly treated not as cops but rogues. The lines have been drawn along race and class, and they are sharp.

The authoritarian presence of Donald Trump only intensified the fraying, for while he did not create the theater, he has determined the characters, taking an ahistorical view for the sake of emotion, positioning the athletes with real concerns about the direction of the country against it. In a sense, what is occurring today is consistent with history. "It's the America 'Love it or leave it' kneejerk from Vietnam all over again," Burns said.

The original elders of the Heritage were once called unpatriotic only to be vindicated by history, but, asked Toni Smith-Thompson, "How much progress have we really made? When you think about it, the response to those who challenge, from the 1960s with Muhammad Ali, Tommie and John, for what Mahmoud and I went through, to Colin Kaepernick today, has been the same. It hasn't changed."

It is unlikely that sports will return to its pre-9/11 dynamics—less nationalism, less crass commercialism, less hero worship—because no one, not fans, not leagues, and not players, is asking it to. The popular culture, sports as well as movies and, to a certain extent, music, has accepted today's template with no plan for rollback. The flags and flyovers, as baseball writer Jack O'Connell said, is similar to the day in the late 1960s when metal detectors showed up at airports and have remained ever since.

"Is it all overdone? Yes. Do we need to do it? No, but who's going to go first?" one baseball executive told me. "Can you imagine the criticism a team is going to face the minute somebody realizes we didn't salute the troops? It would depend on the regional market, but seriously, no one is going to risk that."

Much of the reason is that authoritarianism has already become normalized, embedded. For all the player protest, not one has indicted the militarized spectacle their day jobs have become.

"I think this is who we are. I think this is who we've always been, and 9/11 was just an opportunity to reveal itself," Smith-Thompson said, adding that "9/11 only provided the rare opportunity to show who America is when America is on the receiving end of what it does. We value pretense. America is white supremacy, capitalism, and pretense. We don't care what the reality is. We care more what it looks like. We are proud of plastic surgery when everyone knows it's not our real face."

SKIN IN THE GAME

Even though he did not play a down, the specter of Colin Kaepernick would test NFL players. Before the season began, Goodell had been in communication with Philadelphia Eagles safety Malcolm Jenkins, who had immersed himself in the issues of police community relations after the deaths of Castile and Sterling. Jenkins was not a kneeler, opting to raise a fist during the national anthem, an ode to the black-gloved 1968 Olympic protest of Smith and Carlos. Jenkins began discussing initiatives with Goodell and his player liaison, Troy Vincent. The players created a

massive group chat allowing them to communicate openly and collabora-
tively. The group called itself the Players Coalition. As Trump attacked,
they seemed ready to unify.

Though several of the owners had bankrolled Trump's campaign,
they recognized that the president's "sons of bitches" rhetoric had produced an uprising (and when it comes to labor peace, worker revolts
are generally not awesome), and *even the owners were kneeling*. Before a
Cowboys-Cardinals *Monday Night Football* game on September 25, there
was Cowboys owner Jerry Jones suddenly on one knee looking like a
Freedom Rider—or an informant.

Privately, owners were nervous of what a unified front of players could
do. Would the Kaepernick protest evolve into a unity NFL players had
never had before? Would the NFL represent another proving ground
in the post-Ferguson athletic awakening where, as the NBA players had
done in ousting the LA Clippers' Donald Sterling and the University of
Missouri football team had done in its protest, the athletes would flex and
shift the balance?

In meeting with the owners, players, specifically Josh Norman of the
Washington Redskins, reminded the owners of their million-dollar contributions to the Trump campaign (including one from Daniel Snyder, the
owner of his team). They reminded the owners that they had allowed the
players to be savaged by the public and the president. And they reminded
ownership of another critical detail: "We haven't forgotten Kaep doesn't
have a job," Philadelphia Eagles defensive end Chris Long said. "He deserves a job."

There was one additional problem to this tidy partnership with the
NFL and its new Players Coalition: no NFL team was willing to offer
Kaepernick a chance to play. But the Players Coalition continued negotiating with the league to partner on a social justice platform. Individual
players, such as Michael Bennett of the Seattle Seahawks, Russell Okung
of the Los Angeles Chargers, Eric Reid of the San Francisco 49ers, and
Michael Thomas of the Miami Dolphins, believed Kaepernick being out
of work should have been a priority. But neither the Players Coalition
nor the players' union, the NFLPA, was willing to couple cooperation on
protest initiatives to Kaepernick's employment status, and it was the curious decoupling of him from the owners that gave Reid pause. Why were
players negotiating with the very owners who had denied Kaepernick

employment for the past eight months? Maybe, Reid thought, this wasn't a transformative moment at all. Maybe this was a setup and the owners were playing divide and conquer.

Malcolm Jenkins of the Philadelphia Eagles did not believe in the need for Kaepernick's job status to be coupled to gaining concessions from the owners. The two were separate, he thought. Besides, the movement was bigger than Kaepernick. Kaepernick had said so himself. Jenkins's goal was to secure resources from billionaire owners to create change. Yet to Reid, something was gnawing at him about the whole thing, and it started with a distrust of Jenkins. Reid's first real suspicion was that the coalition was not representative of the players but the hand-picked moderate, alternative to Kaepernick that ownership would use to buy off the protests. The kneelers slowly began to wonder about the coalition's tactics. Reid did not like the direct contact between Goodell and Jenkins, and he believed the movement should be more collaborative. Reid also did not like that Jenkins positioned himself as the leader of the coalition and told Kaepernick so, setting off tension between Jenkins and Kaepernick. When Kaepernick's lawyers asked Jenkins to document his claim that Kaepernick had been invited to meetings, Jenkins sent a message to the group chat on October 28 that read, "Heads up guys. I removed Kap from this chat. His attorneys have been contacting me and it seems clear to me that he is not interested in working under the coalition. I think it's important that we keep him involved in what we do and he will still be invited to meetings that we have. But in regards to our decision making and communications between members of the coalition, I think its [sic] important to keep these things in house in the spirit of solidarity." Okung, who was not a kneeler, sent a message to Jenkins saying that "I support your decision fully and look forward to us being intentional about our purpose."

Reid had been skeptical since the first New York meeting when Buffalo Bills owner Terry Pegula, who also owns the NHL's Buffalo Sabres, said that his hockey team had lost two sponsors due to protest of the Bills. Pegula said owners and players needed a joint plan on social issues, which needed a face—a black face. Why, Reid wondered, would the NFL need to create a "face" for its initiatives when, across the country, Kaepernick was the clear and obvious one? Pegula nominated Anquan Boldin, the former star wide receiver who had finished his career in Buffalo. Reid suggested Kaepernick. "If there's going to be a face to this, it needs to be

Colin," Reid recalled saying in the meeting. "I'm going to keep bringing this back to Colin, and we aren't talking about Colin enough." The room did not respond.

Reid saw the kneelers as the catalyst for the movement, and the ones taking the greatest personal risk with their careers. Kaepernick was out of the league, and his own contract had expired after the season ended. Veteran cornerback Antonio Cromartie, another kneeler, was released by the Chargers after kneeling for the first month of the 2016 season and was never signed by another team. Jenkins would say that it was the work that players had done in their communities for years that got the positive attention of the owners, and he made no distinction in commitment or risk between sitting, raising a fist, or kneeling. As an example, Jenkins pointed to defensive end Damontre Moore, who was cut by Dallas after raising his fist during the national anthem in October 2017. "Talk to security at the stadium and ask them if the public appreciates my gesture," Jenkins said.

Reid thought differently. It was the kneeling and the effect of the kneeling on the business of the NFL that made any financial partnership with owners possible, and yet he felt like he had nominal input and influence. There was only one reason any owner was talking to them—the kneeling had negatively defined football, and the owners were using the Players Coalition to put a stop to it.

It was all about skin in the game, who had it and who didn't. Reid looked at the coalition and saw players—Josh McCown of the Jets and Aeneas Williams, a retired Hall of Famer—in leadership positions. Chris Long was a coalition member who *did* have skin in the game. He was the most outspoken white male player in America, both in his solidarity with black players and in his commitment to fight for an America he saw slipping away. Long was a member of the 2014 Los Angeles Rams when the five black players emerged from the tunnel during the Ferguson protests. With the New England Patriots, he was an outspoken supporter of Kaepernick, and when New England won the Super Bowl over Atlanta, two things happened: Long didn't join the team at the White House in protest of Trump, and his phone didn't ring in the offseason. Long was eventually signed by Philadelphia—because he called them and asked for work. "It wasn't just having won a Super Bowl. I was top five or ten in the league in pressures. I got sixty career sacks. That's most on most teams. I would have understood no calls coming off two injury-ridden seasons in St. Louis—I looked out of gas. But after that year, my phone blew up. After a healthy, productive year in New England? Zero calls."

Reid feared the movement was being hijacked by owners who wanted to control the allocation of money. It all felt like public relations, not an organic grassroots moment. "I'm not here for the owners' money," he would say. Then came the moment that, in Reid's words, made his "head explode," and his suspicions about the coalition were realized. It came November 29 in the form of a text message from Jenkins to the group that, to Reid, read like the bribe he had long been suspected was the owners' intention for the Players Coalition all along: to get the kneelers to stop kneeling.

"Fellas, I'm going to send an email (and copy you in it) to RG [Goodell] and TV [Vincent] asking that we be allowed to contribute to the matching funds from our own foundations and have it count toward player contributions," Jenkins's text read. "I'm also going to ask them how soon will they be ready to act on this commitment. We'd like a donation ASAP for us to act in good faith, as we'd be waiting until March to get the actual commitment for the local matching funds. If they were to agree to this do you think you'd be more comfortable with ending the demonstrations?"

Reid was stunned. He felt misled, sold out. He was already frustrated—that though he had never been elected by the group, Jenkins had appointed himself as the leader of the coalition, and that media continued to paint Jenkins and Boldin as *responsible* and *legitimate*, and Reid and the other kneelers as *unreasonable* and *uncompromising*. And now, not only did the text read to him as if Jenkins were asking for money to stop kneeling but that Jenkins himself (and not the owners) was initiating the idea. By virtue of asking the NFL for a donation, Reid thought, Jenkins was *literally selling out the protest*. Days later, when the Players Coalition and the NFL would announce an $89 million partnership over seven years to support criminal justice reform initiatives, Jenkins said that, though other players were still able to protest, he would cease doing so. There was one other damning detail that made him look like a proxy for the owners: it turned out he owned a Papa John's franchise, the anti-protest and former official "pizza provider" of the NFL. That day, Reid, Thomas, and Peters quit the coalition. Okung did, too, but not before calling it a "farce."

The fracturing of the Players Coalition would often be characterized as a personality clash or, more romantically, as an example of the age-old collision of working within the system against working outside of it. The coalition willingly made a business deal with the power. Instead of taking power, as the players did in the Missouri and Donald Sterling cases, the NFL players were more in a sense like Lewis and Vick, closely tied to the owners' money without sharing any autonomy. The truth is that the players never sufficiently reconciled the specter of Kaepernick. Jenkins resented the charge that the coalition sold out, but by never confronting the owners directly on Kaepernick, they were willing to trade the human cost of Kaepernick's apparent banishment from the NFL not just for money but for ownership's money. Kaepernick hadn't played all season, but his specter overshadowed the NFL. Even when he wasn't there, he was there.

"The reason I have such a cautious view is because [players] never said anything about Colin Kaepernick, and he's in your own profession," Al Sharpton said. "So, you can impress the fans, but I'm looking at it this way: if you're real, if you're really real, how did you let this brother sit there and you didn't say nothing? And the only one who said something was Vick saying he should have cut his afro. How ridiculous was that, no matter how innocently he said it? And why weren't there ten of y'all out there saying it was wrong?"

"YOU OWE BECAUSE YOU RECEIVED"

The Heritage has been reborn, for now, living in heart within the tenuous space reserved for the dissidents and the patriots, the unpopular and the committed. After decades of silence, Kareem Abdul-Jabbar is writing with the free hand of the liberated. In body, however, the Heritage lives within the complicated, conflicting world of super-rich modern athletes, far removed from the proletariat by the zeroes on their paycheck. They are individual corporations and brands, often aligned with the power, yet collectively so powerful that they could halt college athletics with a single movement. Their choice, governed by the billions they impact, is a daily one: peacemakers or protesters.

After immigration and integration, the third act of sports has been the ultimate victory of the dollar, and the mission of this capitalism runs counter to every tenet of dissidence and principle. Paul Robeson knew this. Jackie Robinson and Muhammad Ali knew it—and in a sense so did

OJ, Michael, and Tiger, though they chose to apply that knowledge quite differently.

"I just love the freedom and the flesh and blood of my people more so than I do the money," Muhammad Ali said in 1971. "You can take your show and play it right in Washington, let Nixon hear it. And I'll be happy. So this boldness and telling the truth overshadows sports greatly."

The Heritage was never about sports but about America making sports—quite specifically the black body in this country—so economically and socially important that the people needed the player to be present for them. This is the inheritance of the black athlete, his coat of arms, and no contract or endorsement deal has yet ever been big enough to make that obligation go away. It is a responsibility the black player will carry until America values the black brain over the black body, and the black people, like all the others, rise through education and not touchdowns. Then sports for black people can finally be reduced to what it should have always been in the first place—just a game.

ACKNOWLEDGMENTS

AN ARGUMENT COULD BE made that the research for this book began in February 1993, when I walked into the clubhouse at Scottsdale Stadium, the spring training home of the San Francisco Giants, as a twenty-four-year-old reporter with the *Oakland Tribune*. I had never been in a big-league clubhouse before.

Two things stand out from that day: the sharp voice behind me talking to me only I didn't know who it was, saying, "Get the fuck away from my locker." (It was Barry Bonds.) And a veteran player on an exercise bike motioning me over to introduce himself. It was the outfielder Willie McGee. Of course I knew who he was.

"Good to see you," he said. "And good to see more *of* you. We need more of you." He was talking about African American reporters, and each day I saw him, McGee made it a point to say hello and teach me a little something about the game, the industry I was about to begin covering. It was my first introduction to the Heritage.

There would be others. Ellis Burks, Ron Washington, and the late Don Baylor, and the tight-knit circle of black baseball that all cycles back to Jackie Robinson, both in lineage and sense of responsibility. I am always grateful for their knowledge and generosity, but I'm especially so to Dusty Baker, whose face lit up with pride one day in Rittenhouse Square in Philadelphia when I told him I could take him through the history of black baseball, from 2017 back to 1920, the first days of the Negro Leagues, in just four handshakes, starting with his:

Dusty shook hands with Henry Aaron.
Henry shook hands with Jackie Robinson.

Jackie shook hand with Satchel Paige.
Satchel shook hands with Rube Foster.

That is the Heritage.

Nothing gets done without people taking an interest in your ideas, and as post-9/11 America began to take a form once celebratory, then commercial and later cynical and increasingly authoritarian as it collided with a post-Ferguson America that saw the rise of the black athlete voice against police misconduct, my editors at *ESPN the Magazine*, Scott Burton specifically, along with Jena Janovy, encouraged an explanation of the intersecting of the two. *Stick to sports* was not his mandate. Editors Eric Neel and Becky Hudson were patient and professional during what has been a volatile and relentless collision of sports and politics, and former ESPN president John Skipper has always championed doing the work. So many of the ideas that became this project were tested out on the magazine's pages.

It is always a joy to be able to work with people multiple times, especially in a changing business, but my agent, Deirdre Mullane, and my editor David Kutzmann remained to guide this project and hopefully many more.

Beacon Press published the paperback of my first book, *Shut Out: A Story of Race and Baseball* in 2003. To be able do another project with Helene Atwan and Tom Hallock fifteen years later is very special, as was working with my editor, Rakia Clark, for the first time. Rakia had a passion for this project from the very start. I believed I was in good hands and that remained true throughout.

As any writer will tell you, we live in our heads, and that can spell misery for the world around us, but you need to lean on your people to get anything done. I leaned heavily on Tisa Bryant, Simone Hughes, Christopher Sauceda, Marques Benton, and Janet Pawson to be there, and they were. Glenn Stout, Peg Kern, Dave Zirin, Laura Harrington, and Louis Moore were particularly invaluable in the constant shaping, brainstorming, and conceptualizing of a fast-moving idea, sending me articles and research I may have missed in the dizzying nonstop news cycles. Special thanks also goes out to my old ESPN colleague and friend Amy K. Nelson for researching and reading sections of the manuscript, to Terrina Long for helping sift through US Census data with the ease of a professional, to Gemma Waters at National Public Radio for the relevant books that magically appeared at my doorstep, and especially to William Astore, Cecilia Evans, and Mark Zinno for taking pity on a civilian and being very generous with their time and recollections of their military service.

Lastly, but never least, even with deadlines and chapters piling up, Ilan Bryant always stands as a smiling reminder of what is most important.

NOTES

INTERVIEWS

Conducted in person and by telephone and email between January 2016 and December 2017. Interviews were also conducted during this period with individuals who preferred to remain anonymous.

Eric Adams	Cecilia Evans
Carmelo Anthony	Jeffrey Hammonds
William Astore	John Hickey
George Atallah	Russel Honoré
Dusty Baker	Edwin Jackson
Charles Barkley	Malcolm Jenkins
Billy Beane	Magic Johnson
Todd Boyd	Bomani Jones
Della Britton Baeza	Jacque Jones
Ellis Burks	Colin Kaepernick
Ken Burns	Ann Killion
John Burton	Donna Lieberman
Mary Carillo	Chris Long
Art Carrington	Davey Lopes
Tony Clark	Bruce Maxwell
Cat Collins	Lee Mazzilli
Patrick Courtney	Louis Moore
Chuck D	Sweeny Murti
De Lacy Davis	David Ortiz
Nessa Diab	Eric Reid
Sean Doolittle	C. C. Sabathia
Shawon Dunston	Steve Sayles
Harry Edwards	Al Sharpton

Buck Showalter

John Skipper

DeMaurice Smith

Toni Smith-Thompson

Jimmie Lee Solomon

Etan Thomas

Joe Torre

Gabrielle Union

Ron Washington

Chris Webber

David West

Dave Winfield

Donald Yee

Mark Zinno

Dave Zirin

PROLOGUE: HERE I STAND

"The reason I am here today . . ." Bentley, *Thirty Years of Treason*.

"I am a Negro" . . . Robeson, *Here I Stand*, 1.

"hadn't gotten around to it yet" . . . Tony Manfred, "An NFL Player Has Gone Weeks Without Cashing His $15 Million Signing Bonus Check," *Business Insider*, Aug. 25, 2014.

"Wouldn't you love to see . . ." Donald Trump, speech in Huntsville, AL, Sept. 22, 2017, CNN.

1

STICK TO SPORTS

"I really don't care . . ." Muhammad Ali interview with Michael Parkinson, BBC, 1971.

"According to Barrett Sports Media . . ." "Barrett Sports Media: Top 20 Sports Radio Programs," Barrett Sports Media blog, Jan. 2, 2017.

"For me, I just got to a point . . ." Eric Branch, "Colin Kaepernick: 'This Stand Wasn't For Me,'" *San Francisco Chronicle*, Aug. 28, 2016.

"I found myself remembering . . ." Batuman, *The Idiot*, 86.

"From an early age . . ." Robeson, *Here I Stand*, 20, v. Emphasis added.

"I guess no one bothered . . ." Brian T. Smith, "49ers QB Colin Kaepernick Has Rights, but He's Not Correct," *Houston Chronicle*, Aug. 27, 2016.

"When it was said (and it was said many times) . . ." Robeson, *Here I Stand*, 28.

"I cannot say it in the strongest . . ." Bob Glauber, "Colin Kaepernick Draws Criticism from Boomer Esiason, Praise from Bart Scott," *Newsday*, August 30, 2016.

Since Esiason knew and cared . . . Joe Sexton, "Police, Youths and Toy Guns–1 Hurt, 1 Dead," *New York Times*, Sept. 29, 1994.

"If I was ever involved . . ." "I'll Bench Any Player That Doesn't Stand for the National Anthem," *SportsCenter* interview with John Tortorella, ESPN, Sept. 7, 2016.

"I think that's disrespectful . . ." "Tony La Russa: Colin Kaepernick Protest All Publicity, No Substance," SI.com. Sept. 14, 2016.

"Statement from Kansas City Chiefs Players . . ." Chris Korman, "Kansas City Chiefs Players Stand with Arms Locked in Solidarity During National Anthem," *For the Win* (blog), *USA Today*, Sept. 11, 2016.

"I'm in support of anybody . . ." Charles Curtis, "Bart Scott on Colin Kaepernick: 'I Think the Death of Muhammad Ali Has Stirred the Pot,'" *For the Win* (blog), *USA Today*, August 30, 2016.

"Far from disrespecting our troops . . ." "An Open Letter of Support for Colin Kaepernick from American Military Veterans," Medium.com, Sept. 2, 2016.

"All voting is a sort of gaming . . ." In Thoreau, *Civil Disobedience and Other Essays*.

"It was embarrassing . . ." Mike Coppinger, "Colin Kaepernick: 'Embarrassing' That Donald Trump, Hillary Clinton Are Candidates," *USA Today*, Sept. 27, 2016.

"You know, I think . . ." Jill Martin, "Colin Kaepernick: 'It Would Be Hypocritical of Me to Vote,'" CNN, Nov. 15, 2016.

"I thought it was egregious . . ." Stephen A. Smith, *First Take*, ESPN, Dec. 3, 2016.

"What really fries me . . ." George Skelton, "Colin Kaepernick Chose Not to Vote. He Should Stop Complaining About the System," *Los Angeles Times*, Nov. 21, 2016.

"According to the US Elections Project. . ." Pillsbury and Johannesen, *America Goes to the Polls 2016*.

"In any case . . ." Jean-Paul Sartre, "Elections: A Trap for Fools," in Les *Temps Modernes* 318 (Jan. 1973).

"Why am I going to vote? . . ." Ibid.

"the loss of mission . . ." Rhoden, *Forty Million Dollar Slaves*, 2.

2

THE GOOD AMERICANS

"We are adamant . . ." Robinson, *Baseball Has Done It*, 22.

"'No man,'" Lincoln said . . ." Donald, *Lincoln*, 176.

"I am not nor ever have been . . ." Ibid., 221.

"In music, Harry Dett . . ." Lewis, *W. E. B. Du Bois*, 520.

"It is important to understand . . ." White, *Creating the National Pastime*, 158–59.

"The Nazis often point out . . ." Schaap, *Triumph*, 125.

"Let America Be America Again . . ." Langston Hughes, *Esquire*, July 1936.

"The poster itself suggested Louis' iconic status . . ." Roberts, *Joe Louis*, 219.

"I didn't want to fall prey to the white man's game . . ." Robinson, *I Never Had It Made*, 83.

"The white public should start . . ." Ibid., 84–85.

"Moulder: Mr. Robinson . . ." Smith, "The Paul Robeson—Jackie Robinson Saga and a Political Collision."

"And one other thing the American public . . ." Ibid.

"door-breaker to progress [for] Americans of color . . ." Hartmann, *Race, Culture and the Revolt of the Black Athlete*, xi.

"With the coming of television . . ." Halberstam, *The Fifties*, 692.

"They see me in a suit and tie . . ." Kahn, *The Boys of Summer*, 401.

"Stan was one of the outstanding players . . ." Flood, *The Way It Is*, 52–53.

"The word of the day . . ." Carlos, *The John Carlos Story*, 78.

"Brent Musburger, who would go on . . ." Hartmann, *Race, Culture and the Revolt of the Black Athlete*, 11.

"On July 20, 1968 . . ." Ibid., 145.

"All the scared niggers are dead . . ." Quoted in *Eyes on the Prize II*.

"Perfect tactic . . ." Carlos, *The John Carlos Story*, 78.

"You had a lot of the elder African American 'statesmen' . . ." Ibid., 79.

"He said that our strongest leverage . . ." Ibid., 81.

"I know very well . . ." Hartmann, *Race, Culture and the Revolt of the Black Athlete*, 83.

"false props . . ." Carlos, *The John Carlos Story*, 114.

"My raised right hand stood . . ." Hartmann, *Race, Culture and the Revolt of the Black Athlete*, 6.

"Jim Brown told his biographer . . ." Zirin, *Jim Brown: Last Man Standing*, 118–19.

"The same was true . . ." Bryant, *Shut Out*, 77.

"There's a little 'Uncle Tom' in Roy . . ." Kahn, *The Boys of Summer*, 357.

3

JUICE

"Give me a guy like O. J. Simpson . . ." *Michigan Chronicle*, Oct. 19, 1968.

"By 1969 and into 1970 . . ." Carlos, *The John Carlos Story*, 136–37.

"After the silent protest . . ." Smith, *Silent Gesture*, 180.

"It takes a tremendous amount of courage . . ." Snyder, *A Well-Paid Slave*, 165.

"It seems clear . . ." Ibid., 244.

"Although Mr. Robeson was unwelcome in many quarters . . ." *New York Times*, obituary, Jan. 24, 1976.

"Inevitably, like a mountain peak . . ." Lloyd Brown in Robeson, *Here I Stand*, preface.

"That statement was made . . ." Robinson, *I Never Had It Made*, 86.

"right-wing fantasy . . ." Pauline Kael, *New Yorker*, Jan. 15, 1972.

"The movie clearly and unmistakably . . ." Roger Ebert, RogerEbert.com Archive, Jan. 1, 1972.

"*Dirty Harry* is obviously just a genre movie . . ." Kael, *New Yorker*.

"a physician's warning . . ." Geoffrey R. Stone, "'Our Nation Is Moving Toward Two Societies,'" *Huffington Post*, July 11, 2016.

"what white Americans . . ." Ibid.

In a meeting, the players . . . John Henderson, "Spirit of the Black 14," *Denver Post*, Nov. 9, 2009.

"Every Negro athlete is a potential messenger . . ." "The Black Athlete: An Editorial," *Sports Illustrated*, Aug. 5, 1968.

"In attempting to reverse this past discrimination . . ." University of Illinois at Chicago Circle, Urban-Suburban Investment Study Group, *Redlining and Disinvestment as a Discriminatory Practice in Residential Mortgage Loans*, 4–5.

"Perhaps the most remarkable aspect . . ." Ibid., p. 15.

"I don't think anyone . . ." Robinson, *I Never Had It Made*, 78.

"We answered ads . . ." Kahn, *The Boys of Summer*, 405.

The Color of Wealth in Boston . . . Munoz et al. *The Color of Wealth in Boston*, 20.

"I was driving down the street . . ." Early, *The Muhammad Ali Reader*, 144.

In 1979, his final season . . . Leonard Shapiro, "Simpson Was Paid $806,668 in 1979," *Washington Post*, Feb. 1, 1980.

According to the Bureau of Labor Statistics . . . US Bureau of Labor Statistics, https://www.bls.gov.

4

JUMP, MAN

"They go down in history for just being athletes . . ." Ali interview, BBC, 1971.

A rising Yale-educated lawyer . . . Adam Liptak, "Three Supreme Court Justices Return to Yale," *New York Times*, Oct. 25, 2014.

"As Jordan smiled . . ." Halberstam, *Playing for Keeps*, 146.

"The commercials worked . . ." Ibid., 181.

"It is understood in Natural history . . ." Isenberg, *White Trash*, 100.

"This was the same formula . . ." Ibid.

According to Lincoln biographer . . . Donald, *Lincoln*, 165–67.

In her book *Team of Rivals* . . . Goodwin, *Team of Rivals*, 406.

"In the United States . . ." Newman, Rael, and Lapsansky, *Pamphlets of Protest*, 229.

"In Zaire, *everything* was black . . ." Early, *The Muhammad Ali Reader*, 140.

"The summer of 1990 . . ." Hodges, *Long Shot*, 123–24.

"Michael was unusually image conscious . . ." Smith, *The Jordan Rules*, 184.

the first billionaire athlete . . . Autumn Rose, "11 of the Richest Athletes of All Time," *Huffington Post*, Mar. 15, 2016.

Remember Fuzzy Zoeller's . . . After Woods won his record-setting Masters, the responsibility fell on him to maintain the Masters tradition of the reigning champion choosing the menu for the following year's champions dinner. Zoeller, who won the tournament in 1979, said of Woods's victory, "He's doing quite well, pretty impressive. That little boy is driving well and he's putting well. He's doing everything it takes to win. So, what do you guys do when he gets in here? You pat him on the back and you say congratulations and enjoy it and tell him not to serve fried chicken next year . . . or collard greens or whatever the hell they serve." Woods attempted to diffuse the controversy by accepting Zoeller's apology, but the larger point of the controversy undermined his later position of being "Cablinasian." In the America of his dominance, Woods was African American. There were people at the time who gave Woods credit for his attempt at self-determination; others who saw him as naïve at best, greenwashed at worst, and at very worst another member of the O. J. Simpson camp who recognized early the advantage of distancing himself from anything that would indicate to the world that he identified as African American.

the average salary in baseball and basketball . . . "Average Baseball Salary," ESPN.com, updated Dec. 4, 2008, http://www.espn.com/espn/wire/_/section/mlb/id/3744821.

5

"OUR WAY OF LIFE"

"Eventually, in Life on Earth . . ." Ralph Wiley, "Why We Need Sports Now," ESPN.com, Sept. 11, 2001, http://proxy.espn.com/espn/page2/story?id=1250721.

The trading firm Cantor Fitzgerald . . . Julia La Roche, "The Amazing and Heartbreaking Story of the CEO Who Lived and Rebuilt His Firm After 9/11: Howard Lutnick," *Business Insider*, Sept. 11, 2011, http://www .businessinsider.com/cantor-fitzgerald-9-11-story-howard-lutnick-2011-9.

According to the Centers for Disease Control . . . CDC, "Deaths in World Trade Center Terrorist Attacks—New York City, 2001," *MMWR Weekly Special Issue*, Sept. 11, 2002, https://www.cdc.gov/mmwr/preview /mmwrhtml/mm51SPa6.htm.

Walmart sold more than five hundred thousand . . . Julian E. Barnes, "A Nation Challenged: Proud Spirits; As Demand Soars, Flag Makers Help Bolster Nation's Morale," *New York Times*, Sept. 23, 2001.

"Tonight, as we have done . . ." NBA.com video archive, Oct. 31, 2001.

"They were terrified . . ." "Phil Donahue on His 2003 Firing from MSNBC, When Liberal Network Couldn't Tolerate Antiwar Voices," interview, *Democracy Now*, Mar. 21, 2003.

"What didn't you see? . . ." Timothy Dumas, "Truth and Consequences: Whatever Happened to Ashleigh Banfield?," *New Canaan, Darien & Rowayton*, Jan. 2009.

"I said, 'Yeah . . .'" "Bossier Rally Crushes Dixie Chicks CDs," video by Christopher Fleeger. https://www.youtube.com/watch?v=jLAU4TexJ9s.

"These people may think they are patriotic . . ." "Let Them Hate Us," *Der Spiegel*, July 11, 2006.

6

THE SANITATION DEPARTMENT

"Some officers even . . ." Skolnick and Fyfe, *Above the Law*, 139.

"As a transit cop . . ." Dennis Hevesi, "After Prison, Ex-Officer's Advice on Police Violence: 'Don't Do It!'" *New York Times*, Jul. 12, 1991.

"The public thought it could do . . ." Marcia Chambers, "Judge Is Critical of Transit Police Over 3 Beatings," *New York Times*, May 17, 1984.

"I considered myself the law . . ." Michael Daly, "Dangerous Lure of Street Justice," *New York Daily News*, Aug. 24, 1997.

The show glamorized approaches . . . Ibid.

"It is absolutely a very powerful show . . ." Michelle Lanz, "Cops on TV: The Reality Show 'COPS' Is 'The Best Recruiting Tool for Policing Ever,'" *The Frame*, Aug. 16, 2016, http://www.scpr.org/programs/the-frame/2016 /08/16/51321/cops-on-tv-the-reality-show-cops-is-the-best-recru/.

"Crime-based reality . . ." Theodore O. Prosise and Ann Johnson, "Law Enforcement and Crime on *Cops* and *World's Wildest Police Videos*: Anecdotal

Form and the Justification of Racial Profiling," *Western Journal of Communication* (Winter 2004): 75.

"battle between white officers. . ." Ibid., 76.

"I watch these 'Cops' shows . . ." Kelley Beaucar Vlahos, "'Cops' at 25," *American Conservative*, Jan. 15, 2013, http://www.theamericanconservative .com/articles/cops-at-25/.

"Watching reality police shows . . ." Sarah Eschholz et al., "Race and Attitudes Toward the Police: Assessing the Effects of Watching 'Reality' Police Programs," *Journal of Criminal Justice* 30, no. 4 (2002): 327–41.

"Koon ordered his men . . ." *Report of the Independent Commission on the Los Angeles Police Department* (Christopher Commission report) (Los Angeles, 1991), 6–7.

"Perhaps the greatest single barrier . . ." Ibid., xx.

"Monkey slapping time . . ." Ibid., 72–73.

"Bottoming out meant . . ." "Americans Respect for Police Surges," Gallup News, Oct. 24, 2016, http://www.gallup.com/poll/196610/americans -respect-police-surges.aspx.

"Hey Hodge . . ." Hodges, *Long Shot*, 138.

"I want to stay focused . . ." Ibid., 147.

"What do I need an education for? . . ." Ibid., 140.

"I knew [Bulls] management . . ." Hodges, *Long Shot*, 171–73.

"Having grown up . . ." "Arthur Ashe: More Than a Champion," BBC, 2015.

"What's my advice . . ." Connecticut Forum, Feb. 4, 1993.

"I just feel like something has to be done . . ." "Polynice Ends Hunger Strike," *New York Times*, Feb. 21, 1993.

"What allegedly happened to Abner Louima . . ." Marie Brenner, "Incident in the 70th Precinct," *Vanity Fair*, Dec. 1997.

Volpe bragged . . . "In Surprise, Witness Says Officer Bragged About Louima Torture," *New York Times*, May 20, 1999.

"Dunleavy generally ignores . . ." Jeffrey Toobin, "The Driver," *New Yorker*, June 10, 2002.

7

PROPS

"The new patriotism . . ." Rich, *The Greatest Story Ever Sold*, 38.

"As early as 1983 . . ." Balko, *Rise of the Warrior Cop*, 121.

"This settlement ensures . . ." New York Civil Liberties Union, "Yankees Settle 'God Bless America' Case, Won't Restrict Spectators' Movements During Song," press release, July 7, 2009.

"When the *New York Times* . . ." C. J. Hughes, "At Stadium, Trip to the Bathroom Signals Free Choice," *New York Times*, July 19, 2009.

8

FERGUSON

"Protest can be organized through social media . . ." Snyder, *On Tyranny*, 84.

"With very rare exceptions . . ." Rothstein, *The Color of Law*, 200.

"The captain noted that . . ." US Department of Justice, *Federal Reports on Police Killings*, quotes here and below from pp. 2, 16, 4, 5, 30.

"These people were balancing . . ." Kareem Abdul-Jabbar, interview with Dave Zirin, *Edge of Sports* podcast, Jan. 13, 2016.

In 2011, New York City . . . Henry Goldman, "NYPD Abuse Increases Settlements Costing City $735 Million," *Bloomberg*, Sept. 4, 2012.

"and in 2015. . ." "How Chicago Racked Up a $662 Million Police Misconduct Bill," *Crain's Chicago Business*, Mar. 20, 2016.

"I just think there has to be a change . . ." Adam Howard, "St. Louis Rams Players Show Solidarity with Ferguson Protesters," MSNBC.com, Dec. 1, 2014.

"I know that there are those . . ." Ben Mathis-Lilley, "Spokesman Who Attacked Rams' Ferguson Protest Was Fired from Police Job in 2001 for Misconduct," *Slate*, Dec. 1, 2014.

"I'm ANGRY . . ." Benjamin Watson Facebook post, Nov. 25, 2014, https://www.facebook.com/BenjaminWatsonOfficial/posts/602172116576590.

Arrests without probable cause . . . US Department of Justice, *Federal Reports on Police Killings*, 183.

"If the Baltimore City Council . . ." Brandon M. Scott, "Who Killed Police Reform Bills in Baltimore?" *Baltimore Sun*, Apr. 21, 2017.

"My greater source of personal concern. . ." "Orioles COO John Angelos Offers Eye-Opening Perspectives on Baltimore Protests," *USA Today*, Apr. 27, 2015.

9

A SEAT AT THE TABLE

"The NFL was a 70 percent black league . . ." Forbes.com, Annual valuation of sports teams.

"Do you have to bring them to my games? . . ." Amy Davidson Sorkin, "Donald Sterling's Revealing Racism," *New Yorker*, Apr. 28, 2014.

"million-dollar niggers . . ." Jim McLennan, "Baseball's Greatest Scandals, #8: Marge Schott by Both Sides," *AZ Snake Pit* (blog), SB Nation, May 9, 2011.

"he's got AIDS . . ." "Donald Sterling on Magic Johnson: 'He's Got AIDS,'"
For the Win (blog), *USA Today*, May 12, 2014.

"When I started doing it . . ." "The Rise of Allen Iverson and Reebok Basketball," Nicekicks.com, June 7, 2017.

"It's the best . . ." Ibid.

"Are there impediments . . ." "The Black Athlete," *Sports Illustrated.*

"The NCAA today . . ." Branch, *The Cartel*, 11.

"As the football team . . ." *Concerned Student 1950*, dir. Adam Dietrich,
Varun Bajaj, and Kellan Marvin, prod. Field of Vision, 2016.

"He's backpedaling faster . . ." Joel Anderson, "Mizzou Football's Long,
Fraught History with Racism on Campus," *BuzzFeed*, Nov. 14, 2015.

10
_____

"WHO IS THE PATRIOT?"

"A patriot . . ." Snyder, *On Tyranny*, 114.

***Tackling Paid Patriotism* . . .** McCain and Flake, *Tackling Paid Patriotism*.
Quotes from pp. 1–2, 61, 37, 81, 66, and 14.

the UK *Guardian* newspaper . . . Les Carpenter, "Report Highlights the
Obscene Price of NFL's Paid Patriotism," *Guardian*, Nov. 5, 2015.

During a high school . . . Dan Barry and John Eligon, "'Trump! Trump!
Trump!': How a President's Name Became a Racial Jeer," *New York Times*,
Dec. 16, 2017.

"a white man's sport . . ." Bob Nightengale, "Adam Jones on MLB's Lack
of Kaepernick Protest: 'Baseball Is a White Man's Sport,'" *USA Today*,
Sept. 12, 2016.

EPILOGUE: THE PEACEMAKERS

James pledged over $40 million . . . "LeBron's Foundation to Spend $41M
to Send Kids to College," *FoxSports*, Aug. 13, 2015.

"The four of us . . ." "LeBron James on Social Activism: 'We All Have to Do
Better,'" ESPN.com, July 14, 2016.

As of 2017 . . . "Player Contracts," Basketball Reference, www.basketball
-reference.com.

The *Motley Fool* . . . Keith Noonan, "What Is LeBron James' Net Worth?,"
Motley Fool, Nov. 28, 2016.

"I can no longer stay silent . . ." Michael Jordan, "I Can No Longer Stay
Silent," *The Undefeated*, July 25, 2016.

"Colin Kaepernick began his protest . . ." John Branch, "The Awakening of
Colin Kaepernick," *New York Times*, Sept. 7, 2017.

Michael Vick said . . . Victor Mather, "Michael Vick's Advice for Unemployed Colin Kaepernick: Cut Your Hair," *New York Times*, July 18, 2017.

Ray Lewis said . . . "Ray Lewis to Kaepernick: Stay Quiet About Social Activism!," *TMZ Sports*, Aug. 1, 2017.

"I accept this award . . ." Colin Kaepernick: 'With or Without the NFL's Platform, I Will Continue to Work for the People,'" *Sports Illustrated*, Dec. 5, 2017.

Reid was stunned . . . Author interview with Reid; Howard Bryant, "A Protest Divided," *ESPN the Magazine*, Jan. 26, 2018.

Okung did, too . . . Adam Wells, "Russell Okung Explains Players Coalition Split, Says $89M Donation Plan 'Farce,'" *Bleacher Report*, Dec. 2, 2017.

"I just love . . ." Ali interview, BBC, 1971.

BIBLIOGRAPHY

Balko, Radley. *Rise of the Warrior Cop: The Militarization of America's Armed Forces*. New York: Public Affairs, 2013.

Bass, Amy. *Not the Triumph, but the Struggle: The 1968 Olympics and the Making of the Black Athlete*. Minneapolis: University of Minnesota Press, 2002.

Batuman, Elif. *The Idiot*. New York: Penguin Press, 2017.

Bentley, Eric, ed. *Thirty Years of Treason: Excerpts from Hearings Before the House Committee on Un-American Activities*. Vol. 3. New York: Viking, 1971.

Blackmon, Douglas A. *Slavery by Another Name: The Re-Enslavement of Black Americans from the Civil War to World War II*. New York: Anchor, 2008.

Branch, Taylor. *The Cartel: Inside the Rise and Imminent Fall of the NCAA*. San Francisco: Byliner, 2011.

Bryant, Howard. *Shut Out: A Story of Race and Baseball in Boston*. Boston, Beacon Press, 2002.

Carlos, John, with Dave Zirin. *The John Carlos Story: The Sports Moment That Changed the World*. Chicago: Haymarket Books, 2013.

Donald, David Herbert. *Lincoln*. New York: Simon and Schuster, 1995.

Du Bois, W. E. B. *Black Reconstruction in America, 1860–1880*. Originally published 1935. New York: Free Press, 1962.

Du Bois, W. E. B. *The Souls of Black Folk*. Originally published 1903. New York: Barnes and Noble Classics, 2003.

Early, Gerald, ed. *The Muhammad Ali Reader*. Hopewell, NJ: Ecco Press, 1998.

Flood, Curt, with Richard Carter. *The Way It Is*. New York: Trident Press, 1971.

Goodwin, Doris Kearns. *Team of Rivals: The Political Genius of Abraham Lincoln*. New York: Simon and Schuster, 2005.

Halberstam, David. *The Fifties*. New York: Fawcett Books, 1993.

Halberstam, David. *Playing for Keeps: Michael Jordan and the World He Made*. New York: Broadway Books, 1999.

Hartmann, Douglas. *Race, Culture and the Revolt of the Black Athlete: The 1968 Olympic Protests and Their Aftermath*. Chicago: University of Chicago Press, 2003.

Hodges, Craig, with Rory Fanning. *Long Shot: The Triumphs and Struggles of an NBA Freedom Fighter*. Chicago: Haymarket Books, 2017.

Isenberg, Nancy. *White Trash: The 400-Year Untold History of Class in America*. New York: Penguin, 2016.

Johnson, James Weldon. *Along This Way: The Autobiography of James Weldon Johnson*. Originally published 1933. New York: Da Capo Press, 2000.

Johnson, James Weldon. *The Autobiography of an Ex-Colored Man*. Originally published 1919. New York: Norton Critical Editions, 2015.

Kahn, Roger. *The Boys of Summer*. Originally published 1971. New York: Perennial Library, 1987.

LaFeber, Walter. *Michael Jordan and the New Global Capitalism*. New York: W. W. Norton, 1999.

Lewis, David Levering. *W. E. B. Du Bois: A Reader*. New York: Henry Holt, 1995.

McCain, John, and Jeff Flake. *Tackling Paid Patriotism: A Joint Oversight Report*. Washington, DC: US Senate, 2015.

Moffi, Larry, and Jonathan Kronstadt. *Crossing the Line: Black Major Leaguers, 1947–1959*. Iowa City: University of Iowa Press, 1994.

Munoz, Ana Patricia, et al. *The Color of Wealth in Boston*. Boston: Federal Reserve Bank of Boston, 2015.

Nelson, Jill. *Police Brutality: An Anthology*. New York: W. W. Norton, 2000.

Newman, Richard, Patrick Rael, and Phillip Lapsansky. *Pamphlets of Protest: An Anthology of Early African-American Protest Literature, 1790–1860*. New York: Routledge, 2001.

Orfield, Gary, and Susan Eaton. *Dismantling Desegregation: The Quiet Reversal of Brown v. Board of Education*. New York: New Press, 1996.

Pillsbury, George, and Julian Johannesen. *America Goes to the Polls 2016: A Report on Voter Turnout in the 2016 Election*. Cambridge, MA: Nonprofit Vote and US Elections Project, 2017.

Report of the Independent Commission on the Los Angeles Police Department. Los Angeles: Independent Commission on the Los Angeles Police Department, 1991.

Rhoden, William C. *Forty Million Dollar Slaves: The Rise, Fall, and Redemption of the Black Athlete*. New York: Three Rivers Press, 2006.

Rich, Frank. *The Greatest Story Ever Sold: The Decline and Fall of Truth from 9/11 to Katrina*. New York: Penguin Press, 2006.

Ritchie, Andrea J. *Invisible No More: Police Violence Against Black Women and Women of Color*. Boston: Beacon Press, 2017.

Roberts, Randy. *Joe Louis: Hard Times Man*. New Haven, CT: Yale University Press, 2010.

Robeson, Paul. *Here I Stand*. Originally published 1958. Boston: Beacon Press, 1988.

Robinson, Jackie. *Baseball Has Done It*. Originally published 1964. Brooklyn, NY: Ig Publishing, 2005.

Robinson, Jackie. *I Never Had It Made: The Autobiography of Jackie Robinson*. Originally published 1972. New York: Ecco Press, 1995.

Rothstein, Richard. *The Color of Law: A Forgotten History of How Our Government Segregated America*. New York: Liveright, 2017.

Schaap, Jeremy. *Triumph: The Untold Story of Jesse Owens and Hitler's Olympics*. Boston: Houghton Mifflin, 2007.

Schwartz, Sanford, ed. *The Age of Movies: Selected Writings of Pauline Kael*. New York: Library of America, 2011.

Silber, Irwin. *Press Box Red: The Story of Lester Rodney, the Communist Who Helped Break the Color Line in American Sports*. Philadelphia: Temple University Press, 2003.

Skolnick, Jerome H., and James J. Fyfe. *Above the Law: Police and the Excessive Use of Force*. New York: Free Press, 1993.

Smith, Ronald A. "The Paul Robeson–Jackie Robinson Saga and a Political Collision." *Journal of Sport History* 6, no. 2 (1979): 5–27.

Smith, Sam. *The Jordan Rules: The Inside Story of Michael Jordan and the Chicago Bulls*. New York: Diversion Books, 2012.

Smith, Tommie, with David Steele. *Silent Gesture: The Autobiography of Tommie Smith*. Philadelphia: Temple University Press, 2007.

Snyder, Brad. *A Well-Paid Slave: Curt Flood's Fight for Free Agency in Professional Sports*. New York: Viking, 2006.

Snyder, Timothy. *On Tyranny: Twenty Lessons from the Twentieth Century*. New York: Tim Duggan Books, 2017.

Zirin, Dave. *Jim Brown: Last Man Standing*. New York: Blue Rider Press, 2018.

Thoreau, Henry David. *Civil Disobedience and Other Essays*. New York: Dover Publications, 1993.

University of Illinois at Chicago Circle, Urban-Suburban Investment Study Group. *Redlining and Disinvestment as a Discriminatory Practice in Residential Mortgage Loans*. Washington, DC: US Government Printing Office, 1977.

US Department of Defense. *2015 Demographics: Profile of the Military Community*. Washington, DC: US Department of Defense, 2015.

US Department of Justice, Civil Rights Division. *Federal Reports on Police Killings: Ferguson, Cleveland, Baltimore, and Chicago.* Brooklyn, NY: Melville House, 2017.

US Department of Justice, Civil Rights Division. *Investigation of the Ferguson Police Department.* Washington, DC: US Department of Justice, March 4, 2015.

White, G. Edward. *Creating the National Pastime: Baseball Transforms Itself, 1903–1953.* Princeton, NJ: Princeton University Press, 1996.

INDEX